CAPITAL STRUCTURE

Determination, Evaluation, and Accounting

Ahmed Riahi-Belkaoui

QUORUM BOOKS
WESTPORT, CONNECTICUT • LONDON

Library of Congress Cataloging-in-Publication Data

Riahi-Belkaoui, Ahmed, 1943–
    Capital structure : determination, evaluation, and accounting /
Ahmed Riahi-Belkaoui.
      p. cm.
    Includes bibliographical references and index.
    ISBN 1–56720–234–9 (alk. paper)
    1. Corporations—United States—Finance. 2. Capital. I. Title.
HG4061.R5   1999
658.15—dc21   98–24565

British Library Cataloguing in Publication Data is available.

Library of Congress Catalog Card Number: 98–24565
ISBN: 1–56720–234–9

First published in 1999

Quorum Books, 88 Post Road West, Westport, CT 06881
An imprint of Greenwood Publishing Group, Inc.

Printed in the United States of America

The paper used in this book complies with the
Permanent Paper Standard issued by the National
Information Standards Organization (Z39.48–1984).

10 9 8 7 6 5 4 3 2 1

Copyright Acknowledgments

The author and publisher gratefully acknowledge permission to reprint from the following:

M. Bradley, G. A. Jarrell and E. H. Kim, "On the Existence of an Optimal Capital Structure: Theory and Evidence," from *Journal of Finance* (Blackwell Publishers, July 1984), 857–878.

M. Harris and A. Raviv, "The Theory of Capital Structure," from *Journal of Finance* (Blackwell Publishers, March 1991), 297–355.

Ahmed Riahi-Belkaoui and James W. Bannister, "Multidivisional Structure and Capital Structure: The Contingency of Diversification Strategy," from *Managerial and Decision Economics* 15 (Wiley and Sons, 1994), 267–276.

To My Family Here and Everywhere!

Contents

Exhibits

Preface

Capital structure represents the major claim to a corporation's assets. It includes different types of both equities and liabilities. This mix of debt and equity, also known as capital structure, has long been the subject of debate concerning its determination, evaluation, and accounting. Its determination is based on the assumption that an optimal capital structure can be determined. The book presents first the popular theories underlying the potential optimum capital structure—the most popular being based on agency costs, asymmetric information, product/input market interactions, and corporate control considerations (Chapter 1). The same problem is then presented under either a contingency of diversification (Chapter 2) or a contingency of multinationality and investment opportunity set (Chapter 3).

The evaluation of capital structure rests on the ratings of its bonds. Therefore, the book presents a model that can be used for the prediction of industrial bond ratings (Chapter 4).

Finally, the accounting issues of capital structure involve both accounting for equity (Chapter 5) and accounting for long-term liabilities (Chapter 6).

The book should be of interest to a variety of groups, including financial officers, researchers interested in corporate finance, and graduate and undergraduate students in accounting and finance.

Many people helped in the development of this book. Eric Valentine of Quorum Books is a true professional and has my deepest gratitude. Terry Park brought the book through the production process. A special note of appreciation is extended to my teaching and research assistants Belia Ortega and Dimitra K. Alvertos for their cheerful and intelligent assistance. Finally to Hedi and Janice thanks for making everything worthwhile.

1

On the Existence of an Optimal Capital Structure

INTRODUCTION

Capital structure represents the major claim to a corporation's assets. It includes publicly issued securities, private placements, bank debt, trade debt, leasing contracts, tax liabilities, pension liabilities, deferred compensation to management and employees, performance guarantees, product warrantees, and other contingent liabilities.[1] The importance of capital structure is evident in the size of the external funds generated by U.S. corporations in general. Exhibit 1.1 summarizes the internal and external sources of funds for nonfarm, nonfinancial corporations over the 1947–1994 period. Notice the $229.9 billion of external funds generated in 1988 as compared to $404.3 billion of internal funds generated for the same year. In generating these external fundings, companies use either debt or equity capital, creating a major corporate question as to whether or not there is an optimal mix of debt and equity that firms should seek. This mix is in fact that of debt and equity that is known as the capital structure, piling up the cash flows of the firms to a relatively safe stream going to the debtholders and a riskier one going to the stockholders. Searching for the optimal capital structure has been a major preoccupation of corporate finance, generating scores of capital structure theories, the most popular of which are based on agency costs, asymmetric information, product/input market interactions, and corporate control considerations. As stated by Harris and Raviv, there are four categories of the determinants of capital structure emanating from the desire to

- Ameliorate conflicts of interest among various groups with claims to the firm's resources, including managers (the agency approach);
- Convey private information to capital markets or mitigate adverse selection effects (the asymmetric information approach);

Exhibit 1.1
Sources and Uses of Funds, Nonfarm Nonfinancial Corporate Business, 1947–94

Year or quarter	Sources Total	Internal Total	U.S. undistributed profits	Inventory valuation and capital consumption adjustments	Capital consumption allowances	Foreign earnings retained abroad [1]	External Total	Credit market funds Total	Securities and mortgages	Loans and short-term paper	Other [2]	Uses Total	Capital expenditures [3]	Increase in financial assets	Discrepancy (sources less uses)
1947	27.3	13.3	12.7	-8.7	9.0	0.3	14.0	8.5	5.6	2.9	5.4	26.4	18.1	8.3	0.9
1948	29.7	19.7	14.0	-5.2	10.4	.4	10.1	7.7	6.9	.8	2.4	25.6	20.7	4.9	4.1
1949	20.8	20.0	9.6	-1.0	11.2	.3	.8	3.3	5.2	-1.9	-2.5	18.4	14.9	3.5	2.4
1950	42.7	18.5	14.1	-7.9	12.0	.3	24.2	8.5	4.6	3.9	15.7	40.3	24.0	16.3	2.4
1951	36.6	20.8	10.8	-4.4	13.8	.6	15.9	10.8	6.3	4.5	5.1	37.9	30.6	7.3	-1.3
1952	30.7	22.7	9.1	-2.0	14.8	.8	8.0	8.9	7.7	1.2	-.9	29.8	25.3	4.5	.9
1953	28.9	22.6	9.4	-3.3	15.8	.7	6.3	5.8	6.2	-.3	.5	28.3	26.1	2.2	.5
1954	29.6	24.7	9.3	-1.9	16.7	.5	5.0	5.8	6.2	-.5	-.8	27.8	23.0	4.8	1.8
1955	53.9	30.3	13.7	-2.0	17.8	.8	23.6	10.8	7.0	3.8	12.8	49.0	32.6	16.4	4.8
1956	45.1	30.5	13.1	-3.7	20.0	1.0	14.6	11.8	6.5	5.3	2.8	40.9	37.0	3.9	4.2
1957	44.2	32.4	11.9	-2.7	22.0	1.2	11.8	12.2	10.0	2.2	-.4	39.8	35.7	4.1	4.4
1958	42.3	31.2	8.8	-1.4	23.0	.8	11.1	9.8	9.9	-.1	1.3	38.7	28.0	10.7	3.6
1959	55.3	37.0	13.0	-1.0	24.1	.9	18.3	10.5	6.1	4.4	7.8	51.8	37.8	14.1	3.5
1960	48.1	36.4	10.5	-.4	25.1	1.2	11.7	9.9	5.4	4.5	1.7	41.5	37.7	3.8	6.6
1961	53.5	37.5	10.2	.6	25.8	1.0	16.0	9.7	8.2	1.5	6.3	50.6	36.5	14.1	2.9
1962	59.8	44.0	13.0	3.2	26.8	1.1	15.8	11.0	7.0	4.0	4.8	54.6	42.2	12.3	5.3
1963	68.3	47.8	14.5	4.0	27.9	1.4	20.5	10.7	6.6	4.2	9.8	59.9	44.4	15.5	8.4
1964	76.6	53.0	18.4	4.0	29.3	1.3	23.6	15.3	8.8	6.5	8.3	64.5	49.8	14.7	12.1
1965	95.4	60.1	23.4	4.0	31.3	1.4	35.4	20.3	7.8	12.5	15.1	82.4	60.8	21.6	13.0
1966	100.7	64.3	25.0	3.5	34.1	1.7	36.4	26.0	15.3	10.8	10.3	91.0	74.5	16.5	9.7
1967	97.0	65.3	22.2	4.2	37.3	1.6	31.7	27.2	19.2	8.1	4.4	87.3	71.2	16.2	9.7
1968	116.6	66.7	21.3	1.9	41.1	2.3	49.9	30.3	17.1	13.2	19.6	106.0	75.6	30.5	10.5
1969	124.8	66.5	18.4	.4	45.0	2.8	58.3	37.6	18.3	19.3	20.7	116.5	85.2	31.3	8.3
1970	109.9	64.0	12.6	-1.1	49.4	3.2	46.0	39.3	31.2	8.1	6.7	99.9	81.7	18.3	10.0
1971	131.4	76.1	18.7	.0	54.2	3.2	55.3	39.0	33.9	5.1	16.3	123.5	87.4	36.1	7.8
1972	162.4	88.1	24.6	-1.6	60.5	4.7	74.3	47.4	30.3	17.2	26.8	148.4	99.1	49.4	13.9
1973	221.9	95.5	36.9	-15.2	65.6	8.1	126.4	80.4	47.0	33.4	46.0	192.4	122.6	69.8	29.5
1974	191.8	91.0	45.3	-38.8	76.8	7.7	100.8	59.8	24.8	35.0	41.0	189.7	138.4	51.3	2.1
1975	159.6	125.0	43.4	-18.6	92.2	8.1	34.6	26.6	41.7	-15.2	8.0	155.9	116.2	39.7	3.7
1976	211.7	140.5	56.5	-26.1	102.5	7.6	71.2	51.1	40.1	11.0	20.2	207.4	155.7	51.7	4.3
1977	263.7	162.7	66.9	-27.0	114.8	8.1	100.9	72.4	43.6	28.9	28.5	244.6	184.3	60.3	19.1
1978	323.0	183.6	78.7	-37.8	131.1	11.7	139.4	76.7	39.9	36.8	62.6	327.6	221.9	105.7	-4.6
1979	343.7	198.5	86.4	-58.0	151.6	18.6	145.2	75.0	20.1	54.8	70.2	369.8	242.2	127.6	-26.1
1980	336.1	199.7	69.2	-61.4	173.2	18.7	136.4	78.4	35.9	42.4	58.0	334.5	252.4	82.1	1.6
1981	394.4	238.9	64.2	-44.8	205.3	14.2	155.6	105.8	32.7	73.1	49.8	418.3	309.9	108.4	23.9
1982	331.7	247.5	30.6	-22.4	227.5	11.8	84.1	70.0	11.6	58.4	14.1	343.3	278.8	64.6	-11.7
1383	444.6	292.3	30.5	2.9	240.1	18.8	152.3	101.0	56.2	44.8	.9	410.4	294.0	116.4	34.2
1984	511.4	336.3	46.4	24.1	246.1	19.7	175.0	118.9	-5.6	124.5	56.1	495.4	391.6	103.8	16.0
1985	493.8	351.9	21.7	54.4	256.0	19.8	142.0	84.7	13.2	71.5	57.3	467.2	370.2	97.0	26.7
1986	538.8	336.7	-2.1	53.4	269.2	16.2	202.1	148.1	65.1	83.0	54.0	501.7	344.2	157.5	37.1
1987	564.7	375.9	41.3	30.6	279.2	24.8	188.8	89.3	39.9	49.4	99.4	492.3	361.5	130.9	72.4
1988	634.2	404.3	73.6	15.7	295.1	19.9	229.9	95.0	-4.7	99.8	134.9	575.8	391.0	184.8	58.4
1989	567.9	399.6	32.2	19.8	314.8	32.8	168.2	68.0	-37.6	105.6	100.2	509.4	401.1	108.3	58.4
1990	535.5	411.6	20.5	21.8	326.6	42.8	123.9	48.3	-20.1	68.3	75.6	488.7	402.8	85.9	46.7
1991	471.7	426.0	4.7	35.2	338.6	47.6	45.7	8.7	96.1	-87.4	37.0	435.3	379.8	55.6	36.4
1992	560.5	438.4	29.8	22.0	349.3	37.3	122.2	67.9	67.0	-.9	54.3	527.8	386.0	141.8	32.8
1993	557.4	462.3	17.5	36.5	357.6	50.8	95.1	67.1	81.2	-14.1	28.0	523.4	440.4	83.0	34.0
1992: I	541.3	434.3	28.7	26.7	341.8	37.1	107.0	81.6	94.3	-12.7	25.5	512.8	362.1	150.7	28.4
II	570.7	432.9	37.3	11.8	344.0	39.8	137.8	78.4	95.4	-16.9	59.4	528.7	389.2	139.5	42.0
III	531.2	440.7	26.7	16.9	362.5	34.7	90.5	39.4	31.1	8.3	51.1	522.6	394.1	128.5	8.6
IV	598.9	445.6	26.4	32.4	349.1	37.6	153.3	72.2	47.2	25.0	81.1	547.0	398.7	148.3	51.9
1993: I	443.4	436.4	3.1	23.1	352.6	57.6	7.0	27.5	83.9	-56.4	-20.6	426.1	424.7	1.4	17.3
II	548.8	450.7	20.7	29.6	355.1	45.3	98.1	80.6	68.0	12.7	17.5	530.4	441.5	88.9	18.4
III	600.6	476.4	13.4	47.7	362.4	52.9	124.1	78.6	101.9	-23.3	45.6	550.0	444.1	105.9	50.5
IV	636.8	485.7	32.7	45.3	360.4	47.3	151.1	81.7	71.1	10.6	69.4	587.2	451.2	136.0	49.5
1994: I	653.8	502.9	41.3	38.5	381.3	41.7	150.8	110.3	12.4	97.9	40.5	648.9	474.7	174.2	4.8
II	656.8	500.4	48.6	38.0	372.0	41.8	156.4	114.4	36.7	77.7	42.0	652.0	520.7	131.3	4.8
III	664.5	503.1	59.6	33.2	377.9	32.5	161.5	75.9	-23.7	99.6	85.6	646.2	535.2	111.0	18.3

Source: Economic Report to the President (Washington, D.C.: GPO, 1995), 384.

[1] Foreign branch profits, dividends, and subsidiaries' earnings retained abroad.

[2] Consists of tax liabilities, trade debt, direct foreign investment in the United States, and pension fund contributions payable.

[3] Plant and equipment, residential structures, inventory investment, and access rights from U.S. government.

- Influence the nature of products or competition in the product/input market; or
- Affect the outcome of corporate control contests.[2]

This chapter elaborates on these theories and others as they impact the determination of capital structure.

CAPITAL STRUCTURE AND THE MAXIMIZATION OF FIRM VALUE

Basically, financial risk is the risk placed on the common stockholders as a result of the decision to use debt financing, or financial leverage, in the capital structure. Management is therefore interested in determining the amount of debt or financial risk that maximizes firm value. To illustrate the impact of financial risk on firm value, let us use the following two examples:

Example 1 deals with the XYZ Corporation, which has $200,000 in assets and is all equity financed. Assuming an earnings before taxes (EBIT) of $40,000, the rate of return on equity (ROE) is computed as follows:

EBIT	$40,000
− Interest	0
EBIT	$40,000
Taxes (40%)	16,000
Net income	$24,000
ROE = $24,000/$200,000	12%

Now, assume that the XYZ Corporation decides to issue $100,000 of debt at an interest rate of 10% to be used to retire $100,000 of common stock. The ROE will be as follows:

EBIT	$40,000
− Interest (10% × $100,000)	10,000
EBIT	$30,000
− Taxes (40%)	12,000
Net income	$18,000
ROE = $18,000/$100,000	18%

What appears from the XYZ example is that the use of financial leverage increased ROE from 12% to 18%. One can expect firms to continue to increase leverage and increase the ROE to stockholders. The fact is that the improvement depends on the return on assets, as measured by EBIT/total assets, being higher than on the interest rate of debt. As an illustration, suppose that EBIT was $20,000 rather than $40,000. The ROE would be computed as follows:

EBIT	$20,000
− Interest (10% × $100,000)	10,000
EBIT	$10,000
− Taxes (40%)	4,000
Net income	$6,000
ROE = $6,000/$100,000	6%

With lower rate of return on assets, the ROE with 50% financing declined from 18% to 6%. Although there may be an optimal capital structure that maximizes ROE, the use of financial risk increases the risk faced by equity investors and depends on whether the return on assets exceeds the interest rate on debt.

Example 2 deals with the ABC Corporation, which is all equity financed and has 200 shares selling for $20 a share. ABC plans to issue $2,000 worth of debt and use the proceeds to give a $10 cash dividend per share. Management expects the market value of the firm to either stay the same or increase or decrease by $500. The potential capital structures are as follows:

	No Debt Capital Structure	Debt + Dividends Scenarios		
		1	2	3
Debt	0	$2,000	$2,000	$2,000
Equity	$4,000	2,500	2,000	1,500
Firm value	$4,000	$4,500	$4,000	$3,500

The payoff to stockholders under the three scenarios are as follows:

	1	2	3
Capital gains	−1,500	−2,000	−2,500
Dividends	2,000	2,000	2,000
Net gain or loss to stockholders	500	0	−500

Obviously the capital structure that maximize firm value occurs under scenario 1. If management expected scenario 1 to happen, then the restructuring of capital structure is a good idea. It is a bad idea if scenario 3 was expected.

CAPITAL STRUCTURE THEORY: MODIGLIANI AND MILLER PROPOSITION I (NO TAXES)

Modigliani and Miller (hereafter MM) proved under a very restrictive set of conditions that a firm's value is unaffected by its capital structure.[3] This implies that the financing choice of firms is irrelevant. The assumptions were as follows:

1. Firms with the same degree of business risk are in a homogeneous risk class.

2. Investors have homogeneous expectations about future corporate earnings and their level of riskiness.

3. Securities are traded in perfect capital markets.

4. The interest rate on debt is the risk-free rate.

5. All cash flows are perpetuities.

Proposition I states the value of the firm is unaffected by its choice of capital structure.

To see how proposition I works, let us imagine two identical firms that differ only in their capital structure. Firm X is unleveraged, whereas firm Y is leveraged. For firm X, the total value of its equity (E_x) is equal to the total value of the firm (V_x). For firm Y, the value of the equity (E_y) is equal to the value of the firm (V_y) mixing the value of its debt (D_y): $E_y = V_y - D_y$.

Now consider an arbitrageur who purchases 1% of firm X. The result is

Dollar Investment	Dollar Return
$0.01 V_x$	0.01 Profits

Let us assume in a second scenario that he purchases 10% of the debt and equity of firm Y. The result is

Dollar Investment	Dollar Return
$0.01(D_y + E_y) = 0.01\ V_y$	0.01 Interest + 0.01 (Profits − Interest) = 0.01 Profits

Scenarios 1 and 2 yield the same 0.01 profits, meaning that they are generated by the same value. Therefore $0.01V_x$ is equal to $0.01V_y$. The value of the firm is therefore unaffected by its choice of capital structure.

Let us consider a third scenario where the arbitrageur buys 1% of the equity of the leveraged firm Y. The result is

Dollar Investment	Dollar Return
$0.01E_y = 0.01(V_y - D_y)$	$0.01(\text{Profits} - \text{Interest})$

The fourth scenario is where the arbitrageur borrows $0.01D_y$ as her own account to purchase $0.1V_x$. The result is

Dollar Investment	Dollar Return
$- 0.01D_y + 0.01V_y$	$-0.01\text{Interest} + 0.01\text{Profits}$
$= 0.01(V_x - D_y)$	$= 0.01 \ (\text{Profits} - \text{Interest})$

Again, scenarios 3 and 4 yield the same 0.01 (Profits − Interest), indicating that the investments have the same costs. Therefore $0.01(V_y - D_y) = 0.01 \ (V_x - D_y)$ and $V_y = V_x$. The example indicates that the market value of firm is independent of its capital structure.

CAPITAL STRUCTURE THEORY: MODIGLIANI AND MILLER PROPOSITION II (NO TAXES)

Proposition II states that the expected return on equity is positively related to leverage because the risk of equity increases with leverage.

To develop this proposition, consider the weighted average cost of capital as

$$R_0 = \frac{D}{D + E} \times r_d + \frac{E}{D + E} r_e$$

where

R_0 = Weighted average cost of capital

D = Debt

E = Equity

r_d = Interest rate of cost of debt

r_e = Cost of equity or required return on equity.

If we solve the equation for r_e, then we obtain

$$r_e = r_0 + \frac{D}{E} (r_0 - r_d)$$

In other words, the expected return on equity is a linear function of the firm leverage. As a firm increases its leverage through a higher D/E ratio, it raises the risk of equity and the required rate of the return on equity r_e. The same applies to the beta of equity of a leveraged firm, which is

$$\beta_e = \beta_a + \frac{D}{E} (\beta_a - \beta_d)$$

where

β_e = Beta of equity

β_a = Beta of assets

β_d = Beta of debt.

Both propositions I and II ignore taxes and do not consider bankruptcy costs and agency costs. Releasing these assumptions leads to more interesting results.

CAPITAL STRUCTURE THEORY AND CORPORATE TAXES

The previous analyses ignored taxes. The MM model can be adjusted for the effect of taxes. For a leveraged firm, the following variables can be computed:

Taxable income = EBIT $- r_dD$ (1)

Total taxes = $T_c \times$ (EBIT $- r_dD$), where T_c = tax rate   (2)

Cash flow to stockholders = (EBIT $- r_dD$) $(1 - T_c)$ (3)

Cash flow to stockholders and bondholders = EBIT $(1 - T_c) + T_c r_dD$

For an unleveraged firm, the following variable can be computed:

Earnings after corporate taxes = EBIT $(1 - T_c)$ (4)

Comparing expressions (3) and (4) shows that with leverage, the investors in the leveraged firms receive an extra cash flow equal to $T_c r_dD$, which is the *tax shield from debt*. Given that it has the same risk as the interest on the debt, it can be discovered at the interest rate r_d. Therefore,

$$PV \text{ (tax shield)} + \frac{T_c r_dD}{r_d} = T_cD$$

Therefore MM proposition I with corporate taxes becomes

Value of firm = Value of all equity financed + PV (tax shield)

or

$$\text{Value of firm} = \frac{\text{EBIT} \times (1 - T_c)}{r_0} + \frac{T_c r_dD}{r_d}$$

or

Value of firm $= V_x + T_c D$

In other words, the value of the firm is equal to the value of the firm's cash flows with no debt tax shield (value of an all equity firm) plus the present value of the tax shield in the case of perpetual cash flows.

Similarly, MM proposition II with corporate taxes becomes

$$r_e = r_0 + \frac{D}{E}(r_0 - r_d)(1 - T_c)$$

where r_0 is now computed as

$$r_o = \frac{D}{V}r_d(1 - T_c) + \frac{E}{V}r_e$$

CAPITAL STRUCTURE THEORY: CORPORATE AND PERSONAL TAXES

The MM model with corporate taxes can be improved by the inclusion of personal taxes. Miller introduced such a model where leverage affects the firm's values when both corporate and personal taxes are taken into account.[4] The Miller model is as follows:

$$V_l = V_u + 1 - \left[\frac{(1 - T_c) \times (1 - T_s)}{(1 - T_d)}\right] D$$

where

T_d = Personal tax rate on income from debt

T_c = Corporate tax rate

T_s = Personal tax rate on income from stocks

V_l = Value of the leveraged firm

V_u = Value of the unleveraged firm.

Notice that

1. The bracketed term multiplied by D represents the gain from leverage.

2. If $T_c = T_s = T_d = 0$, the result will correspond to the MM result without taxes.

CAPITAL STRUCTURE THEORY AND COSTS OF FINANCIAL DISTRESS

None of the previous models presented in this chapter consider the potential of financial distress leading to bankruptcy. Financial distress creates both direct and indirect costs to the firm. The costs of financial distress can be broken down as follows:

1. Bankruptcy costs

    (a) Direct costs such as court fees

    (b) Indirect costs reflecting the difficulty of managing a company undergoing reorganization

2. Costs of financial distress short of bankruptcy

    (a) Conflicts of interest between bondholders and stockholders of firms in financial distress may lead to poor operating and investment decisions. Stockholders acting in their narrow self-interest can gain at the expense of creditors by playing ''games'' that reduce the overall value of the firm.

    (b) The fine print in debt contracts is designed to prevent these games. But fine print increases the costs of writing, monitoring, and enforcing the debt contract.[5]

Financial distress is generated by the presence of debt in the sense that the larger the fixed interest charges created by the use of leverage, the greater the probability of decline in earnings and the greater the probability of incurrence of costs of financial distress. The value of the leveraged firm is now made of these parts:

Value of firm = Value of all equity financed + PV(tax shield) − PV(costs of financial distress)

The combination of distress costs and tax effects is shown in Exhibit 1.2. The exhibit shows the determination of capital structure as a result of the trade-off between the tax benefits and the costs of distress. Whereas the inverted U-shaped curve shows the value of the firm with bankruptcy costs, the diagonal straight line shows the same value without the bankruptcy costs. The value of the firm rises as the firm uses more debt up to an optimum, where the present value of tax savings due to additional debt is more than offset by increases in the present value of costs of distress. This is the amount D_2 indicated in Exhibit 1.2. Basically, although the tax shield increases the value of the leveraged firm, the financial distress costs lower it, and both offsetting factors yield an optimal amount of debt. This is the trade-off theory of capital structure.

Exhibit 1.2
Effect of Debt Financing on Value of Firm

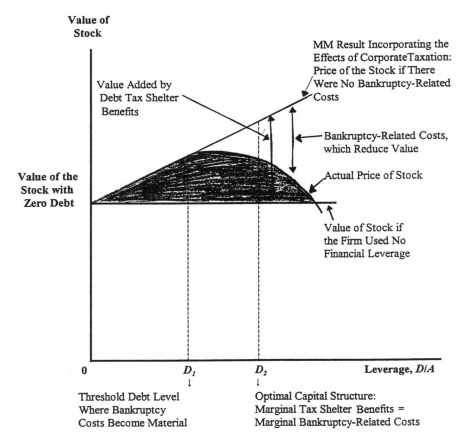

CAPITAL STRUCTURE THEORY AND AGENCY COSTS

None of the models presented earlier include agency costs. More research has been devoted recently to models in which capital structure is determined by agency costs, that is, costs due to conflicts of interest. Two types of conflicts were identified by Jensen and Meckling:[6] conflicts between shareholders and managers arising from the situation of managers holding less than 100% of the residual claim, and conflicts between debtholders and equity holders arising from the debt contract giving the equity holders the incentive to invest suboptimally. Therefore, an optimal capital structure can be obtained by trading off the agency cost of debt against the benefit of debt. The value of the firm is now computed as

Value of the firm = Value of all equity financed + PV (tax shield) − PV (costs of financial distress) − PV (agency costs)

In Exhibit 1.2, the agency costs can be added to financial distress costs, resulting in a more complete trade-off model.

CAPITAL STRUCTURE THEORY AND THE ASYMMETRIC INFORMATION MODEL

The models reviewed earlier did not consider the possibility of asymmetric information whereby firm managers are assumed to know more about the characteristics of the firm's return stream or investment opportunities. As a result the choice of a capital structure by management, signals to outside investors convey some insider information. This asymmetry of information influences the choice of capital structure, in general, and the choice between internal and external financing and between new issues of debt and equity securities, in particular. This choice is based on the following financing *pecking order*:

1. Firms prefer internal finance.

2. They adapt their target dividend payout ratios to their investment opportunities, although dividends are sticky and target payout ratios are only gradually adjusted to shifts in the extent of valuable investment opportunities.

3. Sticky dividend policies, plus unpredictable fluctuations in profitability and investment opportunities, mean that the internally generated cash flow may be more or less than investment outlays. If it is less, the firm first draws down its cash balance or marketable securities portfolio.

4. If external financing is required, firms issue the safest security first. That is, they start with debt, then possibly hybrid securities such as convertible bonds, and perhaps equity as a last resort. In this story, there is no well-defined target debt/equity mix, because there are two kinds of equity, internal and external, one at the top of the pecking order and one at the bottom. Each firm's observed debt ratio reflects its cumulative requirements for external finance.[7]

Therefore profitable firms borrow less because they rely on internal funds. As a result of the preference for internal equity over external equity, firms will use less debt than has been implied by the trade-off theory of taxes and financial distress costs. Firms are therefore more likely to create *financial slack* to be used eventually for internal funding. The fundamental results of the pecking order are

1. Absence of price effects on issuance of (riskless) debt.

2. A negative price effect of an equity issue.

3. A pecking order in the choice of the type of financing.

CAPITAL STRUCTURE THEORY AND PRODUCT/INPUT MARKET INTERACTION

None of the previous theories relied on any of the features of the theory of industrial organization. There are, however, models of capital structure based on product/input market interactions that either (a) exploit the relationships between a firm's capital structure and its strategy when competing in the product market or (b) consider the relationship between capital structure of a firm and the characteristics of its product or input. The strategic variables examined are product price and quantity. The product or input characteristics included the future availability of products, parts, and service; product quality; and the bargaining game between management and input supplies. Some of the results follow:

1. Oligopolists tend to have more debt than monopolists or firms in competitive industries.[8]
2. When tacit collusion is important, debt is limited and debt capacity increases with the elasticity of demand.[9]
3. Firms with products that are unique or require service and/or parts and firms relying on the reputation of their products are expected to have less debt.[10]
4. Finally, highly unionized firms and firms with transferable skilled workers have more debt.[11]

CONCLUSIONS

The answer to the existence of an optimal capital structure is contingent on a consideration of (a) corporate and personal taxes, (b) costs of financial distress, (c) agency costs, (d) existence of asymmetry of information, and (e) product/input market interaction and corporate control considerations.

The studies reviewed in Appendix A point to the ongoing debate on the feasibility of an optimal capital structure and point to the needs for new innovative approaches. Two such innovative approaches are presented in Chapters 2 and 3, with Chapter 2 focusing on the contingency of diversification strategy and Chapter 3 focusing on the contingency of the investment opportunity set.

NOTES

1. Ronald W. Masulis, *The Debt/Equity Choice* (Cambridge, Mass.: Ballinger Publishing Company, 1988), 1.

2. Milton Harris and Artur Raviv, "The Theory of Capital Structure," *Journal of Finance* (March 1991): 299.

3. F. Modigliani and M. Miller, "The Cost of Capital, Corporation Finance and the Theory of Investment," *American Economic Review* 48 (June 1958): 261–297.

4. Merton H. Miller, "Debt and Taxes," *Journal of Finance* 32 (May 1977): 261–275.

5. Richard A. Brealey and Stewart C. Myers, *Principles of Corporate Finance* (New York: McGraw-Hill, 1996), 503.

6. Michael C. Jensen and William Meckling, "Theory of the Firm: Managerial Behavior, Agency Costs and Capital Structure," *Journal of Financial Economics* 3 (October 1976): 305–360.

7. Stewart C. Myers, "The Capital Structure Puzzle," *Journal of Finance* 39 (July 1984): 581.

8. J. A. Brander and T. R. Lewis, "Oligopoly and Financial Structure: The Limited Liability Effect," *American Economic Review* 76 (1986): 956–970.

9. J. Glazer, "Live and Let Live: Collusion among Oligopolists with Long-Term Debt," Working Paper, Boston University, 1989.

10. V. Maksinonic, "Capital Structure in Repeated Oligopolies," *Rand Journal of Economics* 19 (1988): 389–407.

11. O. H. Sharig, "Bargaining with a Corporation as the Capital Structure of the Bargaining Firm," Working Paper, Tel Aviv University, 1988.

SELECTED READINGS

Barclay, M. J., C. W. Smith, and R. L. Watts. "The Determinants of Corporate Leverage and Dividend Policies." *Journal of Applied Corporate Finance* 7 (Winter 1995): 4–19.

Baskin, J. "An Empirical Investigation of the Pecking Order Hypothesis." *Financial Management* 18 (Spring 1989): 26–35.

DeAngelo, H., and R. Masulis. "Optimal Capital Structure Under Corporate Taxation." *Journal of Financial Economics* 8 (March 1980): 5–29.

Durnad, D. "Cost of Debt and Equity Funds for Business: Trends and Problems in Measurement." In *Conference on Research in Business Finance.* New York: National Bureau of Economic Research, 1952, pp. 215–247.

Fama, E. F. "The Effects of a Firm's Investment and Financing Decisions." *American Economic Review* 68 (June 1978): 272–284.

Galai, D., and R. W. Masulis. "The Option Pricing Model and the Risk Factor of Stock." *Journal of Financial Economics* 3 (January–March 1976): 53–82.

Hamada, R. S. "Portfolio Analysis, Market Equilibrium and Corporation Finance." *Journal of Finance* 24 (March 1969): 13–31.

Harris, M., and A. Raviv. "The Theory of Capital Structure." *Journal of Finance* 48 (March 1991): 297–356.

Jensen, Michael C., and W. H. Meckling. "Theory of the Firm: Managerial Behavior, Agency Costs and Ownership Structure." *Journal of Financial Economics* 3 (October 1976): 305–360.

Miller, Merton H. "Debt and Taxes." *Journal of Finance* 32 (May 1977): 261–276.

Modigliani, F., and M. H. Miller. "The Cost of Capital, Corporation Finance and the Theory of Investment." *American Economic Review* 48 (June 1958): 261–297.

Modigliani, F., and M. H. Miller. "Corporate Income Taxes and the Cost of Capital: A Correction." *American Economic Review* 53 (June 1963): 433–443.

Modigliani, F., and M. H. Miller. "Some Estimates of the Cost of Capital to the Electric

Utility Industry, 1954–57." *American Economic Review* 56 (June 1966): 333–391.

Modigliani, F., and M. H. Miller. "Reply to Heins and Sprenkle." *American Economic Review* 59 (September 1969): 592–595.

Myers, S. C. "Determinants of Corporate Borrowing." *Journal of Financial Economics* 5 (1977): 146–175.

Myers, Stewart C. "The Capital Structure Puzzle." *Journal of Finance* 39 (July 1984): 575–592.

Myers, S. C. "Still Searching for Optimal Capital Structure." *Journal of Applied Corporate Finance* 6 (Spring 1993): 4–14.

Myers, S. C., and N. S. Majluf. "Corporate Financing and Investment Decisions when Firms Have Information Investors Do Not Have." *Journal of Financial Economics* 13 (June 1984): 187–222.

Riahi-Belkaoui, Ahmed. "A Canadian Survey of Financial Structure." *Financial Management* (Spring 1975): 74–79.

Riahi-Belkaoui, Ahmed. *Industrial Bond Ratings and the Rating Process.* Westport, Conn.: Greenwood Publishing, 1983.

Riahi-Belkaoui, Ahmed. "Multinationality and Corporate Financing Policies." *Advances in Financial Planning and Forecasting* 7 (1997): 207–215.

Riahi-Belkaoui, Ahmed, and James Bannister. "Multidivisional Structure and Capital Structure: The Contingency of Diversification Strategy." *Managerial and Decision Economics* 15 (1994): 267–276.

Stiglitz, J. E. "On the Irrelevance of Corporate Financial Policy." *American Economic Review* 64 (December 1974): 851–866.

2

The Determination of Capital Structure: The Contingency of Diversification Strategy

INTRODUCTION

This chapter employs a contingency perspective to examine the impact of the implementation of the multidivisional form (M-form) structure on a firm's capital structure given different corporate diversification strategies. Theories of corporate capital structure have often focused on the various roles of debt, including the tax advantage of debt,[1] the choice of debt level to signal firm quality,[2] the use of debt as an antitakeover device,[3] the agency costs of debt,[4] and the usefulness of debt for restricting managerial discretion.[5] These theories and the related empirical work on capital structure have increased our understanding of the issues. There is, however, no consensus about which of the determinants have an impact on the capital structure decision or how they affect performance. We believe that Barton and Gordon's[6] suggestion to employ a strategy perspective will add to the understanding of the capital structure decision.

Specifically, we test whether implementation of the M-form structure is associated with a change in capital structure, and whether such changes vary over firms with different corporate diversification strategies. Williamson[7] discusses a theory of the firm's strategy for financing projects based on the redeployability of the assets involved and the governance structure best suited to those assets. Both concepts are used in this study to motivate the differential capital structures expected from different diversification strategies. Three major categories of corporate diversification strategy are examined: vertical integration, related business diversification, and unrelated diversification.[8] Our central proposition is that the implementation of the M-form structure affects the capital structure decision differently depending on which diversification strategy exists prior to M-form implementation. We investigate the proposition by comparing the capital structure of large multiproduct firms before and after their reorganization.

The chapter proceeds as follows. The next section discusses the multidivisional form and its relation to firm performance. Hypotheses related to the impact of M-form restructuring and diversification strategy on capital structure are presented. The third section details the sample, data collection, and the variables used in the study. Our approach and empirical results are presented in the fourth section. The final section contains a discussion of the results.

BACKGROUND AND HYPOTHESES

Implementation of the Multidivisional Form and Capital Structure

Extending Chandler's[9] work, Williamson[10] argues that as the size and diversity of centralized (U-form) firms increase, managers reach their limits of control and may resort to opportunism, thereby threatening efficiency and profitability. He suggests that the multidivisional form (M-form) of managerial structure can reduce such opportunism. Since M-form implementation requires the firm to be decomposed into distinct divisions, most operating decisions, and some strategic decisions, are decentralized to these divisions. With effective decentralization, middle-management opportunism can be reduced, since responsibility for operating budgets and cost management is shifted to division managers.

Although the M-form may reduce middle-management opportunism, it offers less to control top-management opportunism. One area where top management may display opportunism is in the misuse of free cash flow; namely, cash flow in excess of that required to fund all projects that have positive net present value when discounted at the relevant cost of capital. M-form implementation does not prevent top management from investing free cash flow at below the cost of capital, or wasting it on organizational inefficiencies.

M-form adopters may tend to have free cash flow. Population-ecology theory suggests that as organizations age, they reach higher levels of performance reliability and move to a state of "structural inertia,"[11] which is characterized by substantial free cash flow. Fligstein[12] uses population-ecology theory to explain the adoption of the M-form.

Management that has been retaining free cash flow may be forced to release it when seeking new financing. Jensen[13] theorizes that the capital market may force firms to finance new capital with debt, rather than equity, to reduce management misuse of free cash flow. He argues that debt reduces the agency costs of free cash flow by reducing the cash flow available for discretionary spending by top management. Increased debt financing would act to increase the efficiency of organizations that have large cash flows but few high-return investments by forcing them to disgorge cash to investors.

Two features of M-form implementation suggest that additional financing may be needed by the firm. First, the evidence shows that the size and asset growth of firms increase after implementation of the M-form. Second, costly coordination and information-processing functions may be needed to realize the economic gains associated with the M-form. Following the implementation of the M-form, we expect that firms will seek new financing and be required to use an increased amount of debt to reduce opportunism in the use of free cash flow. Thus, we hypothesize:

H_1: The implementation of the M-form leads to an increase in the firm's debt/equity ratio.

Diversification Strategy and Capital Structure

Galbraith and Nathanson[14] trace the growth of firms in three major categories of corporate diversification strategy: vertical integration, related business diversification, and unrelated business diversification. Each strategy results in different economic benefits or costs and implies different management objectives. Transaction cost economics (TCE) suggests that the economic characteristics of the three diversification strategies may call for different types of financing.

TCE views project financing as a choice between alternative corporate governance structures and cash-flow requirements. Debt financing does not allow the debtholder voting power, but it imposes mandatory cash outflows for interest and principal on the borrower. Equity financing requires shared voting power, but does not involve mandatory cash flows. Since management is assumed to desire as little dilution of its voting power as possible, it will opt for debt financing so long as the project can generate sufficient cash flow. Thus, the choice of debt or equity funding for a project is related to the project specificity of its assets. If a project's assets are redeployable (less project-specific), they can be sold or put to an alternative productive use in the firm, and the cash-flow stream from these assets is less risky. Projects with redeployable (less risky) assets are thus suited to debt financing. Conversely, projects with less redeployable (more risky) assets are suited to equity financing, which has no mandatory cash outflow requirement. The implications of TCE for the three diversification strategies are discussed later.

Vertical integration offers the firm economies due to control of its supply/output markets. The firm's value-added margin for a chain of processing is increased due to increased control over raw materials and/or outlets.[15] Further, market transaction costs, such as opportunistic action by traders or the drafting and monitoring of contingent claims contracts to ensure harmonious trading relationships, can be either eliminated or reduced.[16] Because up- or downstream integration provides cost savings to the firm, redeployment of these assets could tend to reduce the value of the firm disproportionately to their individual value.

Firms pursuing a strategy of related diversification can realize synergistic economies of scope through the joint use of inputs.[17] Exploitation of this synergy is achieved through both tangible and intangible interrelationships. Tangible inter-relationships are created by such devices as joint procurement of raw materials, joint development of shared technologies or production processes, joint sales forces, and joint physical distribution systems. Intangible interrelationships arise from the sharing of know-how and capabilities. Redeployment of assets in a related diversified firm would again imply a disproportionate loss in firm value since synergistic economics could be lost.

A traditional argument for unrelated diversification suggests that the multi-product firm can realize financial economies. The risk pooling of imperfectly correlated income streams created by unrelated diversification is, in principle, assumed to produce an asset with a superior risk/return relationship.[18] The same risk diversification can, however, be more efficiently achieved by the investor with a portfolio of bond holdings.[19] Empirical evidence is also inconsistent with the idea that unrelated diversification reduces risk. Furthermore, unrelated diversification in itself does not imply the achievement of input/output market cost savings or the existence of managerial, technological, or operational synergies. Although Williamson[20] contends that "conglomerate" firms may benefit from improved governance after the adoption of the M-form structure, assets (divisions) of unrelated diversifiers remain highly redeployable through spin-off or outright sale with little synergistic loss to the firm.

TCE argues that as assets become more redeployable, management prefers debt financing over equity financing. The previous discussion suggests that there is differential redeployability of assets among firms that follow different diversification strategies, with unrelated diversifiers holding more redeployable assets than related diversifiers and vertical integrators. In addition, Jensen[21] argues that firms that are generating large free cash flows (and are thus subject to the market discipline of debt financing) often diversify into unrelated areas. We hypothesize that the different diversification strategies employed by firms are associated with cross-sectional differences in capital structure between diversification strategies. More specifically,

H_2: Firms using related diversification or vertical integration strategies have lower debt/equity ratios than firms using an unrelated diversification strategy.

SAMPLE AND DATA COLLECTION

Previous research has identified 62 firms that adopted the M-form during the period 1950–78. Our sample consists of these firms. Each firm was diversified at the time of its restructuring and was classified using a classification method. Firms were classified as having been in one of the three diversification classes—unrelated (16 firms), related (22 firms), or vertical (24 firms). Exhibit 2.1 lists the firms, their classifications, and the year in which the restructuring occurred.

Exhibit 2.1

Diversified Firms Restructuring to the M-Form from the U-Form

Company name	Diversification strategy	Year of restructuring	Company name	Diversification strategy	Year of restructuring
Aluminum Co. of America	V	68	CPC	R	67
BFGoodrich	V	53	Dow Chemical	R	63
Burlington	V	62	General Foods	R	52
City Service	V	66	Heinz	R	67
Continental Can	V	50	Honeywell	R	62
Crown Zellerbach	V	66	IBM	R	65
Getty Oil	V	59	Ingersoll Rand	R	64
Goodyear	V	76	Monsanto	R	71
Hormel	V	66	Phillip Morris	R	67
International Paper	V	73	Procter & Gamble	R	66
Kaiser Aluminum	V	58	Quaker Oats	R	71
Kennecott Paper	V	66	Ralston Purina	R	68
Marathon Oil	V	63	R.J. Reynolds	R	70
Mobil Oil	V	60	J. P. Stevens	R	71
Occidental Petroleum	V	72	White Motor Co.	R	69
Phillips Petroleum	V	75	AMF	U	58
Shell Oil	V	61	Borg Warner	U	70
Standard Oil (California)	V	55	Brunswick	U	69
Standard Oil (Ohio)	V	62	Colt Industries	U	68
Standard Oil (Indiana)	V	61	Dart Industries	U	62
St Regis Paper	V	69	Dayco	U	66
Sun Oil	V	71	Esmark	U	70
Union Oil	V	64	FMC	U	61
Uniroyal	V	60	Gulf & Western	U	67
Allied Chemical	R	72	ITT	U	68
Ashland Oil	R	70	Lear Siegler	U	62
Bendix	R	65	Ogden	U	69
Borden	R	68	Textron	U	60
Burroughs	R	66	US Industries	U	69
Celanese	R	63	Raytheon	U	59
Coca-Cola	R	68	SCM	U	62

Source: Ahmed Riahi-Belkaoui and James W. Bannister, "Multidivisional Structure and Capital Structure: The Contingency of Diversification Strategy," *Managerial and Decision Economics* 15 (1994): 267–276. Reprinted with permission of the editor.

V = vertically diversified, R = related diversification, U = unrelated diversification

Dependent Variable

A longitudinal design was used to capture the effects over time of the implementation of a decentralized multidivisional structure. Data for the measure of capital structure, year-end long-term debt to common equity, was collected for years −5 through +5 (relative to the year of the restructuring). Financial statement data for each firm were collected from Compustat and, in cases where Compustat coverage was incomplete, from *Moody's Industrials Manual*. The data collected for the dependent variable were long-term liabilities (Compustat data item 9) and common equity (item 60).

Control Variables and Covariates

A control factor, early/late adoption of the M-form and three covariates (firm size, growth in total assets, and growth in gross national product [GNP]) are included to control for possible intervening effects. The control factor, early/late adoption of the M-form, is motivated by the belief that late movers learn from the experience of early movers and are thus able to restructure faster and more efficiently.[22] Early/late adoption is measured by the year of restructuring relative to sample median. Firms adopting the M-form prior to 1967 are classified as early movers; those adopting in 1967 or later are classified as late movers.

Firm size, asset growth rate, and GNP growth rate are included as covariates. Their use is motivated by (1) the known relationship between leverage and size, (2) the suggestion that firms may sacrifice profitability in periods of growth, and (3) the need to control for changes in capital structure related to major external shifts in aggregate demand. Firm size is measured as the natural logarithm of average total assets; asset growth rate is measured as the proportional change in total assets. Data for year-end total assets were collected from Compustat (data item 6), or from *Moody's Industrials Manual* when Compustat coverage was incomplete. GNP growth rate is measured as the proportional change in GNP. Data for GNP were collected from the National Income and Product Accounts constructed by the U.S. Department of Commerce. Each of the covariates is measured over the same period as the dependent variable. Exhibit 2.2 gives the means, standard deviations, and correlations for the variables used in the chapter.

DATA ANALYSIS

A longitudinal design is used to capture the effects over time of the implementation of a decentralized multidivisional structure. Years −1, 0, and +1 relative to the year of the restructuring (year 0) were excluded from the analysis to avoid the potential confounding of capital structure measures with events during the transition. An analysis of covariance is used to test the overall rela-

Exhibit 2.2
Means, Standard Deviations, and Correlation Coefficients of Variables by Strategic Type and Stage of M-Form Implementation (Three-Year Window Excluded)

	Means[a]		Correlations[b]			
Variables	Before M-form	After M-form	1	2	3	4
(A) *Vertically integrated firms*						
1. Long-term Debt/Total Equity	0.36	0.42	1.000	0.088	0.209	−0.393
	(0.07)	(0.07)				
2. Size[c]	6.77	7.32	0.054	1.000	0.585	0.019
	(0.98)	(1.00)				
3. Total Growth in GNP[d]	0.21	0.26	−0.058	0.330	1.000	0.223
	(0.06)	(0.07)				
4. Total asset growth[e]	0.29	0.28	0.339	0.224	0.324	1.000
	(0.26)	(0.15)				
(B) *Related diversified firms*						
1. Long-term Debt/Total Equity	0.25	0.46	1.000	−0.006	0.123	0.186
	(0.07)	(0.07)				
2. Size[c]	6.34	7.12	0.161	1.000	0.131	0.169
	(0.69)	(0.67)				
3. Total Growth in GNP[d]	0.22	0.28	−0.014	0.161	1.000	−0.045
	(0.04)	(0.04)				
4. Total Asset Growth[e]	0.30	0.42	0.145	−0.055	0.258	1.000
	(0.23)	(0.21)				
(C) *Unrelated diversified firms*						
1. Long-term Debt/Total Equity	0.59	0.70	1.000	0.075	−0.173	−0.030
	(0.10)	(0.08)				
2. Size[c]	5.19	6.37	−0.091	1.000	0.582	−0.396
	(1.08)	(1.03)				
3. Total Growth in GNP[d]	0.21	0.28	0.066	0.526	1.000	−0.084
	(0.05)	(0.05)				
4. Total Asset Growth[e]	0.65	0.62	−0.351	−0.471	−0.147	1.000
	(0.58)	(0.83)				

[a] Standard deviations are in parentheses.
[b] Correlations in the upper (lower) half of the matrices are from after (before) implementation of the M-form.
[c] Size is computed as ln(Average Total Assets).
[d] Total Growth in GNP is computed as $(GNP_E - GNP_B)/GNP_B$, where B denotes the beginning of a period and E the end of a period.
[e] Total Asset Growth is computed as $(TA_E - TA_B)/TA_B$, where TA = total assets, B denotes the beginning of a period, and E denotes the end of a period.

Source: Ahmed Riahi-Belkaoui and James W. Bannister, "Multidivisional Structure and Capital Structure: The Contingency of Diversification Strategy," *Managerial and Decision Economics* 15 (1994): 267-276. Reprinted with permission of the editor.

Exhibit 2.3
Results of Analysis of Covariance for Long-Term Liabilities/Total Common Equity

Sources	F-Statistic	Pr. > F
Diversification strategy	6.59	0.002
M-form implementation	2.66	0.100
M-form × diversification strategy	0.65	0.526
Control variable		
Early/late adopter	2.85	0.094
Covariates		
Size	0.00	0.948
Total asset growth	0.17	0.679
Total growth in GNP	1.09	0.299

Source: Ahmed Riahi-Belkaoui and James W. Bannister, "Multidivisional Structure and Capital Structure: The Contingency of Diversification Strategy," *Managerial and Decision Economics* 15 (1994): 267-276. Reprinted with permission of the editor.

tionship between (1) organizational structure and capital structure, (2) diversification strategy and capital structure, and (3) the interactive effect of organizational structure and diversification strategy on capital structure. Early/late adoption is a control variable; firm size, asset growth rate, and GNP growth rate are covariates. The effects on capital structure of M-form implementation, diversification strategy, and their interaction are first examined by an F-test of the difference between variances after controlling for the effects of early/late adoption and the covariates.

Exhibit 2.3 presents the results of the analysis of covariance for long-term debt to total common equity for the 62 firms in the sample. The overall analysis of covariance is statistically significant ($F[9,123] = 2.70$, $p = 0.007$, and $R^2 = 0.18$). Further, nondirectional F-tests for differences in variance indicate that (1) the implementation of the M-form leads to a different capital structure and (2) the different diversification strategies employed by the sample firms are associated with cross-sectional differences in capital structure. There is no interactive effect of organizational form and diversification strategy on capital structure. Directional tests of hypotheses related to the main effects are reported below.

Hypothesis H_1 states the implementation of the M-form is associated with an increased use of debt in the firm's capital structure. The impact of the M-form implementation on capital structure is further investigated by performing comparisons of mean debt/equity ratios before and after the M-form for the overall sample, and by strategic type. Exhibit 2.4 presents these results. In agreement with H_1, the exhibit indicates that following the implementation of the M-form, firms in the overall sample significantly increased their debt/equity ratios. Further, the mean debt/equity ratio for firms in each of the strategy types increased.

Exhibit 2.4

Mean Comparisons of Long-Term Liabilities/Total Common Equity by Strategy Type before versus after M-Form Implementation

Strategy type	Before the M-form	After the M-form	t-probability[a]
(1) All strategies	0.4010	0.5276	0.05
(2) Unrelated diversified firms	0.5879	0.7048	0.19
(3) Vertically integrated firms	0.3607	0.4173	0.29
(4) Related diversified firms	0.2542	0.4605	0.03

[a] H_1 predicts that the debt/equity ratio increases after M-form implementation, t-probabilities are one-tailed.

Source: Ahmed Riahi-Belkaoui and James W. Bannister, "Multidivisional Structure and Capital Structure: The Contingency of Diversification Strategy," *Managerial and Decision Economics* 15 (1994): 267-276. Reprinted with permission of the editor.

The analysis indicates, however, that the increase is statistically significant only in the case of firms employing the strategy of related diversification.

Hypothesis H_2 states that firms employing a strategy of unrelated diversification use more debt in their capital structure than do firms employing strategies of related diversification or vertical integration. The impact of diversification strategy on capital structure is further investigated by performing mean comparisons between type of diversification strategy. Exhibit 2.5 presents these results. As suggested by H_2, unrelated diversified firms have long-term debt/equity ratios that are significantly larger than those for vertically integrated firms and related diversified firms. Hypothesis H_2 did not make a projection about the

Exhibit 2.5

Mean Comparison of Long-Term Liabilities/Total Common Equity by Strategy Type

Means for strategy types			t-probability[a]		
Unrelated diversifiers	Vertical integraters	Related diversifiers	U versus V	U versus R	R versus V
0.6463	0.3890	0.3574	0.0025	0.0026	0.6519

[a] U—unrelated diversifiers, V—vertical integraters, R—related diversifiers. H_2 predicts that unrelated diversifiers have higher debt/equity ratios than do related diversifiers or vertical integraters. Thus, the reported t-probabilities for U versus V and U versus R are one-tailed. H_2 makes no prediction about the relationship between R and V firms; the reported t-probability is two-tailed.

Source: Ahmed Riahi-Belkaoui and James W. Bannister, "Multidivisional Structure and Capital Structure: The Contingency of Diversification Strategy," *Managerial and Decision Economics* 15 (1994): 267-276. Reprinted with permission of the editor.

relative use of debt and equity between vertically integrated firms and related diversified firms. A test indicates, however, that there is no significant difference in debt/equity ratios for firms following these strategies.

DISCUSSION

The central proposition of this study was that the implementation of a multi-divisional structure is associated with different capital structures in firms that employ the different strategic diversification approaches of unrelated diversification, vertical integration, and related diversification. The results of this study support the contingency view of the relationship between capital structure and the implementation of the M-form.

Hypothesis 1 was confirmed, the sample firms increased the level of debt used in their capital structure. Although percentage debt usage generally increased for all diversification classes, within diversification classes only related diversified firms made a statistically significant change. An explanation for the general increase in debt is that the implementation of the M-form controls is associated with a reduction in the availability of free cash flow through debt creation. The reduction of opportunism implied as one of the goals of decentralization is further enhanced by the "control" mechanism of debt creation. The increase in debt level following the implementation of the M-form points to the role of debt in reducing the agency costs of free cash flow.

In regard to the significant increase in debt usage for related diversified firms, Hill and Hoskisson[23] suggest that, among the strategies of unrelated diversification, related diversification, and vertical integration, the strategy of related diversification requires higher costs of coordination and information processing to realize potential economic gains. A significant increase in debt level for the related diversified firms, rather than for the unrelated diversified or vertically integrated firms, supports their suggestion that extra funds may have been needed to achieve and exploit economies of scope, which require efficient interdivisional coordination.

The test hypothesis 2 also yielded statistically significant results, suggesting that, in agreement with Williamson's thesis, debt as a governance structure is more suited to projects where assets are highly redeployable and, therefore, that different diversification strategies with different asset redeployabilities are associated with different capital structures. Where the redeployability of assets is high, as in unrelated diversified firms, the use of long-term debt financing in the firm's capital structure is greater than for firms where redeployability of assets is lower, as in related diversified and vertically integrated firms. As a result, although increased costs of coordination may require a significant increase in debt for related diversified firms, the usage of debt in their capital structures after M-form implementation is still lower than in that of unrelated diversified firms.

These results show a link between diversification as a strategy, organizational structure, and capital structure. At the divisional level, diversification strategies influence capital structure strategies. These results complement and add to the strategic-group paradigm.[24] Based on a firm's heterogeneous capabilities and resources, the strategic-group paradigm enables researchers and practitioners to map industrial firms into sets of similar competitors, the so-called strategic groups. Although a more comprehensive review of the literature is provided by McGee and Thomas,[25] Thomas and Venkatraman,[26] and Barney and Hoskisson,[27] the results of this study indicate that the strategic linkages between the divisions of the firm and the rest of the firm need to be taken into account in the formulation of strategic groups. Better strategic groups could be identified by a simultaneous consideration of corporate diversification strategy and divisional strategy.

More research is needed to verify the results of this study and to test the questions that it raises. Replication needs to consider (1) using different data and multiple measures of leverage, (2) relying on recent periods, and (3) imposing a control group of firms not adopting the M-form. Until further research is completed, the results of the leverage effects of a historical shift to an M-form framework must be interpreted with caution.

APPENDIX: CLASSIFICATION OF DIVERSIFICATION STRATEGIES

A framework for the classification categories relies on three ratios: (1) the specialization ratio, (2) the related ratio, and (3) the vertical ratio. Each of the three ratios is based on the proportion of revenues earned from various business activities. The specialization ratio is used to define firms into the primary categories of single business, dominant business, related business, or unrelated business. The related and vertical ratios are then used to subdivide firms into finer classifications.

The specialization ratio (SR) is defined as the proportion of the firm's revenues that is attributable to its largest discrete product-market activity. The related ratio (RR) is defined as the proportion of firm revenues that are related to one another in some way. The vertical ratio (VR) is defined as the proportion of revenues attributable to all the by-products, intermediate products, and final products of a vertically integrated sequence of manufacturing operations.

The primary diversification strategies and their subcategories are (1) single business; (2) dominant business as either (a) dominant vertical, (b) dominant constrained, (c) dominant linked, or (d) dominant unrelated; (3) related business as either (a) related constrained or (b) related linked; and (4) unrelated business as either (a) multibusiness or (b) unrelated portfolio.

A specialization ratio of less than 0.7 defines a business as unrelated. If $0.7 < SR < 0.95$, then the firm is classified as a dominant business. The firm is classified as a single business if $SR \geq 0.95$. A related ratio greater than 0.7 defines a related business. A vertical ratio greater than 0.7 defines a vertically integrated business.

A reduced classification system for the sample firms is used in this study. Each firm is classified as being in one of the three following categories:

1. Primary dominant vertical firms. Vertically integrated firms ($VR \geq 0.7$) producing and selling different end products, no one of which contributes more than 94% of total revenues.

2. Related-constrained firms. Firms with $0.7 \leq SR < 0.95$ and $RR \geq 0.7$, which have diversified by relating new businesses to a specific central skill or resource, wherein each business activity is related to almost all the other business activities of the firm.

3. Unrelated business firm. Firms with $0.7 \leq SR < 0.95$ and $RR < 0.7$ that have aggressive programs for the acquisition of new unrelated business.

NOTES

1. F. Modigliani and M. H. Miller, "Corporate Income Taxes and the Cost of Capital: A Correction," *American Economic Review* 3 (1963): 433–443.

2. S. A. Ross, "The Determination of Financial Structure: The Incentive-Signaling Approach," *Bell Journal of Economics* 8 (1977): 23–40.

3. M. Harris and A. Raviv, "Corporate Control Contests and Capital Structure," *Journal of Financial Economics* 20 (1988): 55–86.

4. S. C. Myers, "Determinants of Corporate Borrowing," *Journal of Financial Economics* 5 (1977): 147–176.

5. M. C. Jensen, "Agency Costs of Free Cash Flow, Corporate Finance, and Takeovers," *American Economic Review* 76 (1986): 323–329.

6. S. L. Barton and P. J. Gordon, "Corporate Strategy: Usefulness Perspective for the Study of Capital Structure?" *Academy of Managerial Review* 12 (1987): 67–75.

7. O. W. Williamson, "Corporate Finance and Corporate Governance," *Journal of Finance* 43 (1988): 567–591.

8. J. R. Galbraith and D. A. Nathanson, "Role of Organizational Structure and Process in Strategy Implementation," in *Strategic Management: A New View of Business Policy and Planning*, ed. by D. Schandel and C. Hofer (Boston: Little, Brown & Co., 1979), 249–283.

9. A. Chandler, *Strategy and Structure* (Cambridge, Mass.: MIT Press, 1962).

10. O. W. Williamson, *Corporate Control and Business Behavior* (Englewood Cliffs, N.J.: Prentice-Hall, 1970).

11. M. Hannan and J. Freeman, "The Population Ecology of Organizations," *American Journal of Sociology* 92 (1977): 929–964.

12. N. Fligstein, "The Spread of the Multidivisional Form among Large Firms," *American Sociological Review* 50 (1985): 377–391.

13. M. C. Jensen, "Agency Costs of Free Cash Flow, Corporate Finance and Takeovers," *American Economic Review* 76 (1986): 323–329.

14. Galbraith and Nathanson, "Role of Organizational Structure and Process in Strategy Implementation."

15. K. R. Harrigan, "Vertical Integration and Corporate Strategy," *Academy of Management Journal* 28 (1985): 397–425.

16. C. W. Hill and R. E. Hoskisson, "Multidivisional Structure and Performance: The Contingency of Diversification Strategy," *Academy of Management Review* 12 (1987): 331–340.

17. D. Teece, "Economies of Scope and the Scope of the Enterprise," *Journal of Behavior and Organization* 1 (1980): 223–247.

18. W. Lewellen, "A Pure Financial Rationale for the Conglomerate Merger," *Journal of Finance* 26 (1971): 521–545.

19. H. Levy and M. Sarnat, "Diversification, Portfolio Analysis and the Uneasy Case for Conglomerate Mergers," *Journal of Finance* 25 (1970): 795–802.

20. O. W. Williamson, *Markets and Hierarchies: Analysis and Antitrust Implications* (New York: Free Press, 1975).

21. Jensen, "Agency Costs of Free Cash Flows, Corporate Finance and Takeovers."

22. E. Mansfield, "How Rapidly Does New Industrial Technology Leak Out?" *Journal of Industrial Economics* 34 (1985): 217–225.

23. Hill and Hoskisson, "Multidivisional Structure and Performance."

24. M. Porter, *Competitive Advantage: Creating and Sustaining Superior Performance* (New York: Free Press, 1985).

25. J. McGee and H. Thomas, "Strategic Groups: Theory, Research and Taxonomy," *Strategic Management Journal* 7 (1986): 141–160.

26. H. Thomas and N. Venkatraman, "Research on Strategic Groups: Progress and Prognosis," *Journal of Management Studies* 25 (1988): 537–555.

27. J. B. Barney and R. E. Hoskisson, "Untested Assertions in Strategic Group Research," *Managerial and Decision Economics* 11 (1990): 187–198.

SELECTED READINGS

Barney, J. B., and R. E. Hoskisson. "Untested Assertions in Strategic Group Research." *Managerial and Decision Economics* 11 (1990): 187–198.

Barton, S. L., and P. J. Gordon. "Corporate Strategy: Usefulness Perspective for the Study of Capital Structure?" *Academy of Managerial Review* 12 (1987): 67–75.

Chandler, A. *Strategy and Structure*. Cambridge, Mass.: MIT Press, 1962.

Fligstein, N. "The Spread of the Multidivisional Form among Large Firms." *American Sociological Review* 50 (1985): 377–391.

Galbraith, J. R., and D. A. Nathanson. "Role of Organizational Structure and Process in Strategy Implementation." In *Strategic Management: A New View of Business Policy and Planning*, edited by D. Schandel and C. Hofer, 249–283. Boston: Little, Brown & Co., 1979.

Hannan, M., and J. Freeman. "The Population Ecology of Organizations." *American Journal of Sociology* 92 (1977): 929–964.

Harrigan, K. R. "Vertical Integration and Corporate Strategy." *Academy of Management Journal* 28 (1985): 397–425.

Harris, M., and A. Raviv. "Corporate Control Contests and Capital Structure." *Journal of Financial Economics* 20 (1988): 55–86.

Hill, C. W., and R. E. Hoskisson. "Multidivisional Structure and Performance: The Contingency of Diversification Strategy." *Academy of Management Review* 12 (1987): 331–340.

Jensen, M. C. "Agency Costs of Free Cash Flow, Corporate Finance, and Takeovers." *American Economic Review* 76 (1986): 323–329.

Levy, H., and M. Sarnat. "Diversification, Portfolio Analysis and the Uneasy Case for Conglomerate Mergers." *Journal of Finance* 25 (1970): 795–802.

Lewellen, W. "A Pure Financial Rationale for the Conglomerate Merger." *Journal of Finance* 26 (1971): 521–545.

Mansfield, E. "How Rapidly Does New Industrial Technology Leak Out?" *Journal of Industrial Economics* 34 (1985): 217–225.

McGee, J., and H. Thomas. "Strategic Groups: Theory, Research and Taxonomy." *Strategic Management Journal* 7 (1986): 141–160.

Modigliani, F., and M. H. Miller. "Corporate Income Taxes and the Cost of Capital: A Correction." *American Economic Review* 3 (1963): 433–443.

Myers, S. C. "Determinants of Corporate Borrowing." *Journal of Financial Economics* 5 (1977): 147–176.

Porter, M. *Competitive Advantage: Creating and Sustaining Superior Performance*. New York: Free Press, 1985.

Ross, S. A. "The Determination of Financial Structure: The Incentive-Signaling Approach." *Bell Journal of Economics* 8 (1977): 23–40.

Teece, D. "Economies of Scope and the Scope of the Enterprise." *Journal of Behavior and Organization* 1 (1980): 223–247.

Thomas, H., and N. Venkatraman. "Research on Strategic Groups: Progress and Prognosis." *Journal of Management Studies* 25 (1988): 537–555.

Williamson, O. W. *Corporate Control and Business Behavior*. Englewood Cliffs, N.J.: Prentice-Hall, 1970.

Williamson, O. W. *Markets and Hierarchies: Analysis and Antitrust Implications*. New York: Free Press, 1975.

Williamson, O. W. ''Corporate Finance and Corporate Governance.'' *Journal of Finance* 43 (1988): 567–591.

3

Capital Structure and Investment Opportunity Set: The Contingency of Multinationality

INTRODUCTION

The study employs a contingency perspective to examine the association between the investment opportunity set and corporate financing given different levels of multinationality. Theories of corporate financing have often emphasized the various roles of debt, including the tax advantage of debt, the choice of debt level to signal firm quality,[1,2] the use of debt as an antitakeover device,[3] the agency costs of debt,[4,5] and the usefulness of debt for restricting a managerial discretion.[6] There is, however, no consensus about which determinants have an impact on the capital structure decision, or how they affect performance.[7] We agree that Barton and Gordon's[8] suggestion to employ a managerial perspective will add to the understanding of the capital structure decision.

Specifically, we test whether the investment opportunity set is associated with corporate financing, and whether such an association varies over firms with different levels of multinationality. The analysis is conducted at the firm level to allow for more powerful tests than are possible at the industry level. In addition, composite measures of multinationality and the investment opportunity set are used to reduce classification errors in both variables. Specifically, a common factor analysis is used to create an index of multinationality (IOM) and an index of investment opportunity set (IOS). A covariance analysis of the market debt/equity ratio of our sample firms suggests that the investment opportunity set creates different corporate financing in firms that vary in terms of multinationality after controlling for size, changes in gross national product (GNP), inflation rate, and the index of business formation. In general, the findings support a contingency view of the association between the investment opportunity set and corporate financing.

BACKGROUND AND HYPOTHESES

Corporate Financing and the Investment Opportunity Set

Firms can be viewed as a combination of assets in place and future investment options. The lower the proportion of firm value represented by assets in place, the higher the growth opportunities. Myers[9] argued that for firms with growth or investment opportunity sets, the existence of risky debt, maturing after the investment option, causes the firm to forego profitable investment, resulting in an underinvestment scenario. Growth firms tend to issue less debt than firms without growth opportunities. As a result, prior empirical research in finance and accounting examining the cross-sectional differences in major corporate policy decisions relied on contracting cost explanations and presented empirical evidence regarding the relationship between the investment opportunity set and financing policies.[10,11] More evidence is provided in this chapter.

H_1: Growth firms have lower debt/equity than nongrowth firms.

Corporate Financing and Multinationality

Firms invest in physical and human capital internationally, thus determining their level of multinationality. Myers's theory can be expanded to explain how international conditions can lead a multinational corporation either to accelerate the shift from one financing method to the next or to rearrange the pecking order. A situation characterized by lower country risk, higher interest rates, expected strength of host county currency, blocked funds, and lower withholding and corporate taxes calls for a higher amount of external debt financing by the parent and a lower amount by the subsidiary, and vice versa. Where internal funding is not available to the parent, the same conditions that encourage use of debt financing by the subsidiary will result in a more debt-intensive capital structure for the multinational firm.[12] Another alternative explanation for the higher debt of multinational firms is that multinational firms, having diversified cash flows, may be able to support more debt. Accordingly,

H_2: High-multinationality firms have higher debt/equity ratios than low-multinationality firms.

METHODOLOGY

Data Analysis

Covariance analysis was used to test the overall relationship between (1) corporate financing and the investment opportunity set; (2) corporate financing and multinationality; and (3) the interaction of corporate financing, multinationality, and the investment opportunity set. The model's control variables are size, annual percentage changes in GNP as well as inflation rate, and the index of business formation.

Selection of Firms

The population consists of firms included in Forbes's Most International 100 U.S. manufacturing and service firms for the 1987 to 1992 period. The sample consists of firms that are either high on multinationality and investment opportunity set or low on both variables. Common factor analyses were used to create an index of multinationality and an index of investment opportunity set. Firm-year observations in the top quartiles of both indices were classified in a high-growth, high-multinationality sample and firm-year observations in the bottom quartile of both indices were classified in a low-growth, low-multinationality sample. The first sample of high-growth, high-multinationality included 80 firm-year observations, whereas the second sample of low-growth, low-multinationality included 121 firm-year observations.

Measuring Multinationality

Previous research has attempted to measure the following attributes of multi-nationality:

1. *Performance*, in terms of what goes on overseas;[13]
2. *Structure*, in terms of resources used overseas;[14] and
3. *Attitude or conduct*, in terms of top management's orientation.[15]

Sullivan[16] developed nine measures of which five were shown to have a high reliability in the construction of a homogeneous measure of nationality: (1) foreign sales as a percentage of total sales (FSTS), (2) foreign assets over total assets (FATA), (3) overseas subsidiaries as a percentage of total subsidiaries (OSTS), (4) top management's international experience (TMIE), and (5) psychic dispersion of international operations (PDIO).

In this study, we follow a similar approach by measuring multinationality through three measures: (1) foreign sales/total sales (FSTS), (2) foreign profits/total profits (FPTP), and (3) foreign assets/total assets (FATA).

Descriptive statistics and correlations among the three multinationality measures are shown in Exhibit 3.1. Correlations among the variables are positive and, with one exception, all significant. The nonsignificant correlation is between FPTP and FATA. The low correlations between FPTP, FSTS, and FATA indicate that each variable can make a unique contribution as a multinationality measure. Thus, a factor analysis of all observations is used to isolate the factor common to the three measures. Exhibit 3.2 reports the results. One common factor appears in the intercorrelations among the three variables, as the first

Exhibit 3.1
Descriptive Statistics and Correlations of Three Measures of Multinationality for Forbes's Most International 100 U.S. Firms for the 1987–92 Period

Panel A: Descriptive Statistics

	FP/TP[a]	FS/TS[b]	FA/TA[c]
Maximum	914.3	93	91
Third Quantile	61.9	47.4	41.4
Median	41.3	36.7	30.5
First Quantile	25	25.7	22.6
Minimum	0.2	6.6	2.7
Mean	52.81	37.45	39.92

	FP/TP	FS/TS	FA/TA
FP/TP	1.000		
FS/TS	0.280	1.000	
FA/TA	0.034	0.193*	1.000

* Denotes p-value < 0.05.
[a] FP/TP = Foreign profits/total profits.
[b] FS/TS = Foreign sales/total sales.
[c] FA/TA = Foreign assets/total assets.

eigenvalue value alone exceeds the sum of the commonalities. The common factor is significantly positively correlated with the three measures. As pointed out earlier, based on these factor scores, high-multinationality firms were chosen from the top 25% of the distribution factor scores, whereas low-multinationality firms were chosen from the bottom 25% of the distribution factor scores.

Measuring the Investment Opportunity Set

Because the investment opportunity set is not observable there has not been a consensus in an appropriate proxy variable. We use a set of three variables to measure the investment opportunity set: market-to-book assets (MASS), market-to-book equity (MQV), and the earnings/price ratio (EP). These variables are defined as follows:

$$MASS = (Assets - Total\ common\ equity + Shares\ outstanding \times Share\ closing\ price)/Assets$$

Exhibit 3.2
Selected Statistics Related to a Common Factor Analysis of Three Measures of Multinationality for Forbes's Most International 100 U.S. Firms for the 1987–92 Period

1. Eigenvalues of the Correlation Matrix:

Eigenvalues	1	2	3
	1.3615	0.9680	0.6705

2. Factor Pattern

    FACTOR1

FS/TS	FP/TP	FA/TA
0.80529	0.50172	0.67918

3. Final Communality Estimates: Total = 1.361489

FS/TS	FP/TP	FA/TA
0.648491	0.251718	0.461280

4. Standardized Scoring Coefficients

    FACTOR1

FS/TS	FP/TP	FA/TA
0.59148	0.36850	0.49885

5. Descriptive Statistics of the Common Factor Extracted from the Three

    Measures of Multinationality

Maximum	2039.24
Third Quartile	74.70
Median	57.03
First Quartile	40.76
Minimum	5.17
Mean	64.35

MQV = (Shares outstanding × Share closing price)/Total
      common equity
EP = [Primary earnings per share (EPS) before extraordinary items]/Share
     closing price

Descriptive statistics and correlation among the three measures of the investment opportunity set are in Exhibit 3.3. Correlations among the three variables
are significant. The low correlations indicate that each variable makes a unique
contribution as a measure of the investment opportunity set. The results of the
factor analysis are shown in Exhibit 3.4. One common factor appears to explain
the interrelations among the three individual measures. Based on these factor
scores, high-growth firms were chosen from the top 25% of the distribution
factor scores, whereas low-growth firms were chosen from the bottom 25% of
the distribution factor scores.

Exhibit 3.3
Descriptive Statistics and Correlation of Three Measures of the Investment
Opportunity Set for Forbes's Most International 100 U.S. Firms for the 1987–92
Period

Panel A: Descriptive Statistics

	MASS	MQV	EP
Maximum	6.4943	60	0.5175
Third Quartile	1.8556	3.1851	0.1081
Median	1.2905	1.9090	0.0713
First Quartile	1.0618	1.2666	0.0482
Minimum	0.8745	4.3333	2.1536
Mean	0.3081	2.7020	0.0638

Panel B: Correlation

	MASS	MQV	EP
Mass	1.000		
MQV	0.0399**	1.000	
EP	0.0158**	0.0230**	1.000

** Denotes p-value < 0.05.
MASS = Market-to-book assets.
MQV = Market-to-book equity.
EP = Earnings/Price ratio.

Exhibit 3.4
Selected Statistics Related to a Common Factor Analysis of Three Measures of the Investment Opportunity Set for Forbes's Most International 100 U.S. Firms for the 1987–92 Period

1.   Eigenvalues of the Correlation Matrix: Total = 3 Average = 1

Eigenvalues	1	2	3
	1.0540	0.9868	0.9592

2.   Factor Pattern

FACTOR1

MASS	MQV	EP
0.62821	0.66411	0.46722

3.   Final Communality Estimates: Total = 1.053994

MASS	MQV	EP
0.394651	0.441045	0.218299

4.   Standardized Scoring Coefficients

FACTOR1

MASS	MQV	EP
0.59603	0.63009	0.44329

5.   Descriptive Statistics of the Common Factor Extracted from the Three

Measures of the Investment Opportunity

Maximum	9.3595
Third Quartile	3.2200
Median	2.0450
First Quartile	1.5085
Minimum	2.5209
Means	1.9812

Corporate Financing

The central corporate financing measure used in this study is a time series of the ratio of market debt to equity over the 1987–92 period, computed as follows:

Market debt/equity = Total liabilities/(Shares outstanding × Share closing price)

Covariates

Covariates included the logarithm of total assets, annual percentage changes in gross national product and in inflation rate, and an index of net business formation. The logarithm of total assets was used to control for size. The other three covariates controlled for changes in corporate financing related to major shifts in aggregate demand. They also resulted in an analysis conditioned by macroeconomic variables. The macroeconomic variables were obtained from the *Economic Report of the President*.[17]

RESULTS

The effects on corporate financing of multinationality, the investment opportunity set and their interaction are first examined by an F-test of the difference between variances after controlling for the covariates.

Exhibit 3.5 presents the results of the covariance analysis for market debt/equity. The overall analysis of covariance is statistically significant ($F[7,200] = 4.30$, $p = 0.0002$, and $R^2 = 0.13$). A further nondirectional F-test for differences in variance indicates that (1) multinationality leads to a different capital structure and (2) the investment opportunity set of the sample firms is associated with cross-sectional differences in capital structure. A third interesting result is the significant interaction effect, which implies the investment opportunity set has a different impact depending on the multinationality level. The significance level of the covariates indicates that only size and the annual percentage changes in inflation are important controls.

Exhibit 3.6 presents the results of the mean comparisons of the debt/equity ratio by growth type and multinationality type. Hypothesis H_1 states that growth firms have a lower debt/equity ratio than nongrowth firms. This is supported by the results in Exhibit 3.6, which show a significant difference between the debt/equity ratio of high-growth firms (6.3886) and the debt/equity ratio of low-growth firms (11.215). Hypothesis H_2 states that high-multinationality firms have a higher debt/equity ratio than low-multinationality firms. This is also supported by the results in Exhibit 3.6, which show a significant difference between the high-multinationality firms (11.6732) and the low-multinationality firms (5.9107).

Exhibit 3.5
Results of Overall Analysis of Covariance for Market Debt/Equity Ratio

Sources	F	P
Multinationality	13.62	0.0003
Investment Opportunity Set	88.06	0.0001
Interaction	10.34	0.0025
Covariates		
Size (Log of Assets)	69.21	0.0001
Annual Percentage Changes in GNP	0.08	0.7715
Annual Percentage Changes in Inflation	2.95	0.0875
Index of Business Formation	0.23	0.6337

Exhibit 3.7 presents the interaction effects of means. The exhibit illustrates that significant differences between the debt/equity ratio of high-growth firms and low-growth firms (as stated in H_1) holds under both high-multinationality and low-multinationality conditions, but at an increased level for high multinationality (as hypothesized in H_2).

DISCUSSION

Our central proposition is that the investment opportunity set is associated with different capital structures in firms that have different levels of multinationality. The results support this contingency view of the relationship between the investment opportunity set and corporate financing.

Hypothesis 1 was confirmed: growth firms have lower debt/equity ratios than nongrowth firms. These results suggest that contracting cost explanations for corporate financing imply these decisions depend on the firm's investment opportunity set. Variation in the investment opportunity set leads to differences in the optimality of corporate financing with growth firms pursuing a lower debt/ equity ratio than nongrowth firms.

Hypothesis 2 was confirmed, high-multinationality firms have higher debt/ equity ratios than low-multinationality firms. Multinational conditions call for more of a debt-intensive capital structure.

Exhibit 3.6
Mean Analysis

Panel A:
By Multinationality

Treatment	Mean	Standard Deviation	t-Probability
1. High Multinationality	11.6732	1.1741	0.0003
2. Low Multinationality	5.9107	1.0340	

Panel B:
By Growth

Treatment	Mean	Standard Deviation	t-Probability
1. High Growth	6.3886	1.3492	0.0164
2. Low Growth	11.2153	1.1889	

The results also show a link between capital structure, the investment opportunity set, and multinationality. At different multinationality levels, different investment opportunity sets influence capital structure strategies.

These results complement and add to the strategic-growth paradigm. Based on a firm's heterogeneous capabilities and resources, the strategic-group paradigm enables researchers and practitioners to consolidate industrial firms into sets of similar competitors, the so-called strategic groups. Although a more comprehensive review of the literature is provided by McGee and Thomas,[18] Thomas and Venkatraman,[19] and Barney and Hoskisson,[20] the results of this study indicate that the strategic linkages between multinationality and the investment opportunity set need to be taken into account in the formation of strategic groups. Better strategic groups could be identified by a simultaneous consideration of multinationality and the investment opportunity set.

Additional research is needed to verify the results of this study and test questions that it raises. Replication needs to consider using different data and different measures of multinationality and investment opportunity set, as well as using a control group of essentially domestic firms. Until further research is

Exhibit 3.7
Mean Comparisons of Market Debt/Equity Means of Multinationality and by Investment Opportunity Sets and *t*-Probabilities

Panel A: Means

Treatments		High Multinationality	Low Multinationality
1.	High Investment Opportunity Set	7.9052	4.8320
2.	Low Investment Opportunity Set	15.4411	6.9895

Panel B: t-Probability of Mean Comparisons

Treatments	1. Low Multinationality/ Low Investment Opportunity Set	2. Low Multinationality/ High Investment Opportunity Set	3. High Multinationality/ Low Investment Opportunity Set	4. High Multinationality/ High Investment Opportunity Set
1. Low Multinationality/ Low Investment Opportunity Set				
2. Low Multinationality/ High Investment Opportunity Set	0.0520			
3. High Multinationality/ Low Investment Opportunity Set	0.0001	0.0002		
4. High Multinationality/ High Investment Opportunity Set	0.0884	0.0870	0.0073	

completed, the results of the leverage differences must be interpreted with caution.

NOTES

1. S. A. Ross, "The Determination of Financial Structure: The Incentive-Signaling Approach," *Bell Journal of Economics* 8 (1977): 23–40.

2. H. Leland and D. Pyle, "Informational Asymmetries, Financial Structure, and Financial Intermediation," *Journal of Finance* 32 (1977): 371–387.

3. M. Harris and A. Raviv, "Corporate Control Contests and Capital Structure," *Journal of Financial Economics* 20 (1988): 55–86.

4. M. C. Jensen and W. H. Meckling, "Theory of the Firm: Managerial Behavior Agency Costs and Ownership Structure," *Journal of Financial Economics* 3 (1976): 305–360.

5. S. C. Myers, "Determinants of Corporate Borrowing," *Journal of Financial Economics* 5 (1977): 147–176.

6. M. C. Jensen, "Agency Costs of Free Cash Flow, Corporate Finance, and Takeovers," *American Economic Review* 76 (1986): 323–329.

7. S. C. Myers, "The Capital Structure Puzzle," *Journal of Finance* 39 (1984): 575–591.

8. S. L. Barton and P. J. Gordon, "Corporate Strategy: Useful Perspective for the Study of Capital Structure?" *Academy of Management Review* 12 (1987): 67–75.

9. Myers, "Determinants of Corporate Borrowing."

10. J. J. Gaver and K. M. Gaver, "Additional Evidence on the Association between the Investment Opportunity Set and Corporate Financial Dividend, and Compensation Policies," *Journal of Accounting and Economics* 16 (1993): 125–160.

11. C. W. Smith and R. L. Watts, "The Investment Opportunity Set and Corporate Financing, Dividend and Compensation Policies," *Journal of Financial Economics* 32 (1992): 236–292.

12. Jeff Madura, *International Financial Management* (St. Paul, Minn.: West Publishing Company, 1995).

13. John H. Dunning, "Reappraising the Electric Paradigm in an Age of Alliance Capitalism," *Journal of International Business Studies* 26 (1995): 461–492.

14. John M. Stopford and Louis T. Wells, *Managing the Multinational Enterprise* (New York: Basic Books, 1972).

15. Howard V. Perlmutter, "The Tortuous Evaluation of the Multinational Corporation," *Columbia Journal of World Business* 4 (January–February 1969): 9–18.

16. D. Sullivan, "Measuring the Degree of Internationalization of a Firm," *Journal of International Business Studies* 25 (1994): 325–342.

17. *Economic Report of the President* (Washington, D.C.: U.S. Government Printing Office, 1995).

18. J. McGee and H. Thomas, "Strategic Groups: Theory, Research and Taxonomy," *Strategic Management Journal* 7 (1986): 141–160.

19. H. Thomas and N. Venkatraman, "Research on Strategic Groups: Progress and Prognosis," *Journal of Management Studies* 25 (1988): 537–555.

20. J. B. Barney and R. E. Hoskisson, "Untested Assertions in Strategic Group Research," *Managerial and Decision Economics* 11 (1990): 187–198.

SELECTED READINGS

Ang, J., J. Chua, and J. McConnell. "The Administrative Costs of Corporate Bankruptcy: A Note." *Journal of Finance* 37 (1982): 219–226.

Barton, S. L., and P. J. Gordon. "Corporate Strategy: Useful Perspective for the Study of Capital Structure?" *Academy of Management Review* 12 (1987): 67–75.

Belkaoui, A. "A Canadian Survey of Financial Structure." *Financial Management* 4 (1975): 74–79.

Gaver, J. J., and K. M. Gaver. "Additional Evidence on the Association between the Investment Opportunity Set and Corporate Financing Dividend, and Compensation Policies." *Journal of Accounting and Economics* 16 (1993): 125–160.

Harris, M., and A. Raviv. "Corporate Control Contests and Capital Structure." *Journal of Financial Economics* 20 (1988): 55–86.

Jensen, M. C. "Agency Costs of Free Cash Flow, Corporate Finance, and Takeovers." *American Economic Review* 76 (1986): 323–329.

Jensen, M. C., and W. H. Meckling. "Theory of the Firm: Managerial Behavior Agency Costs and Ownership Structure." *Journal of Financial Economics* 3 (1976): 305–360.

Leland, H., and D. Pyle. "Informational Asymmetries, Financial Structure, and Financial Intermediation." *Journal of Finance* 32 (1977): 371–387.

Madura, Jeff. *International Financial Management*. St. Paul, Minn.: West Publishing Company, 1995.

Myers, S. C. "Determinants of Corporate Borrowing." *Journal of Financial Economics* 5 (1977): 147–176.

Myers, S. C. "The Capital Structure Puzzle." *Journal of Finance* 39 (1984): 575–591.

Myers, S. C., and N. Majluf. "Corporate Financing and Investment Decisions when Firms Have Information Investors Do Not Have." *Journal of Financial Economics* 13 (1984): 187–221.

Perlmutter, Howard V. "The Tortuous Evaluation of the Multinational Corporation." *Columbia Journal of World Business* 4 (January–February 1969): 9–18.

Ross, S. A. "The Determination of Financial Structure: The Incentive-Signaling Approach." *Bell Journal of Economics* 8 (1977): 23–40.

Scott, J. "Bankruptcy, Secured Debt, and Optimal Capital Structure." *Journal of Finance* 32 (1977): 1–19.

Sullivan, D. "Measuring the Degree of Internationalization of a Firm." *Journal of International Business Studies* 25 (1994): 325–342.

Thomas, H., and N. Venkatraman. "Research on Strategic Groups: Progress and Prognosis." *Journal of Management Studies* 25 (1988): 537–555.

Warner, J. "Bankruptcy Costs: Some Evidence." *Journal of Finance* 32 (1977): 337–347.

4

The Evaluation of Capital Structure: The Prediction of Industrial Bond Ratings

INTRODUCTION

The best known measures of prospective bond quality are the bond ratings assigned by the three agencies: Moody's, Standard and Poor's, and Fitch. Their ratings provide a judgment of the investment quality of a long-term obligation and a measure of default risk. Accordingly, they may affect the interest rate an organization pays on its bonds. Although each rating agency has defined the meaning of its ratings, the agencies have not explicitly specified the process they use to arrive at these ratings. Given the importance of ratings, various authors have attempted to explain and predict them based on the financial and/or statistical characteristics of the bonds and the issuing firms. These rating prediction studies were reviewed in the previous chapter. Although the models derived do an adequate job of capturing the human judgments of bond raters, they suffer from (a) a diversity of approaches used in selecting independent variables for the regression, discriminant, or multivariate probit models; (b) a lack of an "economic rationale" underlying the choice of these variables;[1] (c) a failure to account for the differences among the companies in their accounting for long-term leases; and (d) the confusion of ex ante predictive power with ex post discrimination. Consequently this study corrects for these limitations to develop a multiple discrimination bond-rating model.

ECONOMIC RATIONALE[2]

A bond rating is primarily a judgment of the investment quality of a firm's long-term obligation. It reflects the raters' expectations and estimates of the relevant characteristics of the quality of the investment. To capture the determinants of bond ratings, these characteristics of the investment quality must be identified and rationalized on an economic basis.

The investment quality of a bond is determined by the interaction among three general variables: firm-, market-, and indenture-related variables.

The firm-related variables depict the ability of the firm to provide adequate protection for the bondholders. This ability depends on both size and coverage factors. The size factor allows rating of the bonds in terms of the security it provides. The security itself is a function of the firm's command over total resources. Going from the most aggregate expression to the least aggregate expression, the command over total resources depends on (1) the total size of the firm, (2) the total size of the debt, (3) the long-term capital intensiveness, and (4) the short-term capital intensiveness. Thus, variables expressing each of these determinants of the size factor should be included in a bond-rating model.

The coverage factor allows rating of bonds in terms of the ability of the firm to service the financial changes. Thus, although the size factor is concerned with stock considerations, the coverage factor is concerned with the ability of the firm to service the financial resources. Going from the most aggregate to the least aggregate, the flow of financial resources depends on (1) the total actual liquidity of the firm, (2) the debt coverage, and (3) the future liquidity of the firm. Thus, variables expressing each of these determinants of the coverage factor should be included in any bond-rating model.

The market-related variables depict the ability of the firm to create a favorable market response to all its securities. They reflect the investors' expectations in the aggregate about the firms' performance. Thus, variables expressing measures of investors' expectations about the firm's profitability should be included in any bond-rating model.

The indenture-related variables depict the relevant covenants and terms of the indenture; that is, the basic legal document constituting the contract between the bondholders and the bond issuer. They are deemed very important in bond rating.[3] In spite of the possible difficulties of operationalizing them, variables expressing relevant covenants of the indenture should also be included in any bond-rating model.

DEVELOPMENT OF THE MODEL

Method

To avoid the limitations of the studies surveyed in Chapter 3, the following methodology is used.

First, the bond-rating model is based on a multiple discriminant model. Because bonds convey ordinal information (an AAA bond is more secure than an AA bond, which is more secure than an A bond, etc.), the multiple discriminant and the multivariate probit models are more appropriate than the regression model. And as seen in the Kaplan and Urwitz study,[4] the regression model seems more robust than the multivariate probit model, which leaves the multiple discriminant model as the most appropriate.

Second, to avoid confusing between tests of validation or classification efficiency and tests of prediction the following steps are used.[5]

The first step is to "fit" a discriminant function over a sample of firms A_1 from the data collected in 1981. This sample is the analysis sample.

The second step is to use the linear discrimination function obtained in the first step to classify firms of a time-coincident holdout or validation sample A_2. This sample A_2 of firms with data collected in 1981 is the validation sample. This step has been confused in other studies with prediction. Ex post discrimination may provide a useful foundation for explanation of the past, but it does not provide sufficient evidence for concluding that the future can be predicted.[6]

Assuming successful ex post discrimination, the explanatory significance of the financial variables (independent variables) is investigated using both samples A_1 and A_2 from 1981 data; that is, the samples are recombined to form an estimation sample and a new linear discriminant model for the total 1981 sample, which is estimated. This involves merely a reestimation of the coefficients and not a search for variables.

The next step is to use the linear discriminant model, obtained as just explained, to classify sample B observations from another year, in this case from 1980. As stated correctly: "Prediction thus requires intertemporal validation whereas explanation requires only cross validation."[7]

Both cross-validation (the second step) and intertemporal validation (preceding paragraph) will yield a classification matrix showing the hit rate for the model. Similar to all the previous studies, the success of the prediction is measured by the hit rate; that is, the percentage of industrial bonds correctly classified.

Sample Selection

As explained in the preceding sections, four randomly selected samples of industrial bonds rated B or above by Standard and Poor's are used.[8]

1. An analysis sample of 266 industrial bonds rated B or above by Standard and Poor's in 1981.

2. A validation sample of 115 industrial bonds rated B or above by Standard and Poor's in 1981.

3. An estimation sample of 381 industrial bonds rated B or above by Standard and Poor's in 1981. The estimation sample is a combination of the analysis and validation samples. The year 1981 was used to ensure that all firms represented have a uniform accounting treatment of financial leases following the Financial Accounting Standard Board Statement 13, "Accounting for leases," effective since 1976.

4. A control sample of 388 industrial bonds rated B or above by Standard and Poor's in 1980.[9]

Exhibit 4.1 provides a brief summary of the exact composition of the total sample. Thirty-seven industries are represented in each of the samples (aerospace, airlines, appliances, automotive, beverages, building materials, chemicals, conglomerates, containers, drugs, electrical and electronics, food processing, food and lodging, general machinery, instruments, leisure time industries, metals and mining, miscellaneous manufacturing, natural resources [fuel], office equipment and computers, oil service and supply, paper, personal care products, publishing, radio and TV broadcasting, railroads, real estate and housing, retailing [food], retailing [nonfood], service industries, special machinery, steel textiles and apparel, tire and rubber, tobacco, trucking, and utilities).

Variables in the Multiple Discriminant Model

Nine variables were selected to be included in the multiple discriminant model as representative of the factors identified in the economic rationale section.

X_1 = *Total assets*, included as representative of the total size of the firm.

X_2 = *Total debt*, included as a measure of the total indebtedness of the firm.

X_3 = *Long-term debt/total invested capital*, included as a measure of the long-term capital intensiveness of the firm. By invested capital we mean the sum of the total debt, preferred stock, and common equity (which includes common stocks, capital surplus, and retained earnings).

X_4 = *Short-term debt/total invested capital*, included as a measure of the short-term capital intensiveness of the firm.

X_5 = *Current assets/current liabilities*, included as a measure of the total liquidity of the firm.

X_6 = *Fixed charge coverage ratio*: net income plus total interest expense (adjusted by tax rate)/interest expense (adjusted by tax rate) plus preferred dividend requirement; included as a measure of debt coverage.

X_7 = *Five-year cash flow as percentage of five-year growth needs*: five-year sum of (1) net income available for common stockholders; plus (2) depreciation and amortization; plus (3) income from discontinued operations and extraordinary items net of taxes divided by five-year sum of (a) capital expenditures, plus (b) change in inventories during most recent five years (except utilities), plus (c) common dividends; included as a measure of future liquidity.

X_8 = *Stock price/common equity per share*, included as a measure of investors' expectations.

X_9 = *Subordination* (0–1), included as a measure of the most relevant covenant in the indenture.

These nine variables are, in general, different from the variables used in previous corporate industrial bond-rating models. Exhibit 4.2 presents a comparative analysis of the variables used in these studies. Most of the variables and

Exhibit 4.1
Sample Size of Industrial Corporate Bonds

1980 RATINGS	ANALYSIS SAMPLE 1981		VALIDATION SAMPLE 1981		ESTIMATING SAMPLE 1981		CONTROL SAMPLE	
	Numbers	%	Numbers	%	Numbers	%	Numbers	%
AAA	13	4.88	6	5.21	19	4.98	20	5.15
AA	51	19.17	17	14.78	68	17.84	99	25.51
A	112	42.10	35	30.43	147	38.58	140	36.08
BBB	51	19.17	30	26.08	81	21.25	50	12.88
BB	9	3.38	20	17.39	29	7.61	40	10.30
B	30	11.27	7	6.08	37	9.71	39	10.05
Total	266	100	115	100	381	100	388	100

Exhibit 4.2
Comparative Analysis of Variables Used in Bond-Rating Models

RATIO	THIS STUDY	HORRIGAN	WEST	PINCHES AND MINGO	KAPLAN AND URWITZ
1. Total size of the firm	Total assets	Total assets	Not used	Not used	Total assets
2. Total size of the debt	Total debt	Not used	Bonds outstanding	Not used	Not used
3. Long-term capital intensiveness	Long-term debt as a percentage of total invested capital	Net worth over total debt	Debt equity ratio	Long-term debt over total assets	a. Long-term debt over total assets b. Long-term debt over net worth
4. Short-term capital intensiveness	Short-term debt as a percentage of total invested capital	Not used	Not used	Not used	Not used
5. Actual liquidity	Current ratio	Working capital over sales	Not used	Not used	Not used
6. Debt coverage	Fixed charge coverage ratio	Not used	Not used	Five-year mean of net income plus interest charge over	a. Cash flow before interest and taxes over interest

					interest charge	b. Cash flow before interest and taxes over total debt
7.	Future liquidity	Five-year cash flow as a percentage of five-year growth needs	Not used	Not used	Not used	Not used
8.	Investors' expectations	Stock price as a percentage of book value	Not used	Not used	Not used	Accounting and market betas
9.	Indenture provision	Subordination status	Subordination status	Not used	Subordination status	Subordination status
10.	Others	Not used	Sales over net worth	Period of solving	Years of consecutive dividends	Net income over total assets
11.	Others	Not used	Net operating profit	Nine-year earnings	Net income over total assets	Coefficients of variations of total assets
12.	Others	Not used	Not used	Not used	Issue size	Issue size
13.	Others	Not used	Not used	Not used	Not used	Coefficient of variations of net income

51

factors used in this study are absent in the other models due mainly to the absence of an economic rationale in their choice of variables. For example, measures of investors' expectations and short-term capital intensiveness are used in only two models (this study and Kaplan and Urwitz's); short-term capital intensiveness is used only in this study; actual liquidity is used in only two models (this study and Horrigan's); future liquidity is used only in this study; only long-term capital intensiveness is used in all models.

Discriminant Analysis Results on the Analysis Sample

The overall discriminating power of the model using the analysis sample was accomplished by testing for differences in the group centroids. The overall F value for the model $F = 20.25$ ($p < 0.001$) permits rejection of the null hypothesis that the differences in the group centroids of the six bond rating groups was zero. This result justifies an examination of the discriminating power of each of the nine independent variables. Exhibit 4.3 presents the means and univariate F ratios for all nine variables by bond-rating groups. All the variables were significant. From a univariate point of view and on the basis of the magnitude of the F ratio, we can state that subordination status is the most important variable, followed by short-term debt over invested capital, total assets, fixed change coverage ratio, total debt, long-term debt over total invested capital, stock price over book value, and five-year cash flow over five-year growth needs.

The independent variables were examined for multicollinearity. Exhibit 4.4 shows the correlation matrix for all the variables. The intercorrelations (average $r = 0.0146$) are not judged large enough to produce a basis for the estimation of the parameters of the model.

A stepwise multiple discriminant analysis was used to determine the discriminant functions. The BMDP7M program was used for the task.[10] Exhibit 4.5 shows the obtained six functions. Based on Wilks's lambda and its associated chi square, the six functions were found to be significant. Exhibit 4.6 presents the pairs of values for the test of significance of the Mahalanobias distance between groups.[11] All the F values were significant, which permits one to reject the null hypothesis that the pairs of group centroids are equal at the 0.01 level.

To determine the relative importance of the variables in the model, four criteria were used.[12] The rank ordering of the nine variables according to the univariate F ratio, the forward and backward stepwise methods, and the scale-weighted method are shown in Exhibit 4.7. The univariate F ratio and the stepwise forward methods show subordination to be the most important and the future liquidity ratio to be the least important. The stepwise backward method shows the long-term debt ratio to be the most important, followed by subordination, and the total assets to be the least important. Finally, the scale-weighted method shows the subordination to be the most important, followed by the current ratio, and the total debt to be the least important. Before evaluating the

Exhibit 4.3
Variable Means and Test of Significance (Analysis Sample)*

VARIABLE	BOND RATING						F^{**}
	AAA	AA	A	BBB	BB	B	
X_1	18433.72	5447.61	2056.82	2263.99	716.43	609.71	29.48
X_2	5655.25	1143.26	533.93	757.16	257.67	277.62	8.01
X_3	15.50	20.40	29.33	37.77	37.59	48.81	6.92
X_4	5.33	9.00	4.35	8.93	4.45	6.03	31.21
X_5	1.65	1.60	1.92	1.61	1.98	1.89	2.92
X_6	19.76	8.75	6.93	4.70	5.91	3.79	14.38
X_7	88.19	83.03	82.26	72.36	58.42	69.55	2.88
X_8	132.28	149.13	108.62	89.74	200.37	148.40	5.90
X_9	1.00	1.00	0.99	0.80	0.11	0.00	157.55

* $\alpha = 9.260$.

** All the F values are significant at the 0.05 level of significance.

Exhibit 4.4
Correlation Coefficients over the Nine Variables (Analysis Sample)

VARIABLE	X_1	X_2	X_3	X_4	X_5	X_6	X_7	X_8	X_9
X_1	1.000								
X_2	0.739	1.000							
X_3	-0.068	0.094	1.000						
X_4	0.078	0.002	-0.200	1.000					
X_5	-0.261	-0.202	-0.356	-0.216	1.000				
X_6	-0.030	-0.090	-0.534	-0.203	0.350	1.000			
X_7	0.044	-0.055	-0.346	0.046	0.316	0.304	1.000		
X_8	-0.054	-0.051	-0.048	0.007	0.218	0.291	-0.050	1.000	
X_9	0.206	0.069	-0.358	-0.008	-0.143	0.141	0.163	-0.226	1.000

Exhibit 4.5
Discriminant Functions (Analysis Sample)

			BOND RATING			
VARIABLE	AAA	AA	A	BBB	BB	B
X_1	0.00091	0.00039	0.00025	0.00024	0.00026	0.00024
X_2	0.00028	-0.000020	-0.000022	-0.00009	-0.00015	-0.00024
X_3	0.48955	0.49510	0.59913	0.73207	0.75037	0.92494
X_4	0.68989	0.72489	0.65544	0.86627	0.73371	0.87970
X_5	7.69142	6.89274	8.15657	8.52282	9.35400	10.20789
X_6	1.03822	0.66162	0.64337	0.68019	0.54337	0.58578
X_7	0.02869	0.04225	0.04496	0.04496	0.04309	0.06080
X_8	0.01764	0.02030	0.01049	0.00378	0.01593	0.00386
X_9	28.47068	26.72795	25.09872	18.84681	0.38142	-4.60076
Constant	-48.13343	-34.42768	-36.42350	-35.75230	-129.57942	-38.46189

Exhibit 4.6
Pairs of *F* Values for the Test of Significance of the Mahalanobias Distance between Groups (Analysis Sample)

GROUP	AAA	AA	A	BBB	BB
AA	13.81				
A	24.14	9.85			
BBB	29.25	19.35	11.91		
BB	29.46	24.36	21.30	12.28	
B	67.91	91.85	91.45	43.87	2.54

Degrees of freedom= 9,252.

classification accuracy of the model, the equality of the covariance matrices among the six bond-rating groups was tested using Box's *M* and its associated *F*-test.[13] The resulting *F* value of 1.03 is not significant at the 0.05 level, resulting in the acceptance of the null hypothesis of equal covariance matrices and supporting the use of linear rather than quadratic classification rules. Similarly, we employed equal prior probabilities for classification, based on the belief that the distribution of bonds in the population is either unstable or unknown and that the main objective is evaluation of the importance of the variables included in the model without any consideration of prior probabilities.

Finally, the multiple discrimination model was used to classify the experimental group of bonds from which it was developed, based on the probability of group membership. The classification matrix for the analysis sample is shown in Exhibit 4.8. The total number of correctly classified bonds is obtained by summing the upper left–lower right diagonal of the classification matrix in Exhibit 4.8. This shows that the multiple discriminant analysis correctly classified 72.93% (194/266) of the firms. The model performs better for some of the individual categories, AAA (76.92%), AA (74.51%), A (80.36%), BBB (54.90%), BB (66.67%), and B (73.33%).

Validation

As stated earlier, ex post discrimination or cross-validation consists of classifying firms of a time-coincident holdout or validation sample using the discriminant functions obtained from the analysis sample. Another reason for validation is the need to check for possible biases due to sampling errors and search. Thus, the multiple discriminant model obtained with the analysis sample of 1981 was used to classify firms from a validation sample of 1981. The classified results are shown in Exhibit 4.9. The model correctly rated 67.8% of the firms in the validation sample. Using the *Z* statistic of Mosteller and Bush,[14] the

Exhibit 4.7
Variable Importance Ranked According to Different Criteria

VARIABLE	UNIVARIATE FRATIO	STEPWISE FORWARD	STEPWISE BACKWARD	SCALE WEIGHTED
X_1	3	2	9	8
X_2	5	8	3	9
X_3	2	3	1	5
X_4	6	4	5	4
X_5	8	7	6	2
X_6	4	5	4	3
X_7	9	9	8	2
X_8	7	6	7	7
X_9	1	1	2	1

Exhibit 4.8
Classification Table (Analysis Sample)

FROM GROUP	NUMBER OF OBSERVATIONS (AND PERCENTAGES) CLASSIFIED INTO GROUPS						TOTAL
	AAA	AA	A	BBB	BB	B	
AAA	10 (76.92)	2 (15.38)	1 (7.69)	0 (0.00)	0 (0.00)	0 (0.00)	13 (100.00)
AA	6 (11.76)	38 (74.51)	7 (13.73)	0 (0.00)	0 (0.00)	0 (0.00)	51 (100.00)
A	1 (0.89)	10 (8.93)	90 (80.36)	10 (8.93)	1 (0.89)	0 (0.00)	112 (100.00)
BBB	1 (1.96)	1 (1.96)	12 (23.53)	28 (54.90)	6 (11.76)	3 (5.88)	51 (100.00)
BB	0 (0.00)	0 (0.00)	0 (0.00)	2 (22.22)	5 (66.67)	2 (22.22)	9 (100.00)
B	0 (0.00)	0 (0.00)	0 (0.00)	0 (0.00)	8 (26.67)	22 (73.33)	30 (100.00)

Exhibit 4.9
Classification Table (Validation Sample)

FROM CLASSIFIED INTO GROUPS GROUP	NUMBER OF OBSERVATIONS (AND PERCENTAGES)					
	AAA	AA	TOTAL A	BBB	BB	B
AAA	2 6 (0.00)	4 (0.33) (1.00)	0 (0.67)	0 (0.00)	0 (0.00)	0 (0.00)
AA	0 (0.00)	5 17 (0.29) (1.00)	12 (0.71)	0 (0.00)	0 (0.00)	0 (0.00)
A	0 (0.00)	0 35 (0.00) (1.00)	0 (0.00)	25 (0.71)	0 (0.00)	10 (0.28)
BBB	0 (0.00)	0 30 (0.00) (1.00)	0 (0.00)	3 (0.10)	21 (0.70)	6 (0.20)
BB	3 (0.15)	0 20 (0.00) (1.00)	0 (0.00)	0 (0.00)	4 (0.20)	13 (0.65)
B	5 (0.71)	0 7 (0.00) (1.00)	0 (0.00)	0 (0.00)	0 (0.00)	2 (0.28)

Exhibit 4.10
Comparison of the Validation Classification

STUDY	% CORRECT VALIDATION SAMPLE
Pinches and Mingo	65 and 56
Horrigan	59
West	60
Belkaoui	65.9
This study	67.8

null hypothesis that the results are due to chance is rejected, confirming the previous discriminating power results of the model. Exhibit 4.9 shows the hit rate for the nine categories. A final interesting result appearing in Exhibit 4.10 is the higher validation results presented by this study approach. As stated earlier, validation should not be confused with prediction. Validation merely provides sufficient evidence for concluding that the future can be predicted. Accordingly, in what follows, the discriminant model is reestimated on the basis of the total sample of 1981 (analysis plus validation samples) and is then applied to a sample of 1980 to test its predictive ability.

Estimating the Model's Linear Discriminant Functions

Given the successful ex post discrimination, the explanatory significance of the independent variables is investigated, using both the analysis and the validation samples from 1981. That is, the samples are recombined to form a total 1981 sample, and new linear discriminant functions are fitted. This step is merely a reestimation of the coefficients and not a new search for variables.

The overall discrimination power of the model based on the total 1981 sample was accomplished by testing for differences in the group centroids. The overall F value for the model of $F = 20.32$ ($p < 0.001$) permits rejection of the null hypothesis that the difference in the group centroids of the six bond-rating groups was zero. This result again justifies an examination of the discriminating power of each of the nine independent variables. Exhibit 4.11 presents the means and univariate F ratios for all nine variables by bond-rating group.

All the variables were found to be significant. The nine dependent variables were again examined for multicollinearity. Exhibit 4.12 shows the correlations matrix for all variables. The intercorrelations (average $r = 0.021$) are not judged large enough to produce a bias in the estimation of the parameters of the model.

A stepwise discriminant analysis based on the BMDP7M program was again used to determine the discriminant functions. Exhibit 4.13 shows the multiple discriminant functions for each rating group. Based on Wilks's lambda and its associated chi square, the six functions were found to be significant. Exhibit 4.14 presents the pairs of F values for the test of significance of the Mahalanobias distance between groups. All the F values were significant, which permits one to again reject the null hypothesis that the pairs of group centroids are equal to the 0.01 level.

To determine the relative importance of the variables in the models, four criteria were again used. The rank ordering of the nine variables according to the univariate F ratio, the forward and backward stepwise methods, and the scale-weighted method is shown in Exhibit 4.15. Similar to the analysis performed on the experimental sample, the rank ordering of the nine variables differs from one method to another. Before evaluating the classification accuracy of the model, the equality of the covariance matrices among the six bond-rating groups was tested using Box's M and its associated F-test. The resulting F value

Exhibit 4.11
Variable Means and Tests of Significance (Estimation Sample)

VARIABLE	BOND RATING						F VALUE
	AAA	AA	A	BBB	BB	B	
X_1	13632.415	5541.445	2100.367	1746.706	1084.565	696.059	25.164
X_2	4009.726	1097.522	554.030	581.456	367.962	987.135	7.359
X_3	13.963	18.954	28.224	37.165	41.775	47.856	50.471
X_4	5.952	8.414	4.419	7.816	6.324	5.808	6.250
X_5	1.778	1.564	1.962	1.781	1.962	1.856	2.214
X_6	17.589	10.817	7.099	4.720	4.100	3.775	15.943
X_7	89.373	85.539	81.278	76.912	63.765	67.348	3.302
X_8	144.494	147.080	110.247	102.406	155.813	141.427	4.132
X_9	0.947	0.985	0.911	0.617	0.344	0.054	58.732

Degrees of freedom = 5,375.
F values significant at $\alpha = 0.05$.

Exhibit 4.12
Correlation Coefficients over the Nine Variables (Estimation Sample)

VARIABLE	X_1	X_2	X_3	X_4	X_5	X_6	X_7	X_8	X_9
X_1	1.000								
X_2	0.063	1.000							
X_3	-0.137	0.063	1.000						
X_4	0.051	0.028	-0.155	1.000					
X_5	-0.259	-0.215	-0.271	-0.215	1.000				
X_6	0.102	-0.045	-0.513	-0.184	0.152	1.000			
X_7	0.020	-0.055	-0.361	0.042	0.284	0.251	1.000		
X_8	-0.088	-0.060	-0.022	-0.035	0.074	0.206	-0.0008	1.000	
X_9	0.206	0.108	-0.280	0.069	-0.079	0.008	0.101	-0.185	1.000

63

Exhibit 4.13
Discriminant Functions (Estimation Sample)

VARIABLE	FUNCTIONS					
	AAA	AA	A	BBB	BB	B
X_1	0.000737	0.000431	0.00269	0.000250	0.000265	0.000242
X_2	0.000119	-0.000147	-0.000149	-0.000233	-0.000295	-0.000357
X_3	0.44234	0.48229	0.58069	0.71530	0.76589	0.85499
X_4	0.62823	0.67906	0.60516	0.79864	0.80544	0.84459
X_5	7.26898	6.80279	7.832642	8.35763	9.15411	9.24043
X_6	0.68425	0.54641	0.48850	0.50766	0.48010	0.49208
X_7	0.06102	0.06600	0.06777	0.07116	0.05952	0.06970
X_8	0.01802	0.01687	0.00809	0.00235	0.00705	0.00099
X_9	10.26302	9.76648	8.78782	4.27079	1.69732	-1.73660
Constant	-31.6004	-26.0425	-26.1304	-29.3824	-31.3397	-34.8229

F statistic = 16.492.

of 1.05 is not significant at the 0.05 level, leading to the acceptance of the null hypothesis of equal covariance matrices and supporting the use of linear rather than quadratic classification rules. Similarly, we employed equal probabilities for classification.

Finally, the multiple discriminant model was used to classify the total estimation sample of bonds, from which it was developed, based on the probability of group membership. The classification matrix for the estimation sample is shown in Exhibit 4.16. The total number of correctly classified bonds is obtained by summing the upper left–lower right diagonal of the classified matrix in Exhibit 4.16, which shows that the multiple discriminant analysis correctly classified 67.19% (256/381) of the firms. The model performs differently for the

Exhibit 4.14
Pairs of F Values for the Test of Significance of the Mahalanobias (Estimation Sample)

GROUP	AAA	AA	A	BBB	BB
AA	7.32				
A	19.86	13.79			
BBB	30.86	31.89	16.51		
BB	30.80	29.63	17.71	3.47	
B	48.50	59.90	44.72	13.45	2.51

Degrees of freedom = 9,367.

Exhibit 4.15
Variable Importance Ranked According to Different Criteria (Estimation Sample)

VARIABLE	UNIVARIATE F RATIO	STEPWISE FORWARD	STEPWISE BACKWARD	SCALE WEIGHTED
X_1	3	3	3	8
X_2	5	8	4	9
X_3	2	2	2	5
X_4	6	4	7	4
X_5	9	6	9	2
X_6	4	7	5	3
X_7	8	9	6	6
X_8	7	5	8	7
X_9	1	1	1	1

Exhibit 4.16
Classification Table (Estimation Sample)

FROM GROUP	NUMBER OF OBSERVATIONS (AND PERCENTAGES) CLASSIFIED INTO GROUPS						TOTAL
	AAA	AA	A	BBB	BB	B	
AAA	9 (.47)	10 (.52)	0 (0.00)	0 (0.00)	0 (0.00)	0 (0.00)	19 (1.00)
AA	11 (0.16)	45 (0.66)	11 (0.16)	0 (0.00)	0 (0.00)	0 (0.00)	68 (1.00)
A	1 (0.006)	13 (0.088)	118 (0.80)	9 (0.061)	5 (0.034)	1 (0.0068)	147 (1.00)
BBB	0 (0.00)	0 (0.00)	15 (0.18)	43 (0.53)	8 (0.098)	15 (0.18)	81 (1.00)
BB	0 (0.00)	0 (0.00)	0 (0.00)	7 (0.34)	15 (0.51)	7 (0.24)	29 (1.00)
B	0 (0.00)	0 (0.00)	1 (0.027)	4 (0.108)	6 (0.16)	26 (0.70)	37 (1.00)

individual categories, AAA (47%), AA (66%), A (80%), BBB (53%), BB (51%), and B (70%).

Prediction

Whereas explanation requires only cross-validation, prediction requires inter-temporal validation. That is to say, the discriminant model obtained from the total sample of 1981 must be used to classify a control sample of bonds from another year to test the predictive ability of the model. The control sample chosen was a sample of bonds from 1980. Thus, the multiple discriminant model obtained from the total 1981 estimation sample (Exhibit 4.12) was used to classify firms from the control sample of 1980. The classification or prediction results are shown in Exhibit 4.17. The model correctly rated 63.65% of the firms in the control sample. Again using the Z statistic of Mosteller and Bush, the null hypothesis that the results are due to chance is rejected, confirming the previous discriminating power of the model and establishing the predictive power of the model.

USING THE BOND-RATING MODEL

Model Performance

The methodology used was discriminant analysis to avoid some of the pitfalls of the other techniques. Based on an economic rationale, the discrimination analysis model developed in this study correctly rated 72.93% of the ratings in an analysis sample (1981), 67% of the ratings in a validation sample (1981), 67.19% of the ratings in a total estimation sample (1981), and 63.65% of the ratings in a control sample. Both the validation and predictive abilities of the model were significant. Two results are also noteworthy. First, most misclassified firms were classified in categories adjacent to the true ratings. Second, an examination of the *Credit Watch* list published by Standard and Poor's for five consecutive weeks following the availability of the information on which the study is based showed that seven of the firms put on the list correspond to five of the misclassified firms (see Exhibit 4.18).

The Discriminant Functions

The discriminant model based on the 1981 estimation sample yields a discriminant function for each of the five rating groups. These discriminant functions can be used to explain and/or predict bond ratings. They are as follows:

For an AAA rating:

$$Z = -31.6004 + 0.000737X_1 + 0.000119X_2 + 0.44234X_3$$
$$+ 0.62823X_4 + 7.26898X_5 + 0.68425X_6 + 0.06102X_7$$
$$+ 0.01802X_8 + 10.26302X_9$$

Exhibit 4.17
Classification Table (Control Sample)

FROM GROUP	NUMBER OBSERVATIONS (AND PERCENTAGES) CLASSIFIED INTO GROUPS						
	AAA	AA	A	BBB	BB	B	TOTAL
AAA	9 (.45)	8 (.40)	3 (.15)	0 (0.00)	0 (0.00)	0 (0.00)	20 (1.00)
AA	7 (0.07)	62 (0.62)	30 (0.30)	0 (0.00)	0 (0.00)	0 (0.00)	99 (1.00)
A	0 (0.00)	31 (0.22)	99 (0.70)	10 (0.07)	0 (0.00)	0 (0.00)	140 (1.00)
BBB	0 (0.00)	0 (0.00)	12 (0.24)	35 (0.70)	3 (0.06)	0 (0.00)	50 (1.00)
BB	0 (0.00)	0 (0.00)	0 (0.00)	7 (0.17)	18 (0.45)	15 (0.37)	40 (1.00)
B	0 (0.00)	0 (0.00)	0 (0.00)	0 (0.00)	15 (0.38)	24 (0.61)	39 (1.00)

Exhibit 4.18
Firms Misclassified and Also on the *Credit Watch* List

	Sample(s) in Which Misclassification Occurred	*CREDIT WATCH RATING*				
		March 29, 1982	April 5, 1982	April 12, 1982	April 19, 1982	April 26, 1982
Utilities, transportation						
Arizona Public Service Company	Analysis sample	/	/	/	/	Negative
Industrial retailing						
Brunswick Corp.	Estimating sample Validation sample	Negative	Negative	Negative	Negative	Negative
Coca-Cola Co.	Estimating sample Validation sample	Negative	Negative	Negative		
Columbia Pictures Inds. Inc.	Estimating sample Validation sample	Positive	Positive	Positive	Positive	Positive
Lone Star Industries Inc.	Estimating sample Validation sample	Negative	Negative	Negative	Negative	Negative
Murphy (G.C.) Co.	Estimating sample Validation sample	Negative	Negative	/	/	/
Resorts International Inc.	Estimating sample Validation sample	Negative	Negative	Negative	/	/

69

For an AA rating:

$$Z = -26.0425 + 0.000431X_1 - 0.000147X_2 + 0.48299X_3$$
$$+ 0.67906X_4 + 6.80279X_5 + 0.54641X_6 + 0.06600X_7$$
$$+ 0.01687X_8 + 9.76648X_9$$

For an A rating:

$$Z = -26.1304 + 0.000269X_1 - 0.000149X_2 + 0.58069X_3$$
$$+ 0.60516X_4 + 7.83642X_5 + 0.48850X_6 + 0.06777X_7$$
$$+ 0.00809X_8 + 8.18782X_9$$

For a BBB rating:

$$Z = -29.3824 + 0.000250X_1 - 0.000233X_2 + 0.71530X_3$$
$$+ 0.79864X_4 + 8.35763X_5 + 0.50766X_6 + 0.07116X_7$$
$$+ 0.00235X_8 + 4.27079X_9$$

For a BB rating:

$$Z = -31.3397 + 0.000265X_1 - 0.000295X_2 + 0.76589X_3$$
$$+ 0.80544X_4 + 9.15411X_5 + 0.48010X_6 + 0.05952X_7$$
$$+ 0.00705X_8 + 1.69732X_9$$

For a B rating:

$$Z = -34.8229 + 0.000242X_1 - 0.000357X_2 + 0.85499X_3$$
$$+ 0.84459X_4 + 9.24043X_5 + 0.49208X_6 + 0.06970X_7$$
$$+ 0.00099X_8 - 1.73660X_9$$

where

X_1 = *Total assets*, included as a representative of the total size of the firm (in millions).

X_2 = *Total debt*, included as a measure of the total indebtedness of the firm (in millions).

X_3 = *Long-term/total invested capital*, included as a measure of the long-term capital intensiveness of the firm. By invested capital we mean the sum of the total debt, preferred stock, and common equity (which includes common stock, capital surplus, and retained earnings).

X_4 = *Short-term debt/total invested capital*, included as a measure of the short-term capital intensiveness of the firm.

X_5 = *Current assets/current liabilities*, included as a measure of the total liquidity of the firm.

X_6 = *Fixed charge coverage ratio*, included as a measure of debt coverage.

X_7 = *Five-year cash flow as a percentage of five-year growth needs*, included as a measure of future liquidity.

X_8 = *Stock price/common equity share*, included as a measure of investors' expectations.

X_9 = *Subordination*, 1 for subordination and 0 for others; included as a measure of the most relevant covenant in the indenture.

The Classification Procedure

The classification method consists simply of using the discriminant functions on new data as follows: For each firm that needs to be classified into a bond-rating category, compute the classification score for each rating category from the discriminant function coefficients (multiply the data by the coefficients and add the constant term). The firm is then classified into the group in which the classification score is highest.

To illustrate the classification procedure, we use the following 1980 data for Frontier Airlines (the ratings given by Standard and Poor's was B):

X_1 = \$312.8 (in millions)
X_2 = 116.1 (in millions)
X_3 = 48.7
X_4 = 4.1
X_5 = 0.9
X_6 = 3.5
X_7 = 52.8
X_8 = 104.7
X_9 = 1 (subordinated debt)

The classification scores for each rating category from the discriminant functions obtained by multiplying the coefficients by the data and adding the constant term are the following:

Z_{AAA} = 18.50916
Z_{AA} = 26.208
Z_A = 30.37737
Z_{BBB} = 38.72666
Z_{BB} = 41.09244
Z_B = 43.51933

Given that Z_B gives the highest classification score, the firm is classified by the model in the bond-rating category B.

Given the sample classification procedure outlined in the previous paragraphs, the model can be useful to all those interested in explaining, predicting, and/or justifying bond ratings and evaluating the investment quality of bonds.

The issuing firm can use the classification procedure to explain the ratings assigned to its industrial bonds. Firms may be at a loss as to why their bonds have been assigned a given rating, and the classification procedure provides a direct and easy way to check on their ratings. Conflicts between the ratings assigned by the rating agencies and this book's classification procedure may indicate that the rating agencies are concerned about qualitative factors not included in the model. Examples of such factors include quality of management, growth plans, and so forth.

The issuing firm can use the classification procedure to predict the ratings that may be assigned to a new issue. Firms are generally at a loss when attempting to determine these ratings, and the classification procedure outlined in this chapter provides a first idea of the ratings that may be assigned to them. Based on the results of the classification, firms can elect to go on with the new issue or attempt to first improve their financial conditions.

Investors can use the classification procedure to assess the investment quality of bonds. The model provides a direct and inexpensive way to classify bonds into five possible categories without resorting to cumbersome and time-consuming univariate analysis. The issuing firm can use the classification procedure to continuously check on their investment quality and to prevent being put on the *Credit Watch* list.

CONCLUSIONS

Based on the economic rationale, the discriminant analysis model developed in this study correctly rated 72.93% of the ratings in an analysis sample, 67.8% of the ratings in a validation sample, 67.19% of the ratings in a total estimation sample, and 63.65% of the ratings in a control sample. Both the validation and the predictive abilities of the model were significant. Most misclassified firms were rated in categories adjacent to the true ratings. Such a model can be useful to the rating agencies themselves if it helps them to reduce inconsistencies among individual ratings, to form a preliminary rating of a bond, or to capture and evaluate the judgments of their raters. The model can be useful to investors when corporate bonds are not rated by Fitch, Moody's, and/or Standard & Poor's. Above all, the findings should be useful to those who pay to have bonds rated. Hence, managers can form an opinion of eventual ratings and take sound actions to improve some of the financial dimensions outlined in this study to achieve a better rating. The implementations of the model are briefly explained in the next chapter.

NOTES

1. George Foster, *Financial Statement Analysis* (Englewood Cliffs, N.J.: Prentice-Hall, Inc., 1978), 443. One exception is provided in Stewart C. Myers, ''Determinants

of Corporate Borrowing,'' *Journal of Financial Economics* (November 1977): 147–176. Myers argues that corporate borrowing is inversely related to the proportion of market value accounted for by ''real opportunities or growth opportunities.'' These growth opportunities are contingent on discretionary future investment by the firm. So, issuing risky debt reduces the present market value of a firm holding growth opportunity by inducing a suboptimal investment strategy or by leading the firm and its creditor to bear the costs of avoiding the suboptimal strategy. However, as Myers admits, a general measure of this concept is difficult to derive from accounting data.

2. This economic rationale was first presented in Ahmed Belkaoui, ''Industrial Bond Ratings: A New Look,'' *Financial Management* (Autumn 1980): 45–46.

3. H. C. Sherwood, *How Corporate and Municipal Debt is Rated* (New York: John Wiley & Sons, Inc., 1976).

4. Robert S. Kaplan and Gabriel Urwitz, ''Statistical Models of Bond Ratings: A Methodological Inquiry,'' *The Journal of Business* 52, no. 2 (1979): 231–261.

5. This procedure was suggested in O. Maurice Joy and John O. Tollefson, ''On the Financial Applications of Discriminant Analysis,'' *Journal of Financial and Quantitative Analysis* (December 1975): 726–727.

6. Ibid., 727.

7. Ibid., 728.

8. Bonds with C ratings were not included because of difficulties of ensuring adequate and sufficient representation (and also to reduce the number of categories to manageable levels).

9. The reader may be interested in testing the model on a control sample of industrial bonds rated B or above in future years, whenever information on the independent variables in those years becomes available.

10. W. J. Dixon, *BMDP Statistical Software 1981* (Berkeley and Los Angeles: University of California Press, 1981).

11. B. J. Winer, *Statistical Principles in Experimental Design*, 2nd ed. (New York: McGraw-Hill Book Company, 1971), p. 845.

12. Robert A. Eisenbeis, Gary G. Gilbert, and Robert B. Avery, ''Investigating the Relative Importance of Individual Variables and Variable Subsets in Discriminant Analysis,'' *Communications in Statistics* (September 1973): 205–219.

13. William M. Cooley and P. R. Lohnes, *Multivariate Data Analysis* (New York: John Wiley & Sons, Inc., 1971).

14. F. Mosteller and R. R. Bush, ''Selecting Quantitative Techniques,'' in *Handbook of Social Psychology*, vol. 1, ed. G. Undzey (Reading, Mass.: Addison-Wesley, 1954), 289–334.

SELECTED READINGS

Belkaoui, Ahmed. ''Industrial Bond Ratings: A New Look.'' *Financial Management* (Autumn 1980): 44–51.

Belkaoui, Ahmed. *Accounting Theory*. New York: Harcourt Brace Jovanovich, 1981.

Belkaoui, Ahmed. *Industrial Bonds and the Ratings Process*. Westport, Conn.: Greenwood, 1983.

Cooley, William M., and P. R. Lohnes. *Multivariate Data Analysis*. New York: John Wiley & Sons, Inc., 1971.

Dixon, W. J. *BMDP Statistical Software 1981*. Berkeley and Los Angeles: University of California Press, 1981.

Eisenbeis, Robert A., Gary G. Gilbert, and Robert B. Avery. "Investigating the Relative Importance of Individual Variables and Variable Subsets in Discriminant Analysis." *Communications in Statistics* (September 1973): 205–219.

Foster, George. *Financial Statement Analysis*. Englewood Cliffs, N.J.: Prentice-Hall, Inc., 1978.

Horrigan, J. O. "The Determinant of Long-Term Credit Standing with Financial Ratios." In *Empirical Research in Accounting: Selected Studies*, supplement to *Journal of Accounting Research* (1966): 44–62.

Joy, O. Maurice, and John O. Tollefson. "On the Financial Applications of Discriminant Analysis." *Journal of Financial and Quantitative Analysis* (December 1975): 723–763.

Mosteller, F., and R. R. Bush. "Selecting Quantitative Techniques." In *Handbook of Social Psychology*, vol. I, edited by G. Undzey, 289–334. Reading, Mass.: Addison-Wesley, 1954.

Pinches, G. E., and K. A. Mingo. "A Multivariate Analysis of Industrial Bond Ratings." *Journal of Finance* (March 1973): 1–18.

West, R. R. "An Alternative Approach to Predicting Corporate Bond Ratings." *Journal of Accounting Research* (Spring 1970): 118–127.

Winer, B. J. *Statistical Principles in Experimental Design*. 2nd ed. New York: McGraw-Hill Book Company, 1971.

5

Accounting for Stockholders' Equity: Contributed Capital and Retained Earnings

THE NATURE AND CHANGES IN EQUITY

The interest in this chapter is with publicly traded corporations, owned by stockholders who have limited liability, and governed by *articles of incorporation* or corporate charters. The firm's capital is measured by the difference between the firm's assets and liabilities. This difference or *residual interest*, known as the *owners' or stockholders' equity*, is equal to the cumulative net contribution of stockholders plus the plowed-back profit. The changes in equity include

A. Changes in equity affecting assets and liabilities that
   1. Affect net income through revenues, expenses, gains, or losses.
   2. Affect transfers between equity and owners through investment by owners and distributions to owners.
B. Changes in equity not affecting assets or liabilities, such as
   1. Issuance of stock dividends and splits.
   2. Conversion of preferred stocks to common stocks.

Stockholders' equity is, in fact, the capital of the firm composed of *contributed capital* (par value of outstanding capital stock, premium less discounts on issuance, amount paid on subscription agreements, and additional assessments) and *earned capital* (plowed-back earnings). In most states, the *par value or stated value* of stock issued constitute the *legal capital*. Finally, the total corporation of stockholders' equity is as follows:

A. *Contributed capital*

    1. *Capital stock* = a designated dollar amount per share established in the articles of incorporation × number of shares outstanding.

    2. *Additional paid-in capital* = the excess of the value over the par or stated value of the stock × number of shares outstanding.

B. *Unrealized capital* is increases in stockholders' equity not related to the issuance of stock or to retained earnings, such as *donated capital* and *revaluation capital* (writeup or writedown of assets from cost).

C. *Retained earnings* is income not distributed but reinvested in the firm or plowed back.

It is appropriate to note that additional paid-in capital is a summary account for the following transactions:

1. Discounts on capital stock issued (debit).
2. Sale of treasury stock below cost (debit).
3. Absorption of a deficit in a recapitalization (quasi-reorganization) (debit).
4. Declaration of a liquidating dividend (debit).
5. Premium on capital stock issued (credit).
6. Sale of treasury stock above cost (credit).
7. Additional capital arising in recapitalizations or revisions in the capital structure (quasi-reorganization) (credit).
8. Additional assessments on stockholders (credit).
9. Conversion of convertible bonds or preferred stock (credit).
10. Declaration of a ''small'' (ordinary) stock dividend (credit).

Other items may be presented as contra or adjunct equity items, generally as adjustments to or below retained earnings. Examples of the items include

1. Foreign currency translation adjustments.
2. Unrealized holding gains and losses for available-for-sale securities.
3. Excess of additional pension liability over unrecognized prior service cost.
4. Guarantees of employee stock option plan (ESOP) debt.
5. Unearned or deferred compensation related to employee stock award plans.
6. Others.

ACCOUNTING FOR THE ISSUANCE OF CAPITAL STOCK

Various transactions are used in the issuance of capital stock. They are examined next.

Issuance of Capital Stock for Cash

When capital stock with a par value is issued for cash, the differences between the proceeds and the par value of the stock issued is accounted for as an *additional paid-in capital on common stock*. For example, let us assume that the Ortega Company issued 1,000 shares of its $20 par common stock for $30 per share. The entry to record the issuance is as follows:

Cash ($30 × 1,000)	$30,000	
Common stock ($20 × 1,000)		$20,000
Additional paid-in capital on common stock		10,000

The same entry would be used if the stock were no-par stock with a stated value of $20 (the $20 value is a minimum value below which it cannot be issued). If the stock was in fact a no-par stock, with no per share amount printed in the stock certificate, the entry would be as follows:

Cash ($30 × 1,000)	$30,000	
Common stock no-par value		$30,000

The costs of issuing stock are treated either as a reduction of the amounts paid in (a debit to paid-in capital in excess par) or as an organization cost to be capitalized as an intangible asset and amortized over a period not to exceed 40 years.

Issuance of Capital Stock on a Subscription Basis

Capital stock may be issued on a subscription basis, namely on an installment basis, accounted for by a credit to *common or preferred stock subscribed* for the amount of stock the firm is obliged to issue, and a debit to *subscription receivable* for the amount to be collected before the subscribed stock is issued.

To illustrate, let us assume that the Albertos Company offered stocks on a subscription basis to its employees, that allows them to purchase 5,000 shares of $8 per common stock at $20 per share if they put down $5 per share and pay the remaining $15 at the end of the month. The entry at the date of issuance is as follows:

Cash ($5 × 5,000)	$25,000	
Subscriptions receivable: common stock ($15 × 5,000)	75,000	
Common stock subscribed (5,000 × $8)		$40,000
Additional paid-in capital on common stock ($12 × 5,000)		60,000

Subscriptions receivable may be reprinted in the current asset section of the balance sheet or as a declaration from stockholders' equity. The Securities and Exchange Commission (SEC) requires the contra equity approach, which explains its popularity in practice.

At the end of the month, when the Albertos Company received payment for and issued 4,000 shares, the following entries are made:

Cash ($15 × 4,000)	$60,000	
Subscription receivable		$60,000

and

Common stock subscribed	$32,000	
Common stock ($8 × 4,000)		$32,000

Assuming that the subscriber to the remaining 1,000 shares defaulted on the contract, the following entry is made:

Common stock subscribed (1,000 × $8)	$ 8,000	
Additional paid-in capital (1,000 × $12)	12,000	
Subscription receivable (1,000 × $15)		$15,000
Additional paid-in capital for subscription default (1,000 × $5)		5,000

Issuance of Capital Stock in a Nonmonetary Exchange

Capital stock may sometimes be issued for services or property other than cash. The general rule is to record the exchange at the fair market value of either the stock or the property or services, depending on whichever is readily determinable and more reliable. For example, let us assume that a corporation issued 20,000 shares of $10 par value for a patent when the stock was at $30. The transaction is recorded as follows:

Patent	$600,000	
Common stock (20,000 × $10)		$200,000
Paid-in capital in excess of par (20,000 × $20)		400,000

If the fair market value of neither the stock nor the property or services were easily determinable or were not reliable, the board of directors is responsible for the determination of the fair market value of the exchange. Two likely situations are (a) an overvaluation of the property or services received, resulting in an overvaluation of stockholders' equity, a phenomenon referred to as *watered stock*, or (b) an undervaluation of stockholders' equity, a phenomenon referred to as *secret reserves*.

ACCOUNTING FOR TREASURY STOCK

Treasury stock represents the stock reacquired by a firm for various reasons including the following:

1. To use for stock option, bonus, and employee purchase plans.
2. To use in the conversion of convertible preferred stocks or bonds.
3. To use as excess cash and help maintain the market price of its stock.
4. To use in the acquisition of other companies.
5. To reduce the number of shares outstanding and thereby increase the earnings per share.
6. To reduce the number of shares held by outside shareholders and thereby reduce the likelihood of being acquired by another company.
7. To use for the issuance of a stock dividend.[1]

Firms may also buy back all their stock and go private, a procedure referred to as an LBO (leveraged buyout).

Two methods can be used to account for treasury stock, namely, (a) the *cost method* and (b) the *par value method*.

A. The cost method accounts for the treasury stock at the reacquisition cost. When reissued, the treasury shares are credited to paid-in capital from treasury stock if the reissuance price exceeds the acquisition price, and are debited to paid-in-capital from treasury stock then to retained earnings if the reissuance price is less than the acquisition price. The treasury stock is reported as a deduction from total paid-in-capital and retained earnings.

B. The par value method accounts for the treasury stock at the par value. At reacquisition, treasury stock at par value and paid-in-capital in excess of par are debited. Retained earnings is debited if the acquisition price is higher than the issuance price. Paid-in-capital from treasury stock is credited if the acquisition price is less than the issuance price. Finally, the treasury stock is reported as a deduction from capital stock only.

To illustrate assume that the Share Corporation is authorized to issue 10,000 shares of $10 par common stock and enters into the following treasury stock transactions:

1. If Share Corporation issued 3,000 shares of $10 par common stock at $15 per share:

A. Under the cost method and the par value method the following entry is made:

Cash (3,000 shares × $15)	$45,000	
Common stock ($10 par × 3,000 shares)		$30,000
Additional paid-in capital on common stock ($5 × 3,000)		15,000

2. If Share Corporation reacquired 500 shares of common stock at $16 per share:
   A. Under the cost method

Treasury stock (500 shares × $16)	$8000	
Cash		$8,000

   B. Under the par value method:

Treasury stock (500 shares at $10)	$5,000	
Additional paid-in capital (500 shares × $5)	2,500	
Retained earnings	500	
Cash		$8,000

3. If Share Corporation reissued 200 shares of treasury stock at $20 per share:
   A. Under the cost method:

Cash (200 shares × $20)	$4,000	
Treasury stock (200 shares × $16)		$3,200
Additional paid-in capital on common stock (200 shares × $4)		800

   B. Under the par value method:

Cash (200 shares × $20)	$4,000	
Treasury stock (200 shares × $10)		$2,000
Additional paid-in capital on common stock (200 shares × $10)		2,000

4. If Share Corporation reissued another 50 shares at $7 per share:
   A. Under the cost method:

Cash ($7 × 50 shares)	$350	
Additional paid-in capital from treasury stock ($9 × 50 shares)	450	
Treasury stock (50 shares × $16)		$800

   B. Under the par value method:

Cash (50 shares × $7)	$350	
Additional paid-in capital in common stock	$150	
Treasury stock (50 shares × $10)		$500

5. If Share Corporation reissued another 200 shares of treasury stock at $10 per share:
   A. Under the cost method:

Cash (200 shares × $10)	$2,000	
Additional paid-in capital from treasury stock	350	
Retained earnings	850	
Treasury stock (200 shares × $16)		$3,200

B. Under the par value method:

Cash	$2,000	
Treasury stock (200 shares × $10)		$2,000

6. If Share Corporation retired the last 50 shares of treasury stock:
   A. Under the cost method:

Common stock ($10 par × 50 shares)	$500	
Additional paid-in capital on common stock	250	
Retained earnings	50	
Treasury stock (50 shares × $16)		$800
($15,000 × 50)/3,000		

B. Under the par value method:

Common stock, $10 par	$500	
Treasury stock (50 shares × $10)		$500

ACCOUNTING FOR PREFERRED STOCK

Preferred stock allows the holder to have rights not available to the common stockholders. One important right is a *preference to dividends* expressed as a *percentage of par value* if the preferred stock is issued with a par value, or as a *specific dollar amount* if the preferred stock is a no-par preferred stock. Other features include the following:

Cumulative Preferred Stock

Holders of cumulative preferred stocks are owed *dividend in arrears* for years the dividend is not declared, that is, not passed. For example, holders of 5,000 shares of 10%, $100 par cumulative preferred stocks are entitled to a $10 annual dividend per share. If dividend is passed for two years, the preferred shareholders are entitled to dividend in arrears of $100,000 ($10 × 5,000 shares × two years) and $50,000 for the third year. The amount paid in the third year is $150,000.

Participating Preferred Stock

Holders of participating preferred stock are entitled to share either fully (fully participating preferred stock) of partially (partially participating preferred stock) in any dividend available after the preferred stockholders have been paid at a rate equal to that paid for preferred stock. If preferred stock are paid at 10%, any amount in excess of 10% paid to common shareholders is shared between the preferred and common stockholders.

Convertible Preferred Stock

Holders of convertible preferred stock have the option to exchange their preferred shares for a specified number of common stock.

Callable Preferred Stock

Callable preferred stock allows the corporation to call or redeem at its option the outstanding preferred shares under conditions specified by the stock contract.

At issuance of the callable preferred stock, the difference between the market and par value is credited to the additional paid-in capital on preferred stock. At recall, the difference is not treated as a gain or loss and two situations arise.

A. If the call price exceeds the contributed capital (preferred stock plus additional paid-in capital associated with the recalled preferred stock), the difference or "loss" is debited to retained earnings like a dividend distribution.

B. If the call price is less than the contributed capital, the difference or "gain" is credited to additional paid-in capital from recall of preferred stock.

For example, let us assume that the XYZ Corporation has 5,000 shares of $100 par callable preferred stock issued at $120 per share.

A. Assuming a call price of $130, the following entry is made at the recall:

Preferred stock ($100 par × 5,000)	$500,000	
Additional paid-in capital or preferred stock	100,000	
Retained earnings ($650,000 − $600,000)	50,000	
Cash ($130 × 5,000)		$650,000

B. Assuming a call price of $110, the following entry is made at recall:

Preferred stock ($100 par × 5,000)	$500,000	
Additional paid-in capital on preferred stock	100,000	

Cash ($110 × 5,000)	550,000
Additional paid-in capital from recall of preferred stock ($600,000 − $550,000)	50,000

Preferred Stock with Stock Warrants

Preferred stocks may be issued with stock warrants offering the holder not only preference as to dividends but also rights to purchase additional shares of common stock at a specified price over some future period. Given these dual rights, the proceeds from the issuance of preferred stock with attachable warrants is to be allocated to preferred stockholders' equity and common stockholders' equity on the basis of the relative fair values of the two securities at the time of issuance. To illustrate, let us assume that the XYZ Company issues 5,000 shares of $100 par value preferred stock at a price of $130 per share with a detachable warrant that allows the holder to purchase for each preferred share one share of $20 par common stock at $50 per share. Following the issuance, the preferred stock was selling ex rights (without the warrants) at a market price of $120, while the warrant was selling for $8 each. The following computations are required:

1. Market value of preferred stock ($120 × 5,000)   = $600,000
2. Market value of warrants ($8 × 5,000)   =   40,000
3. Total market value ($600,000 + $40,000)   =   640,000
4. Issuance value ($130 × 5,000)   =   650,000
5. Allocation to preferred stock (650,000 × $600,000/$640,000) =   609,375
6. Allocation to warrants ($650,000 × $40,000/$640,000)   =   40,625

At the time of issuance the following entry is made:

Cash ($130 × 5,000)	$650,000	
Preferred stock, $100 par (5,000 × $100)		$500,000
Additional paid-in capital on preferred stock		109,375
Common stock warrants		40,625

When the warrants are exercised, the following entry is made:

Cash ($5,000 × $50)	$250,000	
Common stock warrants	40,625	
Common stock, $20 par		$100,000
Additional paid-in capital on common stock		190,625

RETAINED EARNINGS

Notice the following basic accounting equations:

Assets = Liabilities + Owners' equity + Retained earnings
Net profit = Revenues − Expenses

From these two equations, retained earnings appears as the main link between the balance sheet and profit equations. Retained earnings is subject to increases of credits and decreases of debits.

Some of the increases in debits include

1. Net income.
2. Prior period adjustments.
3. Adjustments due to quasi-reorganization.

Some of the decreases or debits include

1. Loss.
2. Prior period adjustments and certain changes in accounting principles.
3. Cash or scrip dividends.
4. Property dividends.
5. Some treasury earning stock transactions.

ACCOUNTING FOR DIVIDENDS

As stated earlier, the decrease in retained earnings follows the distribution of dividends. The types of dividends include (1) cash, (2) property, (3) scrip, (4) liquidation, and (5) stock. With the exception of stock dividends, all the other dividends reduce the stockholders' equity in the corporation.

Cash Dividends

Firms distribute as cash dividends a certain percentage of annual earnings in payout rates. Four dates are crucial to accounting for cash dividends as follows:

1. The *date of declaration* is the date a resolution to pay cash dividends to stockholders of record on a specific future date is approved by the board of directors. At that date, the firm incurs a liability, prompting the recognition of a short-term debt, dividends payable, and the debit to either retained earnings or cash dividend declared.
2. The *ex-dividend date* is the date the stock stops selling with dividends attached. The period between the date of declaration and the ex-dividend date is used by the firm to update its stockholders' ledger.

3. The *date of record* is the date at which the stockholders figuring in the stockholders' ledger are entitled to the cash dividend. No entry is required.

4. The *date of payment* is the date at which the firm distributes the dividend checks and eliminates the dividend payable as a liability.

For example, let us assume that on March 15, 1996, the Natsumura Corporation declared a cash dividend of $1 per share on 2,000,000 shares payable June 1, 1996, to all stockholders of record as of April 15. The following entries are required:

1. Date of declaration, March 15, 1996:

Retained earnings (cash dividend declared)	$2,000,000	
Dividends payable		$2,000,000

2. Date of record, April 15, 1996:
   Memorandum entry that the firm will pay a dividend to all stockholders of record as of today, the date of record.

3. Date of payment, June 1, 1996:

Dividends payable	$2,000,000	
Cash		$2,000,000

It is appropriate to note that cash dividend declared is closed at year-end to retained earnings.

Property Dividends

Firms may elect to declare a property dividend that is payable in nonmonetary assets rather than declaring a cash dividend. Because a property dividend can be classified as a *nonreciprocal nonmonetary transfer to owners*, the property distributed is restated at fair market value at the date of declaration and a gain or loss is recognized.

For example, let us assume that the ABC Corporation declares a property dividend, payable in bonds of company XYZ being held to maturity and costing $500,000. At the date of declaration, the bonds had a market value of $600,000. The following entries are required:

A. Date of declaration:

Investments in Company XYZ bonds	$100,000	
Gain on appreciation of bonds ($600,000 − $500,000)		$100,000
Retained earnings (property dividend declared)	$600,000	
Property dividends payable		$600,000

B. Date of distribution:

Property dividends payable	$600,000	
Investments in Company XYZ bonds		$600,000

Scrip Dividends

Firms may find themselves with sufficient retained earnings to declare a dividend but not enough liquidity for distribution. In such a case, firms may elect to declare a scrip dividend—a dividend payable in scrip—by issuing promissory notes requiring them to pay the dividends at a later date. The accounting treatment at the date of declaration consists of debiting retained earnings or scrip dividends declared and crediting notes payable to stockholders or scrip dividend payable. At the date of distribution, the firm debits the note payable or scrip payable, and the related interest expense and credit cash. For example, let us assume that on June 17, 1996, the Bannos Company declared a scrip dividend in the form of a three-month promissory notes amount to $1 a share on 3,000,000 shares outstanding. The interest rate on the notes is 10% per year. The following entries are required:

1. At the date of declaration, June 17, 1996:

Retained earnings (scrip dividends declared)	$3,000,000	
Notes payable to stockholders (scrip dividends payable) ($1 × 3,000,000)		$3,000,000

2. At the date of payment, September 17, 1996:

Note payable to stockholders	$3,000,000	
Interest expense ($3,000,000 × 0.10 × 3/12)	75,000	
Cash		$3,075,000

Liquidating Dividends

Dividends paid based on other than retained earnings are called liquidating dividends, as a return of contributed capital rather than a distribution of retained earnings. They are treated as a reduction of contributed capital, either additional paid-in capital or a special contra-contributed capital account, designated as contributed capital distributed as a liquidating dividend.

For example, let us assume that the Weigandt Company issued dividend to its common stockholders of $2,500,000 of which $1,000,000 is considered income and the rest is considered a return of contributed capital. The following entries are required:

A. At the date of declaration:

Retained earnings	$1,000,000	
Additional paid-in capital	1,500,000	
Dividends payable		$2,500,000

B. At the date of payment:

Dividends payable	$2,500,000	
Cash		$2,500,000

Stock Dividends

A firm with adequate retained earnings but insufficient liquidity may elect to issue stock dividends by a pro rata distribution of additional shares of the firm's own stock to its stockholders. The transaction is made by a capitalization of retained earnings, resulting in a reduction of retained earnings and an increase in some contributed capital accounts. No corporate assets are distributed, and the value of the total stockholders' equity remains unchanged as does each stockholder's percentage ownership in the firm. Accounting for stock dividends differs depending on the size of the issue:

A. For a *small stock dividend*, that is, less than 20–25% of the common shares outstanding at the time of the dividend declaration, *fair market value* is used to capitalize retained earnings and an increase in capital stock and additional paid-in capital.

B. For a *large stock dividend*, that is, more than 20–25% of the common shares outstanding at the time of the dividend declaration, *par value* is issued to capitalize retained earnings, resulting in a reduction of retained earnings and an increase in capital stock.

To illustrate the accounting for a small stock dividend, let us assume a corporation that has the following stockholders' equity prior to the issuance of a small stock dividend:

Common stock, $20 par (30,000 shares issued and outstanding)

	$600,000	
Additional paid-in capital		$ 300,000
Retained earnings		600,000
Total stockholders' equity		$15,000,000

Let us also assume that the firm issued a 20% stock dividend on a date when the stock was selling at $25 per share. The fair value for the 6,000 shares is $150,000. The following entries are required:

A. At the date of declaration:

Retained earnings	$150,000	
Common stock dividend distributable	120,000	
Additional paid-in capital from stock dividend		$30,000

B. At the date of issuance:

Common stock dividend distribution	120,000	
Common Stock, $20 par		120,000

Following the issuance the stockholders' equity is as follows:

Common Stock, $20 par (36,000 shares issued and outstanding)	$720,000
Additional paid-in capital	330,000
Retained earnings	450,000
Total stockholders' equity	$1,500,000

Let us now assume that the firm issued instead a 50% stock dividend. The following entries are required at the time of declaration.

Retained earnings (50% × 30,000 shares × $20)	$300,000	
Common stock dividend distributable		$300,000

At the time of distribution the following entry is required:

Common stock dividend distributable	$300,000	
Common stock, $20 par		$300,000

Following the issuance the stockholders' equity is as follows:

Common stock, $20 par (45,000)	$900,000
Additional paid-in capital	300,000
Retained earnings	300,000
Total stockholders' equity	$1,500,000

Note that the large stock dividend is treated as a stock split, that is, *a split effected in the form of a dividend*. In fact, for a stock split, no entry is required except a memorandum noting the increase in the number of shares and the decrease in the par value. For example, a two-for-one split of 6,000 shares at $10 par value results in a common stock of 16,000 shares at $5 par value.

APPROPRIATIONS OF RETAINED EARNINGS

To advise that retained earnings can be used for more than the declaration and payment of dividends, firms may appropriate (restrict) retained earnings, "provided that it is shown within the stockholders' equity section of the balance sheet and is clearly identified as an appropriation of retained earnings."[2] The appropriation may be motivated by (a) legal restrictions, (b) contractual restrictions, (c) the existence of possible or expected loss, and (d) protection of working capital position.[3] Note, however, that Financial Accounting Standards Board (FASB) Statement Number 5 clearly states that "Costs or losses shall not be charged to an appropriation of retained earnings, and no part of the appropriation shall be transferred to income."[4]

To illustrate the formal entries associated with appropriation of retained earnings let us assume that the XYZ Company is required by a debt covenant to make an appropriation for a sinking fund or that an appropriation for bond indebtedness is to be created by the transfer from retained earnings of $500,000 a year for the 10-year life of the bonds. Therefore the entry for each year is:

Retained earnings	$500,000	
Retained earnings appropriated for sinking fund		$500,000

At the end of 10 years and assuming the bonds are retired, the following entry is required:

Retained earnings appropriated for sinking fund	$5,000,000	
Retained earnings		$5,000,000

NOTES

1. Loren A. Nikolai and John D. Baley, *Intermediate Accounting*, 6th ed. (Cincinnati, Ohio: South-Western Publishing Co., 1994), 852.
2. Financial Accounting Standards Board (FASB), "Accounting for Contingencies," *FASB Statement of Financial Accounting Standards, Statement Number 5* (Stamford, Conn.: FASB, 1975), par. 15.
3. Donald E. Kieso and Jerry J. Weygandt, *Intermediate Accounting*, 4th ed. (New York: John Wiley & Sons, Inc., 1995), 786.
4. FASB, par. 15.

SELECTED READINGS

Kieso, Donald E., and Jerry J. Weygandt. *Intermediate Accounting*, 4th ed. New York: John Wiley & Sons, 1995.

Riahi-Belkaoui, Ahmed. *Accounting Theory*, 3rd ed. London: Academic Press, 1992.

Riahi-Belkaoui, Ahmed. *Critical Financial Accounting Problems: Issues and Solutions*. Westport, Conn.: Quorum Books, 1998.

6

Accounting for Long-Term Liabilities

INTRODUCTION

Firms issue long-term bonds and long-term notes as part of their financing strategies. This chapter covers the main issues associated with accounting and reporting of long-term liabilities. The focus is on the generally accepted accounting principles (GAAP) governing accounting for long-term liabilities.

ACCOUNTING FOR THE ISSUANCE OF BONDS

Bonds Payable

A bond payable is a long-term debt governed by a contract known as a *bond indenture* whereby the firm promises to pay the holder (a) the face value at the maturity date and (b) periodic interest on the face value. Common characteristics of a bond include

a. A face value, par value, principal amount, or maturity value.
b. A stated coupon, nominal, or contract rate.

However, given the general market condition a *yield (or effective rate)* may prevail in the determination of the bond prices. Three situations may result:

1. The yield is equal to the contract rate and the bonds are sold at par. In such a case, the interest expense is equal to the interest paid.
2. The yield is higher than the contract rate and the bonds are sold at a *discount* (the price of the bond is lower than the face value). In such a case, the interest expense is higher than the interest paid.

3. The yield is lower than the contract rate and the bonds are sold at a *premium* (the price of the bond is higher than the face value). In such a case, the interest expense is lower than the interest paid.

To illustrate the potential difference between the bond price and face value, let us assume that the Katori Company issues $200,000 in bonds, due in five years at a contract rate of 9% per year payable at the end of the year. The market rate for the bonds at the time of issuance was 11%. The bond price is the present value of the principal of $200,000 plus the present value of the five-year-end annual payments of $18,000. In other words, the selling price or present value of the bonds is as follows:

Present value of the principal ($200,000 × 0.59345)	$118,690.00
Present value of the interest payments ($18,000 × 3.6959)	66,526.20
	$185,216.20

Given that the face value of the bond is $200,000, the bonds are selling at a discount of $14,783.80 ($200,000 − $185,216.20), or more explicitly they were sold for 92.6 (185,216.20/200,000) or 92.6 of par. If the bond price was $220,000, then there would be a premium of $20,000 and the bonds were sold for 110 or 110 of par. The accounting for the three cases of selling at par, selling at a discount, and selling at a premium is illustrated next.

Issuance of Bonds at Par on Interest Rate Date

If the bonds are issued at par on the interest rate date, only the cash received and the face value of the bonds are recorded. If we assume that on January 1, 1996, the Katori Company issued $200,000 in bonds, due in five years at a contract rate of 9% per year payable semiannually, and the market rate was also 9%, then the following entries are made:

1. On January 1, 1996, to record the issuance:

Cash	$200,000	
Bonds payable		$200,000

2. On July 1, 1996, to record the first semiannual interest payment of $9,000 ($200,000 × 9% × ½):

Bond interest expense	$9,000	
Cash		$9,000

3. On December 31, 1996, to record the second semiannual interest payment of $9,000:

| Bond interest expense | $9,000 | |
| Cash | | $9,000 |

Issuance of Bonds at Discount or Premium on Interest Rate Date

If we assume that on January 1, 1996, the Katori Company issued $200,000 in bonds, due in five years at a contract rate of 9% and the market rate of 11%, then the bonds are sold at a discount of $14,783.80 (as computed earlier), and the following entry is made:

Cash	$185,216.20	
Discount on bonds payable	14,783.80	
Bonds payable		$200,000

If instead, the bonds were sold for $220,000 at a premium of $20,000, then the following entry is made on January 1, 1996:

Cash	$220,000	
Bonds payable		$200,000
Premium on bonds payable		20,000

In both cases of selling at a discount or premium, the discount on bonds payable or the premium on bonds payable should be amortized using the *straight-line method* or the *effective interest method*.

If the straight-line method is used the entries would have been:

A. In the case of the bonds selling at a discount of $14,783.80, the annual amortization would be $2,956.76 ($14,783.80/5) and the entry at the end of 1996 is as follows:

| Bond interest expense | $2,956.76 | |
| Discount on bonds payable | | $2,956.76 |

B. In the case of bonds selling at a premium of $20,000, the annual amortization would be $4,000 ($20,000/5), and the entry at the end of 1996 is as follows:

| Premium on bonds payable | $4,000 | |
| Bond interest expense | | $4,000 |

The effective interest method is illustrated later in the chapter.

Issuance of Bonds between Interest Payment Dates at Par

Bonds are usually issued at their authorization date. They are sometimes sold after their authorization date and between interest payment dates. Bond interest payments are made semiannually. If the bonds are issued between interest payment dates a problem arises of how to treat the *interest accrued from the last interest payment date to the date of the issue.* An effective solution that reduces record keeping for the first interest payment is to add the interest accrued to the selling of the bonds, making the buyer pay for the interest accrued. On the next semiannual interest payment date, the buyer receives a full six-month interest payment.

To illustrate, assume that on March 1, 1996, the XYZ Corporation issues $160,000 of 10-year bonds dated January 1, 1996, at par and bearing interest at an annual rate of 12% payable semiannually on January 1 and July 1. The journal entry on March 1, 1996, to record the bond issuance is as follows:

Cash	$163,200	
Bonds payable		$160,000
Interest expense ($160,000 × 0.12 × 2/12)		
(interest payable may be credited instead)		3,200

On July 1, 1996, the following entry is made:

Interest expense ($160,000 × 0.12 × 6/12)	$9,600	
Cash		$9,600

or

Interest expense ($160,000 × 0.12 × 4/12)	$6,400	
Interest payable	3,200	
Cash		$9,600

Effective Interest Method and Bonds Issued at a Discount

The issuance of bonds at a discount raises the need for the amortization of the bond discount. The *effective interest method*, also called the *present value amortization*, is used. To illustrate assume that on January 1, 1996, the Teta Company issued $200,000 of five-year bonds paying semiannual interest with a stated rate of 12% and an effective interest rate of 14%. The discount may be computed as follows:

Present value of principal ($200,000 × 0.508349)	$101,669.80
Present value of interest ($12,000 × 7.023582)	84,282.98

Selling price	$185,952.78
Face value	200,000.00
Discount (face value − selling price)	$14,047.22

The journal entry to record the issuance of the bonds follows:

Cash	$185,952.78	
Discount on bonds payable	14,047.22	
Bonds payable		$200,000.00

The amortization of discount on bonds payable using the effective interest method or present value amortization is computed at every interest payment date as follows:

Amortization amount = Bond interest expense − Bond interest paid

where:

Bond interest expense = Carrying value of bonds at the beginning of the period × Effective interest rate

Carrying Value = Face Value minus any unamortized discount plus any un-amortized premium

Bond Interest Paid = Face Amount of Bonds × Stated Interest Rate

The computation of the bond interest expense and discount amortization schedule is shown in Exhibit 6.1. It is used on June 30, 1996, to make the following entry:

Bond Interest Expense	$13,016.69	
Discount on Bonds Payable		$ 1,016.69
Cash		12,000.00

The following entry is made on December 31, 1996:

Bond Interest Expense	$13,087.86	
Discount on Bonds Payable		$ 1,087.86
Cash		12,000.00

Effective Interest Method and Bonds Issued at a Premium

To illustrate, assume that on January 1, 1996, the Smith Company issued $200,000 of five-year bonds paying semiannual interest with a stated rate of

Exhibit 6.1
Teta Company: Schedule of Bond Discount Amortization, Effective Interest Method—Semiannual Interest Payments for 12% Bonds Sold to Yield 14%

Date	Cash Paid (a)	Interest Expense (b)	Discount Amortized (c)	Book Value of Bonds (d)
01/01/96				$185,952.78
06/30/96	$12,000	$13,016.69	$1,016.69	$186,969.47
12/31/96	$12,000	$13,087.86	$1,087.86	$188,057.33
06/30/97	$12,000	$13,164.01	$1,164.01	$189,057.33
12/31/97	$12,000	$13,245.49	$1,254.49	$190,466.83
06/30/98	$12,000	$13,332.67	$1,332.67	$191,799.50
12/31/98	$12,000	$13,425.96	$1,425.96	$193,225.46
06/30/99	$12,000	$13,525.78	$1,525.78	$194,751.24
12/31/99	$12,000	$13,632.58	$1,632.58	$196,383.82
06/30/00	$12,000	$13,746.86	$1,746.86	$198,130.68
12/31/00	$12,000	$13,869.14	$1,869.14	$200,000.00

(a) $200,000 (face value) $\times$ 0.12 (stated rate) $\times$ ½ year.
(b) Previous book value $\times$ 0.14 (effective rate) $\times$ ½ year.
(c) (b) − (a).
(d) Previous book value + (c).

12% and an effective interest rate of 10%. The premium can be computed as follows:

Present value of principal ($200,000 $\times$ 0.613913)	$122,782.60
Present value of interest ($12,000 $\times$ 7.721735)	92,660.82
Selling price	$215,443.42
Face value	200,000.00
Premium	$ 15,443.42

The journal entry to record the issuance of the bonds is as follows:

Cash	$215,443.42	
Premium on bonds payable		$ 15,442.42
Bonds payable		200,000.00

Exhibit 6.2
Smith Company: Schedule of Bond Premium Amortization, Effective Interest Method—Semiannual Interest Payments for 12% Bonds Sold to Yield 10%

Date	Cash Paid (a)	Interest Expense (b)	Premium Amortized (c)	Book Value of Bonds (d)
01/01/96				$215,443.42
06/30/96	$12,000	$10,772.17	$1,227.83	$214,215.59
12/31/96	$12,000	$10,710.77	$1,289.22	$212,926.37
06/30/97	$12,000	$10,646.31	$1,353.68	$211,572.69
12/31/97	$12,000	$10,578.63	$1,421.36	$210,151.33
06/30/98	$12,000	$10,507.56	$1,492.43	$208,658.90
12/31/98	$12,000	$10,432.94	$1,567.05	$207,091.85
06/30/99	$12,000	$10,354.59	$1,645.40	$205,466.45
12/31/99	$12,000	$10,272.32	$1,727.67	$203,718.78
06/30/00	$12,000	$10,185.93	$1,814.06	$201,904.72
12/31/00	$12,000	$10,095.23	$1,904.76	$200,000.00

(a) $200,000 (face value) $\times$ 0.12 (stated rate) $\times$ ½ year.
(b) Previous book value $\times$ 0.14 (effective rate) $\times$ ½ year.
(c) (b) $-$ (a).
(d) Previous book value $-$ (c).

The computation of the bond interest expense and premium amortization schedule is shown in Exhibit 6.2. It is used on June 30, 1996, to make the following entry:

Bond interest expense	$10,772.17	
Premium on bonds payable	1,227.83	
Cash		$12,000.00

Accruing Bond Interest

When interest payment dates and the date of the financial statements issuance are not the same, there is a need for accounting for accrual of interest and a partial premium or discount amortization to be made at the end of the fiscal year. For example let us assume that the previous example of the Smith Company includes a need to report the financial statements by the end of March 1996. In that case, the matching concept dictates a proration over three months of interest and premium amortized as follows:

Premium amortized ($1,227.83 × 3/6)	$ 613.915
Interest expense ($10,772.17 × 3/6)	5,386.085
Interest payable ($12,000 × 3/6)	6,000.000

The journal entry at the end of March 1996 to record the accrual is as follows:

Interest expense	$5,386.085	
Premium on bonds payable		613.915
Interest payable		$6,000.000

Costs of Issuing Bonds

Various expenditures may be required for the issuance of bonds, including legal and accounting fees, printing costs, and registration fees. The present GAAP requirement is to defer the costs of issuing bonds and amortize over the life of the bond issue by the straight-line method. To illustrate, assume that on January 1, 1996, Tucker Company issued five-year bonds with a face value of $10,000,000 and a price of $10,500,000. Expenditures connected with the issue amounted to $250,000. The journal entry to record the issue is as follows:

Cash ($10,500,000 − $250,000)	$10,250,000	
Unamortized bond issue costs	250,000	
Premium on bonds payable		$ 500,000
Bonds payable		10,000,000

The journal entry on December 31, 1996, to record the amortization is as follows:

Bond interest expense	$50,000	
Unamortized bond issue costs ($250,000 / 5)		$50,000

The unamortized bond issue costs are to be disclosed as a deferred charge on other assets.

Bonds Issued with Detachable Warrants

Bonds issued with detachable warrants allow the bondholder to acquire a specific number of common shares at a given price and at a given time. The bonds are known as bonds with stock warrants or stock rights. The proceeds of the bonds are allocated to both the bonds and the warrants as follows:

Amount allocated to bonds

$$= \frac{\text{Market value of bonds without warrants}}{\text{Market value of bonds without warrants} + \text{Market value of warrants}}$$
$\times$ Issuance price

Amount allocated to warrant

$$= \frac{\text{Market value of warrant}}{\text{Market value of bonds without warrants} + \text{Market value of warrants}}$$
$\times$ Issuance price

To illustrate, let us assume that the Dimitra Company sold $400,000 of 12% bonds at 101 or $404,000. Each $1,000 bond is issued with 10 detachable warrants that entitle the holder to acquire one share of $10 par common stock for $30 per share. Following the issuance the bonds without the rights attached (ex rights) were quoted at 99 and the warrants at $3 each. The proceeds of the bonds are allocated as follows:

1. Amount allocated to bonds $= \dfrac{\$990 \times 400}{(990 \times 400) + (3 \times 400 \times 10)}$
$\times \$404,000 = \$392,117.68$

2. Amount allocated to warrant $= \dfrac{\$3 \times 400 \times 10}{(990 \times 400) + (3 \times 400 \times 10)}$
$\times \$404,000 = \$11,882.396$

As a result, the following entry may be made:

Cash	$404,000.00	
Discount on bonds payable ($400,000 − $392,117.68)	7,882.32	
Bonds payable		$400,000.00
Common stock warrants		11,882.32

The value of each warrant is $2.96 (11,882.32/4,000). Assuming 100 warrants were exercised, the following entry will be made:

Cash ($30 × 100)	$3,000.00	
Common stock warranty (2.97 × 100)	297.00	
Common stock (10 × 100)		$1,000.00
Additional paid-in capital on common stock		2,297.00

If all the remaining warrants expire, the following entry is made:

Common stock warrants	$12,585.32	
Additional paid-in capital on common stock		$11,585.32

Accounting for Convertible Bonds and Preferred Stock

Convertible bonds are bonds that can be converted into common stocks, allowing the bondholder (a creditor) to become a stockholder by exchanging the bonds for a specified number of shares. Issuance of convertible bonds may be motivated by making an increase in equity later, or an increase in bonds now, more attractive through the conversion feature. Other factors that may motivate a firm to issue convertible bonds are related to its desire to

1. Avoid the downward price pressure on its stock that placing a large new issue of common stock on the market would cause.
2. Avoid the direct sale of common stock when it believes its stock currently is undervalued in the market.
3. Penetrate that segment of the capital market that is unwilling or unable to participate in a direct common stock issue.
4. Minimize the costs associated with selling securities.[1]

The first accounting problem facing convertible debts is the accounting at the time of issuance. Following *APB Opinion Number 14*,[2] accounting for convertible debt at the time of issuance treats it solely as a debt, with the discount or premium amortized to its maturity date. The second accounting problem arises at the time of conversion. Two methods can be used for recording the conversion.

1. *Book value method.* Under this method the stockholders' equity (common stock and additional paid-in capital) is credited at the book value of convertible bonds on the date of conversion, resulting in no gain or loss being recognized.
2. *Market value method.* Under this method the stockholders' equity (common stock and additional paid-in capital) is credited at the market value of the shares issued on the date of conversion, resulting in the recognition of a gain or loss to be included as ordinary rather than extraordinary income.

To illustrate both methods let us assume that the Bulls Corporation has issued $20,000 worth of convertible bonds that now have a book value of $21,000. Each $1,000 bond is convertible into 20 shares of common stock (par value $40). At the time of conversion, interest had been paid on the debt, and the market value of the common stock is $60 per share. The entries under both methods would be:

A. Under the book value method:

Bonds payable	$20,000	
Premium on bonds payable	1,000	
Common Stock ($40 × 20 × 20)		$16,000

Additional paid-in capital from bond conversion ($21,000 − $16,000)		5,000

B. Under the market value method:

Bonds payable	$20,000	
Premium on bonds payable	1,000	
Loss on conversion ($48,000 − $21,000)	27,000	
Common stock ($40 × 20 × 20)		$16,000
Additional paid-in capital from bond conversion ($40 × 20 × 40)		32,000

Let us assume that in the previous example, the firm has agreed to pay an extra $5,000 to the bondholders to induce conversion. The following entry under the book value method will be made:

Debt conversion expense	$ 5,000	
Bonds payable	20,000	
Premium on bonds payable	1,000	
Common stock		$16,000
Additional paid-in capital		5,000
Cash		5,000

The cash used to induce conversion is treated as an ordinary expense of the current period.

Upon retirement of a convertible debt, the difference between the cash acquisition price of the debt and its carrying amount is treated as an extraordinary gain or loss on extinguishment of debt.[3] The book value is generally preferred because it avoids the type of manipulation of income through gain or loss that is permitted under the market value method. However, for convertible preferred stock, *only the book value method is permitted for conversion, where*:

a. Convertible preferred stock and additional paid-in capital is debited.

b. Common stock and additional paid-in capital (in case an excess exists) is credited.

c. Retained earning is debited if the par value of the common stock exceeds the par value of preferred stock.

To illustrate, let us assume that the Green Company issued 5,000 shares of common stock (par value $10) upon conversion of 5,000 shares of preferred stock (par value $5) that has been previously used with a premium of $800. The entry is as follows:

Convertible preferred stock (5,000 × $5)	$25,000	
Paid-in capital in excess of par (premium on preferred stock)	800	
Retained earnings ($50,000 − $25,800)	24,200	
Common stock (5,000 × $10)		$50,000

Some states, however, require that the additional return used to induce conversion should be debited to paid-in capital.

ACCOUNTING FOR EXTINGUISHMENT AND DEFEASANCE

Long-term debt can be retired either through an extinguishment of debt (reacquisition of debt) or a defeasance of debt (in-substance defeasance of debt). Both practices are examined next.

Reacquisition of Debt

Bonds can be reacquired at maturity or prior to maturity. If the bonds are reacquired at maturity, the premium or discount and issue costs are fully amortized, and the face value of the bond is equal to the market value at the time, resulting in no gain or loss.

If the bonds are retired before maturity or replaced with a new issue (refunding), a different situation arises. First, the *net carrying amount* of the bonds is adjusted for amortized premium, discount, and cost of issuance. Second, the difference between the net carrying amount and the *reacquisition price (call price)* is either a gain or loss from extinguishment. All material gains and losses from debt extinguishment (both retirements and refunding) are classified as extraordinary items in the year of cancellation.

To illustrate let us assume that the Mavrides Corporation had issued $200,000 worth of 10-year bonds paying 12% at 97 on January 1, 1995. The bonds, paying interest on January 1 and July 1, and callable at 105 plus accrued interest, were recalled on June 30, 2000. Two entries are required. The first entry, used to record the current interest expense as well as the amortization of the expired discount, is as follows:

Interest expense	$12,300	
Discount on bonds payable ($6,000/10) × ½		$ 300
Interest payable ($200,000 × 0.12 × ½)		12,000

The second entry, used to record the reacquisition of debt, is as follows:

Bonds payable	$200,000	
Interest payable	12,000	

Extraordinary loss on bond redemption	12,700	
Discount on bonds payable		$ 2,700
Cash		222,000

where

a. The discount on bonds payable is computed as:

The original discount	$6,000
Amortized on a straight-line basis for 5½ years (5.5 × $600)	(3,300)
Unamortized discount	$2,700

b. Cash is $200,000 × 1.05 + 12,000.
c. Extraordinary loss on bond redemption:

Call price (excluding interest)		$210,000
Less face value unamortized discount	$200,000	
	(2,700)	(197,300)
		$ 12,700

In-Substance Defeasance

In-substance defeasance of debt is an arrangement whereby the debtor places cash or purchased securities in an irrevocable trust to be used solely to pay off the interest and principal of debt. To illustrate in-substance defeasance of debt, let us assume that on January 1, 1996, the Das Company issued $100,000 of five-year, 12% bonds that yield 10%. On December 31, 1998, when the book value of the bonds is $103, 545.92, the Das Company purchased $96,545.92 in $100,000 12% U.S. government bonds to service the bond interest and principal and extinguish its debt. The journal entry to record this extinguishment is as follows:

Bonds payable	$100,000.00	
Premium on bonds payable	3,545.92	
Cash		$96,545.92
Extraordinary gain on bond Extinguishment		7,000.00

LONG-TERM NOTES PAYABLE

Long-term notes differ from short-term notes on the basis of different maturities. They differ from long-term bonds in terms of tradability on organized public securities markets. Like a bond, a note payable is recorded at the present value of its future interest and principal cash flows, with any discount or premium amortized over the life of the note. Similarly, interest expense is recorded over the life of the note on the basis of the effective interest method. Examples of issuance of long-term notes payable follow.

Issuance of Note at Face Value

Let us return to the case of the Katori Company earlier in this chapter and assume the same facts for the Katori Company except that the firm issued long-term notes rather than bonds. Because the stated rate and the effective rate are the same, the present value of the note and its face value at the time of issuance are the same, resulting in no premium or discount. Accordingly, the entry at the time of issuance is as follows:

Cash	$200,000	
Notes payable		$200,000

On July 1, 1996, to record the first semiannual interest payment of $9,000 ($200,000 × 9% × ½):

Interest expense	$9,000	
Cash		$9,000

Issuance of a Note at Other than Face Value and at Zero Interest

Notes issued at other than face value and at zero interest are known as zero coupon bonds. The difference between the face value and the cash received (present value) is either a discount or premium to be amortized to interest expense over the life of the note. To illustrate let us assume that the Ignacius Corporation issued three-year, $20,000, zero coupon bonds for $15,443.60, that is, with a discount of $4,556.40. The present value of the note is $15,443.60. Therefore $15,443.60 equals the present value of three years at an interest rate (i) of $20,000.

$$\text{Present value at interest rate } (i) \text{ for three years} = \frac{\$15,443.60}{\$20,000.00} = 0.77218$$

The present value table shows that 0.77218 is the present value of $1 for three periods at 9%. Therefore the implicit interest rate is 9%. Exhibit 6.3 shows the amortization of the note discount using the effective interest method. The two main entries follow:

Exhibit 6.3
Schedule of Note Discount Amortization, Effective Interest Method for 0% Note Discounted at 9%

	Cash Paid	Interest Expense	Discount Amortized	Carrying Amount of Note
Date of Issue				$15,433.60
End of Year 1	$ ---0---	$1,389.924 (a)	$1,389.924 (b)	$16,833.524
End of Year 2	$ ---0---	$1,515.017	$1,515.017	$18,348.541
End of Year 3	$ ---0---	$1,651.458	$1,651.458	$20,000.00

(a) $15,443.60 × 0.09 = $1,389.924.
(b) (a) − 0.
(c) $15,443.60 + $1,389.924.
(d) Rounded.

1. At the time of issuance

Cash	$15,443.60	
Discount on notes payable	4,556.40	
Notes payable		$20,000.00

2. At the end of the first year

Interest expense	$1,389.924	
Discount on notes payable		$1,389.924

Issuance of Note at Other than Face Value and with Interest

Let us assume that the Ignacius Corporation now issues a $20,000, three-year nonbearing note at stated interest of 10%. The market rate for a similar note is 12%.

The present value of the note is equal to:

The present value of the principal ($20,000 [0.7118])	$14,326.00
The present value of the interest ($2,000 [2.40183])	4,803.66
The present value of the note	$19,039.66
The face value of the note is equal to	20,000
The discount is equal to ($20,000 − $19,039.66)	$ 960.34

Therefore at the time of issuance, the following entry is made:

Cash	$19,039.66
Discount on notes payable	960.34
Notes payable	$20,000

Exhibit 6.4 shows the amortization of the note discount using the effective interest method. The entry at the end of the year is as follows:

Interest expense	$2,284.759
Discount on bonds payable	$ 284.759
Cash	2,000.000

Issuance of Notes in Exchange for Cash and Rights or Privileges

Notes can be issued for cash and include special rights or privileges. One example of rights or privileges is the right of the holders of the note to buy certain goods from the company at lower than the prevailing prices. The difference between the present value of the note and the amount of cash received is recorded as a discount on the note to be debited and an unearned revenue to be credited. The discount is to be amortized as a charge to interest expense using the effective interest method. The unearned revenue is amortized as revenue over the life of the contract on the basis of appropriate revenue recognition criteria, for example, in the same proportion as the period sales to total sales to the customers.

Let us assume that the Clinton Company borrowed $200,000 by issuing a three-year, non-interest-bearing note to a customer, that allows the customer to buy an equal amount of goods from the Clinton Company at reduced prices

Exhibit 6.4
Schedule of Note Discount Amortization for 10% Note Discount at 12%

	Cash Paid	Interest Expense	Discount Amortized	Carrying Amount of Note
Date of Issue				$19,039.66
End of Year 1	$2,000 (a)	$2,284.759 (b)	$284.759 (c)	$19,324.419
End of Year 2	$2,000	$2,318.930	$318.930	$19,643.349
End of Year 3	$2,000	$2,357.201	$357.201	$20,000.00

(a) $20,000 × 0.10 = $2,000.
(b) $19,039.66 × 0.12 = $2,284.759.
(c) (b) − (a).
(d) $19,039.66 + (c).

over a 10-year period. The company's incremental borrowing rate is 12%. Therefore the present value of the note is $142,356 ($200,000 × 0.71180). The following entries are made:

A. At the time of issuance:

Cash	$200,000	
Discount on notes payable ($200,000 − $142,356)	57,664	
Notes payable		$200,000
Unearned revenue		57,644

B. At the end of the first year:

Interest expense ($142,356 × 0.12)	$17,082.72	
Discount on notes payable		$17,082.72
Unearned revenue ($57,644/10)	$ 5,764.40	
Sales revenue		$ 5,764.40

C. At the end of the second year:

Interest expense [($142,356 + $17,082.72) × 0.12]	$19,132.646	
Discount on notes payable		$19,132.646
Unearned revenue	$ 5,764.40	
Sales revenue		$ 5,764.40

Issuance of Notes in Exchange for Property, Goods, or Services

Notes can be issued in exchange for property, goods, or services. The stated interest rate is presumed fair unless:

1. No interest rate is stated,
2. The stated interest rate is unreasonable, or
3. The face value of the note is materially different from the current cash sales price of the property, goods, or service, or from the current market value of the note.

In this case, the fair market value of the note is used as the present value of the note. When there is no stated interest rate, the interest element is the difference between the face value of the note and the fair value of the property.

To illustrate, let us assume that on January 1, 1996, the Weygandt Company purchased equipment, with a useful life of five years, from the Zribi Company for a non-interest-bearing $30,000 five-year note. The Weygandt Company's incremental borrowing rate is 12%. Therefore, the present value of $30,000 to be repaid at the end of five years at 12% is $17,022.81 ($30,000 × 0.567427). The following entries are made:

1. At the date of issuance:

Equipment	$17,022.81	
Discount on notes payable	12,977.19	
Notes payable		$30,000.00

2. At the end of the first year:

Interest expense [($30,000 − $12,977.19) × 0.12]	$ 2,042.73	
Discount on notes payable		$ 2,042.73
Depreciation expense	$ 3,404.56	
Accumulated depreciation		$ 3,404.56

3. At the end of the second year:

Interest expense [($30,000 − ($12,977.19 − $2,042.73)) × 0.12]	$ 2,287.86	
Discount on notes payable		$ 2,287.86
Depreciation on expense	$ 3,404.56	
Accumulated depreciation		$ 3,404.56

Issuance of Notes with Imputed Interest

If the stated interest rate is found to be unreasonable, an imputed interest rate is required, leading to a discount or a premium to be amortized. For example, let us assume that on December 31, 1996, the Pegg Company issued a note to the Alvertos Company for the purchase of a building, with a face value of $600,000, a due date of December 1,2000, and a stated interest rate of 2%. The market conditions dictated that an 8% interest rate should be imputed for the case.

A. The present value of the note is equal to:

Present value of $600,000 due in five years at 6% per year = $600,000 × 0.68058	$408,348.00
Present value of $12,000 interest payable per year for five years at 8% = $12,000 × 3.99271	47,912.52
Present value of the note	$456,260.52

B. The face value of the note is equal to   600,000.00

C. The discount of the note is equal to ($600,000 − $456,260.52) $143,739.48

Therefore the entry at the date of issuance is as follows:

Building	$456,260.52	
Discount on notes payable	143,739.48	
Notes payable		$600,000.00

Exhibit 6.5 shows the schedule of note discount amortization using the effective interest method. At the end of the first year, the entry for the first year's interest and discount amortization is as follows:

Interest expense	$36,508.84	
Discount on notes payable		$24,500.84
Cash		12,000.00

ACCOUNTING FOR LOAN IMPAIRMENTS

Loan impairment arises when it is probable that the creditor may not be able to collect all of the principal and interest due on a loan. For example, let us assume that on December 31, 1996, the Gore Company issued a $1,000,000, five-year, non-interest-bearing note to the First Security Bank, yielding 10% per

Exhibit 6.5
Schedule of Note Discount Amortization with Imputed Interest

Date	Cash Paid (2%)	Interest Expense (8%)	Discount Amortized	Carrying Amount of Note
12/31/96				$456,260.52
12/31/97	$12,000 (a)	$36,500.841 (b)	$24,500.841 (c)	$480,761.36
12/31/98	$12,000	$38,460.908	$26,460.908	$507,222.26
12/31/99	$12,000	$40,577.78	$28,577.78	$535,800.04
12/31/00	$12,000	$42,864.003	$30,864.003	$566,664.04
12/31/01	$12,000	$45,333.123	$33,333.123	$600,000.00

(a) $600,000 × 2% = $12,000.
(b) $456,260.52 × 8% = $36,500.841.
(c) $36,500.841 − $12,000 = $24,500.841.

Exhibit 6.6
First Security Bank: First Loan Amortization Schedule

Date	Cash Received	Interest Revenue (10%)	Discount Amortized	Carrying Amount of Note
12/31/96				$620,920.00
12/31/97	$ ---0---	$62,092.00 (a)	$62,092.00	$683,012.00 (b)
12/31/98	$ ---0---	$68,301.20	$68,301.20	$751,313.20
12/31/99	$ ---0---	$75,131.32	$75,131.32	$856,444.52
12/31/00	$ ---0---	$82,644.452	$82,644.452	$909,088.97
12/31/01	$ ---0---	$90,908.897	$90,908.897	$1,000,000.00

(a) $620,920 × 0.10 = $62,092.
(b) $620,920 + $62,092 = $683,012.00.

year. At the date of the issuance the Gore Company paid $620,920 ($1,000,000 × 0.62092). The following entries were made:

A. By the creditor, the First Security Bank:

Notes receivable	$1,000,000	
Discount on notes receivable		$379,080
Cash		620,920

B. By the debtor, the Gore Company:

Cash	$620,920	
Discount on notes payable	379,080	
Notes payable		$1,000,000

Exhibit 6.6. shows the note discount amortization using the effective interest method.

Now, let us assume that because of bad economic conditions for the Gore Company, the First Security Bank estimates on December 31, 1998, that only $800,000 is collectable at the end of the five years. Therefore, it estimates its loss due to impairment as follows:

Carrying amount of the loan, December 31, 1998	$751,312.20
Present value of $800,000 due in three years at 10% compounded annually ($800,000 × 0.75132)	601,056.00
Loss due to impairment ($751,312.20 − $601,056)	$150,256.20

Exhibit 6.7
First Security Bank: Second Loan Amortization Schedule

Date	Cash Received	Interest Revenue (10%)	Discount Amortized	Carrying Amount of Note
12/31/98				$601,056.00
12/31/99	$ ---0---	$60,105.60 (a)	$60,105.60	$661,161.60 (b)
12/31/00	$ ---0---	$66,116.16	$66,116.16	$727,277.76
12/31/01	$ ---0---	$72,727.776	$72,727.776	$800,000.00

(a) $601,056.00 × 10% = $60,105.60.
(b) $601,056.00 + $60,105.60 = $661,161.60.

Therefore, the First Security Bank made the following entry:

Bad debt expense	$150,256.20	
Allowance for doubtful accounts		$150,256.20

The Gore Company does not make an entry. The First Security Bank prepares a new schedule of discount amortization based on the new carrying amount of $601,056, which is shown in Exhibit 6.7. The following entries are made on December 31, 1999:

A. By the First Security Bank

Discount on notes receivable	$75,131.32	
Interest revenue		$60,105.60
Allowance for doubtful accounts		15,025.72

B. By the Gore Company

Interest expense	$75,131.32	
Discount on notes payable		$75,131.32

At the maturity date, on January 1, 2000, the Gore Company pays $800,000 and the following entries are made:

A. By the First Security Bank

Cash	$800,000	
Allowance for doubtful accounts	200,000	
Notes receivable		$1,000,000

B. By the Gore Company

Notes payable	$1,000,000	
Cash		$800,000
Gain on extinguishment		200,000

ACCOUNTING FOR TROUBLED DEBT RESTRUCTURINGS

As stated in *FASB Statement No. 15* a troubled debt restructuring crisis occurs when a creditor "for economic or legal reasons related to the debtor's financial difficulties grants a concession to the debtor that it would not otherwise consider." The troubled debt restructuring can take one of two forms:

1. Settlement of debt at less than its carrying amount.
2. Modification of terms of the debt.

Settlement of Debt

A debt can be settled by an equity or asset exchange. In either case, the equity or the asset should be valued at its fair market value.

For example, let us assume that on December 31, 1996, the Kurk Company exchanges 40,000 of its own shares to a bank holding a note payable and accrued interest totaling $1,800,000. The accrued interest amounts to $800,000. The shares have a par value of $10 per share and a market price of $30 per share. At the date of equity exchange, the following entry is initiated by the Kurk Company:

Notes payable	$1,000,000	
Interest payable	800,000	
Common stock (40,000 × $10)		$400,000
Additional paid-in capital (40,000 × $20)		800,000
Extraordinary gain on debt restructure		600,000

At the same date, the following entry is made by the bank:

Investment in Kurk	$1,200,000	
Loss on restructured loan	600,000	
Notes receivable		$1,000,000
Interest receivable		800,000

Let us now assume that instead of exchanging equity, the Kurk Company decided to exchange land it bought five years ago for $800,000 and that has a current market value of $1,000,000. In such a case, the Kurk Company initiates the following entry:

Notes payable	$1,200,000	
Interest payable	600,000	
Extraordinary gain on debt restructure		$800,000
Gain on disposal of land		200,000
Land		800,000

At the same date, the following entry is made by the bank:

Land	$1,000,000	
Loss on restructured loan	800,000	
Notes receivable		$1,000,000
Interest receivable		800,000

In both the asset and equity exchanges, the bank would have to change the loss (or gain) on the restructured loan to allowance for doubtful accounts if an allowance was available.

Modifications of Terms

The debtor can ask for a modification of terms. Some of the possible modifications include

a. Deduction of the stated interest rate.
b. Extension of the maturity date.
c. Reduction of the face amount of the debt.
d. Reduction of accrued interest.

The accountings for modification of terms differ between the debtor and the creditor. The debtor computes the new loan on the basis of *undiscounted* future cash payments (principal plus interest) specified by the new terms, whereas the creditor relies on *discounted amounts*. Two situations may arise for the debtor:

Situation 1: When the undiscounted restructured cash flows are higher than (or equal to) the carrying value of the liability, no gain is recognized by the debtor, the carrying value of the liability is not reduced, and a new effective rate is used to record the interest expense in future periods.

Situation 2: When the undiscounted restructured cash flows are lower than the carrying value of the liability, a gain is recognized by the debtor, the carrying value of the liability is reduced, and no interest expense is recognized in future periods.

Both situations are examined next.

No Gain Is Recognized by Debtor

To illustrate situation 1 where no gain is recognized by the debtor, let us assume that on December 31, 1996, the Mario Company restructures a $12,671,092 debt with its bank that includes a principal of $12,000,000 and accrued interest of $671,092. The new terms include:

1. Forgiving the $671,092 accrued interest.
2. Reducing the principal by $2,000,000.
3. Extending the maturity date from December 31, 1996, to December 31, 2000.
4. Reducing the interest rate from 12% to 10%.

The total future cash payments resulting from the new terms are $15,000,000 (principal of $10,000,000 at the end of five years and interest of $5,000,000 at the end of each year for five years). Because the undiscounted amount of principal and interest of $15,000,000 is higher than the carrying value of the liability of $12,671,052, no gain is recognized and the carrying value of the liability is not reduced. However, the difference of $2,328,908 is recognized as interest expense using the effective interest method. The effective interest rate is obtained by solving for i in the following formula:

$$\$12,671,092 = \frac{1}{(1 + i)^5} \times 1,000,000 + 1 - \frac{1}{(1 + i)^5/i} \times 1,000,000$$

Solving the equation leads to $i = 4\%$.

Therefore, on December 31, 1995, the Mario Company makes the following entry to transfer the accrued interest payable balance to the notes payable account as follows:

Interest payable	$671,092	
Notes payable		$671,092

Exhibit 6.8 shows the computation of the interest expense. Therefore, on December 31, 1997 (and at the end of each year), the Mario Company makes the following entry:

Notes payable	$493,156.40	
Interest expense	506,842.60	
Cash		$1,000,000

At the end of the year 2000, the following entry will be made:

Exhibit 6.8
Mario Company, Schedule of Interest Computation

Date	Cash Paid (10%)	Interest Expense (4%)	Reduction of Carrying Amount	Carrying Value of the Note
12/31/95				$12,671,092
12/31/96	$1,000,000 (a)	$506,843.68 (b)	$493,156.40	$12,177,936 (d)
12/31/97	$1,000,000	$487,117.44	$512,882.60	$11,665,054
12/31/98	$1,000,000	$466,602.16	$533,397.90	$11,131,657
12/31/99	$1,000,000	$445,266.28	$554,733.80	$10,576,924
12/31/00	$1,000,000	$423,076.96	$10,576,924	$ ---0---

(a) $10,000,000 × 0.10.
(b) $12,671,092 × 0.04.
(d) $12,671,092 − $493,156.40.

Notes payable	$10,576,924	
Interest expense	423,076	
Cash		$11,000,000

The situation is different for the bank. It computes the loss on restructuring as follows:

A. Present value of restructured cash flows:

Present value of $10,000,000 due in five years at 12% ($10,000,000 × 0.56743)	$5,674,300
Present value of $1,000,000 interest payable annually for five years at 12% ($1,000,000 × 3.60478)	3,604,780
Present value of restructured value	$9,279,080

B. Prerestructure value	12,671,092
C. Loss on restructuring ($12,671,092 − $9,279,080)	$3,392,012

Accordingly, the bank makes the following entry on December 31, 1995:

Allowance for doubtful accounts	$3,392,012	
Notes receivable		$3,392,012

Exhibit 6.9 shows the computation of interest revenue. Therefore, on December 31, 1997, the bank makes the following entry:

Exhibit 6.9
Schedule of Computation of Interest Revenue

Date	Cash Received (a) 10%	Interest Expense (b) 12%	Discount Amortized (c)	Carrying Value of the Note
12/31/95				$9,279,080
12/31/96	$1,000,00	$1,113,489.60	$113,489.60	$9,392,569.60 (d)
12/31/97	$1,000,000	$1,127,108.30	$127,108.30	$9,519,677.90
12/31/98	$1,000,000	$1,142,361.30	$142,361.30	$9,662,039.20
12/31/99	$1,000,000	$1,159,444.70	$159,444.70	$9,821,483.90
12/31/00	$1,000,000	$1,178,578.00	$178,578.00	$10,000,000.00

(a) $10,000,000 × 10%.
(b) $9,879,080 × 12%.
(c) $1,113,489.60 − $1,000,000.
(d) $9,279,080 + $113,489.60.

Cash	$1,000,000.00	
Notes receivable	113,489.60	
Interest revenue		$1,113,489.60

At maturity the following additional entry is made:

Cash	$10,000,000	
Notes receivable		$10,000,000

A Gain Is Recognized by the Debtor

To illustrate situation 2, let us assume the same facts as in the previous example except that the bank reduced the principal by $6,000,000. In such a case, the total future cash payments resulting from the new terms are $9,000,000 (principal of $6,000,000 at the end of five years and interest of $3,000,000 at the end of each year for five years). Because the undiscounted amount of principal and interest of $9,000,000 is less than the carrying value of the liability of $12,671,092, the Mario Company will reduce its liability by $3,671,092 and recognize an extraordinary gain of $3,671,092. However, the bank computes its loss on restructuring as follows:

A. Present value of restructured cash flows:

Present value of $6,000,000 due in five years at 12% $3,404,580
($6,000,000 × 0.56743)

Exhibit 6.10
Schedule of Interest Revenue Computations

Date	Interest Received (10%)	Interest Revenue (12%)	Increase in Carrying Amount	Carrying Amount of the Note
12/31/95				$5,567,448.00
12/31/96	$600,000 (a)	$668,093.76 (b)	$68,093.76 (c)	$5,635,541.70
12/31/97	$600,000	$676,265.00	$76,256.00	$5,711,806.70
12/31/98	$600,000	$685,416.80	$85,416.80	$5,797,223.50
12/31/99	$600,000	$695,666.82	$95,666.82	$5,892,890.30
12/31/00	$600,000	$707,146.83	$107,141.83	$6,000,000.00

(a) $6,000,000 × 0.10.
(b) $5,567,488 × 0.12.
(c) $668,093.76 − $600,000.00.

Present value of $600,000 interest payable annually for five years at 12% ($600,000 × 3.60478)	2,162,868
Present value of restructured cash flows	$5,567,448
B. Prerestructure value	12,671,092
C. Loss on restructuring ($12,671,092 − $5,567,448)	$7,103,644

The following entries are made on December 31, 1996:

A. By the Mario Company

Notes payable	$3,671,092	
Gain on restructuring of debt		$3,671,092

B. By the Bank

Allowance for doubtful accounts	$7,103,644	
Notes receivable		$6,000,000
Discount on notes receivable		1,103,644

Exhibit 6.10 shows the schedule of interest revenue computation for the bank. The following entries are made:

A. By the Mario Company

December 31, 1997, 1998, 1999, 2000

Notes payable	$600,000	
Cash		$600,000

December 31, 2000

Notes payable	$6,000,000	
Cash		$6,000,000

B. By the Bank

December 31, 1997

Cash	$600,000.00	
Discount on notes receivable	68,093.76	
Interest revenue		$668,093.76

December 31, 2000

Cash	$6,000,000	
Notes receivable		$6,000,000

CONCLUSION

This chapter covered the main techniques associated with accounting for long-term liabilities in conformity with generally accepted accounting principles.

NOTES

1. Loren A. Nikolai and John D. Bazely, *Intermediate Accounting*, 6th ed. (Cincinnati, Ohio: South-Western Publishing Co., 1994), 543.

2. Accounting Principles Board, "Accounting for Convertible Debt and Debt Issued with Stock Purchase Warrants," *APB Opinion Number 14* (New York: AICPA, 1969), par. 12.

3. Accounting Principles Board, "Early Extinguishment of Debt," *Opinion of the Accounting Principles Board No. 26* (New York: AICPA, 1977).

SELECTED READINGS

Accounting Principles Board. "Early Extinguishment of Debt," *Opinions of the Accounting Principles Board*. New York, AICPA, 1972.

Accounting Principles Board. "Interest on Receivables and Payables," *Opinions of the Accounting Principles Board Number 21*. New York: AICPA, 1971.

Duke, J. C., and H. G. Hunt III. "An Equicial Examination of Debt Covenant Restrictions and Accounting Related Debt Proxies." *Journal of Accounting and Economics* (January 1990): 52.

Financial Accounting Standards Board. "Balance Sheet Classification of Short-Term Obligations Expected to be Refinanced," *FASB Statement of Financial Accounting Standard Number 6*. Stamford, Conn.: FASB, 1975.

Financial Accounting Standards Board. "Reporting Gains and Losses from Extinguishment of Debt," *Statement of Financial Accounting Standards Number 4*. Stamford, Conn.: FASB, 1975.

Financial Accounting Standards Board. "Elements of Financial Statements of Business Enterprises," *Statements of Financial Accounting Concepts Number 3*. Stamford, Conn.: FASB, 1980.

Financial Accounting Standards Board. "Disclosure of Long-Term Obligations," *Statement of Financial Accounting Standards Number 47*. Stamford, Conn.: FASB, 1981.

Financial Accounting Standards Board. "Extinguishment of Debt," *Statements of Financial Accounting Standard Number 76*. Stamford, Conn.: FASB, 1983.

Financial Accounting Standards Board. "Disclosure of Information about Financial Instruments with Off-Balance Sheet Risk and Financial Instruments with Concentrations of Credit Risk," *Statements of Financial Accounting Standards Number 105*. Norwalk, Conn.: FASB, 1990.

Financial Accounting Standards Board. "Disclosure about Derivative Financial Instruments and Fair Value of Financial Instruments," *Statement of Financial Accounting Standards Number 119*. Norwalk, Conn.: FASB, 1994.

Forsyth, T., S. Fletcher, and R. Turpen. "Corporate Borrowing: Cash Flow Implications of In-Substance Defeasance." *CPA Journal* (October 1994): 62–63.

Leftwich, R. "Accounting Information in Private Market: Evidence from Private Lending Agreements." *Accounting Review* (January 1983): 23–42.

Samuelson, Richard A. "Accounting for Liabilities to Perform Services." *Accounting Horizons* (September 1993): 32–45.

Appendix A

The Theory of Capital Structure

Source: M. Harris and A. Raviv, ''The Theory of Capital Structure,'' *Journal of Finance* (March 1991), pp. 297–355. Reprinted with permission.

MILTON HARRIS and ARTUR RAVIV*

ABSTRACT

This paper surveys capital structure theories based on agency costs, asymmetric information, product/input market interactions, and corporate control considerations (but excluding tax-based theories). For each type of model, a brief overview of the papers surveyed and their relation to each other is provided. The central papers are described in some detail, and their results are summarized and followed by a discussion of related extensions. Each section concludes with a summary of the main implications of the models surveyed in the section. Finally, these results are collected and compared to the available evidence. Suggestions for future research are provided.

THE MODERN THEORY OF capital structure began with the celebrated paper of Modigliani and Miller (1958). They (MM) pointed the direction that such theories must take by showing under what conditions capital structure is irrelevant. Since then, many economists have followed the path they mapped. Now, some 30 years later it seems appropriate to take stock of where this research stands and where it is going. Our goal in this survey is to synthesize the *recent* literature, summarize its results, relate these to the known empirical evidence, and suggest promising avenues for future research.[1]

As stated, however, this goal is too ambitious to result in a careful understanding of the state of capital structure research. Consequently, we have chosen to narrow the scope of our inquiry. First, we focus on the *theory* of capital structure. Although we discuss the empirical literature as it relates to the predictions of theory, we make no attempt to give a comprehensive survey of this literature. We simply take the empirical results at face value and do not review or criticize the methods used in these papers. Second, we

* Harris is Chicago Board of Trade Professor of Finance and Business Economics, Graduate School of Business, University of Chicago. Raviv is Alan E. Peterson Distinguished Professor of Finance, Kellogg Graduate School of Management, Northwestern University. We gratefully acknowledge the financial support of the Bradley Foundation. Professor Harris wishes to acknowledge partial financial support from Dimensional Fund Advisors. We also thank seminar participants at the University of Chicago, UCLA, and Tel Aviv University and Michael Fishman, Robert Hansen, Ronen Israel, Steven Kaplan, Robert McDonald, Andrei Shleifer, René Stulz (the editor), Robert Vishny, an anonymous referee, and especially Vincent Warther whose tireless research assistance was invaluable.

[1] Some other recent surveys include Taggart (1985), Masulis (1988), Miller (1988), Ravid (1988), and Allen (1990) and comments on Miller (1988) by Bhattacharya (1988), Modigliani (1988), Ross (1988), and Stiglitz (1988). Taggart (1985) and Masulis (1988) are general surveys. Allen (1990) focuses on security design, and Ravid (1988) concentrates on interactions between capital structure and the product market.

arbitrarily exclude theories based primarily on tax considerations. While such theories are undoubtedly of great empirical importance, we believe that they have been adequately surveyed.[2] Moreover, tax-based research is not our comparative advantage. Third, we systematically exclude certain topics that, while related to capital structure theory, do not have this theory as their central focus. These include literature dealing with the call or conversion of securities, dividend theories, bond covenants and maturity, bankruptcy law, pricing and method of issuance of new securities, and preferred stock. In short, we concentrate on nontax-driven capital structure theories.

Although the above considerations exclude many papers, a fairly large literature remains. To highlight the current state of the art, we consider mainly papers written since 1980. The only exception to this statement is the inclusion of papers written in the mid-to-late 1970's that serve as the foundation for the more recent literature. A diligent search of both published and unpublished research meeting the above criteria for inclusion resulted in over 150 papers. Obviously, we could not survey all these papers here in detail. Consequently, we were forced to pick and choose those papers that, in our opinion, are the most important or the most representative of a given stream of research. Naturally, this selection process is biased by our own tastes and interests. Thus, we tend to emphasize papers based on the economics of information, incentives, and contracting. We apologize to those authors whose papers were omitted or were not given the attention the authors believe them to deserve.

In organizing the survey, several options were available. One approach which has proved fruitful in other areas is to construct or identify a very general model and then examine how existing models specialize this framework. This approach has the advantage of showing clearly the interrelationships among models. In the case of capital structure, however, the set of features one must include in such a general model is so large and complicated that the resulting structure would not yield clear insights. A related approach is to ask what issues might be resolved by theories of capital structure. This "wish list" would include questions such as what the effect is on capital structure of changes in the volatility of cash flows, firm size, elasticity of demand for the product, the extent of insider private information, etc. The survey would then proceed to document the answers available in the literature. The problem with organizing the survey in this way is that often a single model addresses several issues. Such a model would then require discussion in several places. Moreover, a closely related model focusing on a different issue would be presented separately, making a comparison of the two models difficult to exposit. Because of these difficulties, we have chosen instead to organize our survey based on the forces that determine capital structure.

Grouping models based on the force driving capital structure allows discussion of the model to be consolidated in one place and facilitates an examina-

---

[2] In addition to those surveys mentioned in footnote 1, see Bradley, et al. (1984).

tion of the relationships among similar models. We have identified four categories of determinants of capital structure. These are the desire to

- ameliorate conflicts of interest among various groups with claims to the firm's resources, including managers (the agency approach),
- convey private information to capital markets or mitigate adverse selection effects (the asymmetric information approach),
- influence the nature of products or competition in the product/input market, or
- affect the outcome of corporate control contests.

Each of these four categories is discussed in a separate section. Many of the papers we survey fit well in more than one category. We include these in the category corresponding to the most important driving force of the model.

In each topic, we first give a brief overview of the papers surveyed and their relation to each other. We then describe in some detail the central papers and their results. This is generally followed by a discussion of related extensions. Note that we do not exposit all the subtleties of even the models on which we focus the most attention. Instead we try to present the main idea in its most stripped-down form. Each section concludes with a summary of the main implications of the models surveyed in the section. Finally, we collect these results and compare them to the available evidence. Since each section is self-contained, readers not interested in the entire survey can pick and choose sections. Moreover, the summary subsection in each of Sections I through IV can also be read independently. Readers interested only in the overall summary and conclusions should read Sections V and VI.

In this survey, we consider only papers that deal with the determination of the relative amounts of debt and equity, taking these securities as exogenous. There is, however, an incipient literature that considers the more fundamental question of why corporate securities are designed the way they are. Many of these papers attempt to explain the allocation of both cash flows and control rights across securities. We review security design models in a separate paper (Harris and Raviv (1990b)).

Briefly, our conclusions are as follows. First, the models surveyed have identified a large number of *potential* determinants of capital structure. The empirical work so far has not, however, sorted out which of these are important in various contexts. Second, the theory has identified a relatively small number of "general principles." Several properties of the debt contract have important implications for determining capital structure. These are the bankruptcy provision, convexity of payoffs of levered equity, the effect of debt on managerial equity ownership, and the relative insensitivity of debt payoffs to firm performance. Third, the empirical evidence is largely consistent with the theory, although there are a few instances where the evidence seems to contradict certain models. These inconsistencies cannot, however, be regarded as conclusive, because the empirical studies were not designed specifically to test the models and were, therefore, not careful about satisfying the *ceteris paribus* conditions. With regard to further theoretical work, it appears that models relating to products and inputs are underexplored, while the asymmetric information approach has reached the point of diminishing returns. Finally, with regard to further empirical work, it seems essential that empirical studies concentrate on testing particular models or classes of models in an attempt to discover the most important determinants of capital structure in given environments.

The plan of the paper is as follows. In Section I, we discuss models based on agency costs. Models using asymmetric information are considered in Section II. Interactions of capital structure with behavior in the product or input market or with characteristics of products or inputs are taken up in Section III. Section IV surveys models based on corporate control considerations. In Section V, we summarize the theoretical results and compare them with the evidence. Finally, our conclusions are presented in Section VI.

I. Models Based on Agency Costs

A significant fraction of the effort of researchers over the last 10 years has been devoted to models in which capital structure is determined by agency costs, i.e., costs due to conflicts of interest. Research in this area was initiated by Jensen and Meckling (1976) building on earlier work of Fama and Miller (1972).

Jensen and Meckling identify two types of conflicts. Conflicts between shareholders and managers arise because managers hold less than 100% of the residual claim. Consequently, they do not capture the entire gain from their profit enhancement activities, but they do bear the entire cost of these activities. For example, managers can invest less effort in managing firm resources and may be able to transfer firm resources to their own, personal benefit, e.g., by consuming "perquisites" such as corporate jets, plush offices, building "empires," etc. The manager bears the entire cost of refraining from these activities but captures only a fraction of the gain. As a result managers overindulge in these pursuits relative to the level that would maximize firm value. This inefficiency is reduced the larger is the fraction of the firm's equity owned by the manager. Holding constant the manager's absolute investment in the firm, increases in the fraction of the firm financed by debt increase the manager's share of the equity and mitigate the loss from the conflict between the manager and shareholders. Moreover, as pointed out by Jensen (1986), since debt commits the firm to pay out cash, it reduces the amount of "free" cash available to managers to engage in the type of pursuits mentioned above. This mitigation of the conflicts between managers and equityholders constitutes the benefit of debt financing.[3]

---

[3] Another benefit of debt financing is pointed out by Grossman and Hart (1982). If bankruptcy is costly for managers, perhaps because they lose benefits of control or reputation, then debt can create an incentive for managers to work harder, consume fewer perquisites, make better investment decisions, etc., because this behavior reduces the probability of bankruptcy.

Conflicts between debtholders and equityholders arise because the debt contract gives equityholders an incentive to invest suboptimally.[4] More specifically the debt contract provides that if an investment yields large returns, well above the face value of the debt, equityholders capture most of the gain. If, however, the investment fails, because of limited liability, debtholders bear the consequences. As a result, equityholders may benefit from "going for broke," i.e., investing in very risky projects, even if they are value-decreasing. Such investments result in a decrease in the value of the debt. The loss in value of the equity from the poor investment can be more than offset by the gain in equity value captured at the expense of debtholders. Equityholders bear this cost to debtholders, however, when the debt is issued if the debtholders correctly anticipate equityholders' future behavior. In this case, the equityholders receive less for the debt than they otherwise would. Thus, the cost of the incentive to invest in value-decreasing projects created by debt is borne by the equityholders who issue the debt. This effect, generally called the "asset substitution effect," is an agency cost of debt financing.[5]

Jensen and Meckling argue that an optimal capital structure can be obtained by trading off the agency cost of debt against the benefit of debt as previously described.[6] A number of implications follow. First, one would expect bond contracts to include features that .attempt to prevent asset substitution, such as interest coverage requirements, prohibitions against investments in new, unrelated lines of business, etc. Second, industries in which the opportunities for asset substitution are more limited will have higher debt levels, *ceteris paribus*. Thus, for example, the theory predicts that regulated public utilities, banks, and firms in mature industries with few growth opportunities will be more highly levered. Third, firms for which slow or even negative growth is optimal and that have large cash inflows from operations should have more debt. Large cash inflows without good investment prospects create the resources to consume perquisites, build empires, overpay subordinates, etc. Increasing debt reduces the amount of "free cash" and increases the manager's fractional ownership of the residual

---

[4] Obviously, conflicts between security holders do not arise if each investor holds all securities in proportion to their values, i.e., if each investor holds a "strip." Consequently, this literature assumes that equityholders are disjoint classes of investors.

[5] Myers (1977) points out another agency cost of debt. He observes that when firms are likely to go bankrupt in the near future, equityholders may have no incentive to contribute new capital even to invest in value-increasing projects. The reason is that equityholders bear the entire cost of the investment, but the returns from the investment may be captured mainly by the debtholders. Thus larger debt levels result in the rejection of more value-increasing projects. This agency cost of debt yields conclusions about capital structure similar to those of Jensen and Meckling.

[6] Several authors have pointed out that agency problems can be reduced or eliminated through the use of managerial incentive schemes and/or more complicated financial securities such as convertible debt. See Barnea et al. (1985), Brander and Poitevin (1989), and Dybvig and Zender (1989). For a counter view, see Narayanan (1987) and the reply by Haugen and Senbet (1987).

claim. According to Jensen (1989) industries with these characteristics today include steel, chemicals, brewing, tobacco, television and radio broadcasting, and wood and paper products. The theory predicts that these industries should be characterized by high leverage.

All the theories based on agency problems surveyed in the remainder of this section use one of the conflicts introduced by Jensen and Meckling as a starting point. Consequently, we classify these papers into two subsections corresponding to the conflict between equityholders and managers and the conflict between equityholders and debtholders.

A. Conflicts between Equityholders and Managers

The two papers surveyed in this subsection share a common concern with manager-shareholder conflicts but differ according to the specific way in which this conflict arises. More importantly, they also differ in how debt alleviates the problem and in the disadvantages of debt.

In Harris and Raviv (1990a) and Stulz (1990), managers and investors disagree over an operating decision. In particular, in Harris and Raviv managers are assumed to want always to continue the firm's current operations even if liquidation of the firm is preferred by investors. In Stulz, managers are assumed to want always to invest all available funds even if paying out cash is better for investors. In both cases, it is assumed that the conflict cannot be resolved through contracts based on cash flow and investment expenditure. Debt mitigates the problem in the Harris and Raviv model by giving investors (debtholders) the option to force liquidation if cash flows are poor. In Stulz, as in Jensen (1986), debt payments reduce free cash flow. Capital structure is determined by trading off these benefits of debt against costs of debt. In Harris and Raviv, the assertion of control by investors through bankruptcy entails costs related to the production of information, used in the liquidation decision, about the firm's prospects. The cost of debt in Stulz's model is that debt payments may more than exhaust "free" cash, reducing the funds available for profitable investment. This comparison of Harris-Raviv and Stulz is summarized in Table I where the relationship of these two models to Jensen and Meckling (1976) and Jensen (1986) is also shown.[7]

The optimal capital structure in Harris and Raviv trades off improved liquidation decisions versus higher investigation costs. A larger debt level improves the liquidation decision because it makes default more likely. In the absence of default, incumbent management is assumed not to liquidate the firm even if the assets are worth more in their next best alternative use.

[7] Another approach that involves manager-investor conflicts is taken by Williamson (1988). In his view, the benefits of debt are the incentives provided to managers by the rules under which debtholders can take over the firm and liquidate the assets. The costs of debt are that the inflexibility of the rules can result in liquidation of the assets when they are more valuable in the firm. Thus, Williamson concludes that assets that are more redeployable should be financed with debt.

Table I
Comparison of Agency Models Based on Manager-Shareholder Conflicts

Model	Conflict	Benefit of Debt	Cost of Debt
Jensen and Meckling (1976)	Managerial perquisites	Increase managerial ownership	Asset substitution
Jensen (1986)	Overinvestment	Reduce free cash	Unspecified
Harris and Raviv (1990a)	Failure to liquidate	Allows investors option to liquidate	Investigation costs
Stulz (1991)	Overinvestment	Reduce free cash	Underinvestment

Following a default, however, investors control the liquidation decision, and they expend resources to obtain additional information pertinent to this decision. Since investors choose an optimal liquidation decision based on their information, default improves this decision. More frequent default, however, is more costly as resources are expended investigating the firm when it is in default.

The Harris and Raviv model predicts that firms with higher liquidation value, e.g., those with tangible assets, and/or firms with lower investigation costs will have more debt and will be more likely to default but will have higher market value than similar firms with lower liquidation value and/or higher investigation costs. The intuition for the higher debt level is that increases in liquidation value make it more likely that liquidation is the best strategy. Therefore, information is more useful and a higher debt level is called for. Similarly, decreases in investigation costs also increase the value of default resulting in more debt. The increase in debt results in higher default probability. Harris and Raviv also obtain results on whether a firm in bankruptcy is reorganized or liquidated. They show that the probability of being reorganized decreases with liquidation value and is independent of investigation costs. Using a constant-returns-to-scale assumption they show that the debt level relative to expected firm income, default probability, bond yield, and the probability of reorganization are independent of firm size. Combining these results, Harris and Raviv argue that higher leverage can be expected to be associated with larger firm value, higher debt level relative to expected income, and lower probability of reorganization following default.

The optimal capital structure in Stulz is determined by trading off the benefit of debt in preventing investment in value decreasing projects against the cost of debt in preventing investment in value increasing projects. Thus, as in Jensen (1986), firms with an abundance of good investment opportunities can be expected to have low debt levels relative to firms in mature, slow-growth, cash-rich industries. Moreover, Stulz argues that, in general, managers will be reluctant to implement the optimal debt levels but are more likely to do so the greater is the threat of takeover. Thus, firms more likely to be takeover targets can be expected to have more debt, *ceteris paribus*, while firms with anti-takeover measures will have less debt. Finally, firms whose value-increasing investment opportunities create more value than the value-decreasing ones destroy will have less debt than firms in the opposite situation. The reason is that such firms are primarily concerned with not losing the value-creating opportunities.[8]

B. Conflicts between Equityholders and Debtholders

This subsection surveys two papers in which reputation moderates the asset substitution problem, i.e., the incentive of levered equityholders to choose risky, negative net-present-value investments.[9] Diamond (1989) and Hirshleifer and Thakor (1989) show how managers or firms have an incentive to pursue relatively safe projects out of reputational considerations.[10]

Diamond's model is concerned with a firm's reputation for choosing projects that assure debt repayment. There are two possible investment projects: a safe, positive NPV project and a risky, negative NPV project. The risky project can have one of two payoffs ("success" or "failure"). Both projects require the same initial investment which must be financed by debt. A firm can be of three, initially observationally equivalent types. One type has access only to the safe project, one type has access only to the risky project, and one type has access to both. Since investors cannot distinguish the firms *ex ante*, the initial lending rate reflects their beliefs about the projects chosen by firms on average. Returns from the safe project suffice to pay the debtholders (even if the firm is believed by investors to have only the risky project), but returns from the risky project allow repayment only if the project is successful.

Because of the asset substitution problem, if the firm has a choice of projects, myopic maximization of equity value (e.g., in a one-period situation) would lead the firm to choose the risky project. If the firm can convince lenders it has only the safe project, however, it will enjoy a lower lending rate. Since lenders can observe only a firm's default history, it is possible for a firm to build a reputation for having only the safe project by not defaulting.

---

[8] A similar approach is taken by Hart and Moore (1990) with similar results. In particular, Hart and Moore (1990) also focus on the agency problems of overinvestment by managers. There are two major differences between the approach of Hart and Moore (1990) and that of Stulz (1990). First, Hart and Moore derive debt as an optimal security in this setting (see Harris and Raviv (1990b)). Second, debt does not prevent overinvestment in the Hart and Moore approach by reducing available free cash flows. Instead, the existence of senior debt constrains the amount of external funds that can be raised since the outstanding debt represents a prior claim on all assets, including new investments. For further discussion of the effects of seniority rules on the under-and overinvestment incentives, see Berkovitch and Kim (1990).

[9] Another literature considers factors that alleviate the underinvestment cost of debt pointed out by Myers (1977) (see footnote 5). Stulz and Johnson (1985) focus on collateral, John and Nachman (1985) focus on reputation, and Bergman and Callen (Forthcoming) consider renegotiation with debtholders. Berkovitch and Kim (1990) and Kim and Maksimovic (Forthcoming) show how debt can be used to trade off the overinvestment and underinvestment effects.

[10] Green (1984) offers another method of mitigating this agency cost. He points out that convertible bonds and warrants "reverse the convex shape of levered equity over the upper range of the firm's earnings" (p.115) and therefore reduce the asset substitution problem.

The longer the firm's history of repaying its debt, the better is its reputation, and the lower is its borrowing cost. Therefore, older, more established firms find it optimal to choose the safe project, i.e., not engage in asset substitution to avoid losing a valuable reputation. Young firms with little reputation may choose the risky project. If they survive without a default, they will eventually switch to the safe project. As a result, firms with long track records will have lower default rates and lower costs of debt than firms with brief histories. Although the amount of debt is fixed in Diamond's model, it is plausible that an extension of the model would yield the result that younger firms have less debt than older ones, other things equal.

Managers may also have an incentive to pursue relatively safe projects out of a concern for *their* reputations. Hirshleifer and Thakor (1989) consider a manager who has a choice of two projects, each with only two outcomes—success or failure. Failure means the same for both projects, but from the point of view of the shareholders, the high-risk-high-return project yields both higher expected returns and higher returns if it succeeds. Suppose that from the point of view of the manager's reputation, however, success on the two projects is equivalent, i.e., the managerial labor market can only distinguish "success" *versus* "failure." Thus the manager maximizes probability of success while shareholders prefer expected return. If the safer project has a higher probability of success, the manager will choose it even if the other project is better for the equityholders. This behavior of managers reduces the agency cost of debt. Thus, if managers are susceptible to such a reputation effect, the firm may be expected to have more debt than otherwise. Hirshleifer and Thakor argue that managers of firms more likely to be takeover targets are more susceptible to the reputation effect. Such firms can be expected to have more debt, *ceteris paribus*. Conversely, firms that have adopted anti-takeover measures will use less debt, other things equal.

C. Summary of Section I

Agency models have been among the most successful in generating interesting implications. In particular, these models predict that leverage is positively associated with firm value (Hirshleifer and Thakor (1989), Harris and Raviv (1990a), Stulz (1990)), default probability (Harris and Raviv (1990a)), extent of regulation (Jensen and Meckling (1976), Stulz (1990)), free cash flow (Jensen (1986), Stulz (1990)), liquidation value (Williamson (1988), Harris and Raviv (1990a)), extent to which the firm is a takeover target (Hirshleifer and Thakor (1989), Stulz (1990)), and the importance of managerial reputation (Hirshleifer and Thakor (1989)). Also, leverage is expected to be negatively associated with the extent of growth opportunities (Jensen and Meckling (1976), Stulz (1990)), interest coverage, the cost of investigating firm prospects, and the probability of reorganization following default (Harris and Raviv (1990a)). Some other implications include the prediction that bonds will have covenants that attempt to restrict the extent to which equityholders can pursue risky projects that reduce the value of the debt

(Jensen and Meckling (1976)) and that older firms with longer credit histories will tend to have lower default rates and costs of debt (Diamond (1989)). Finally, the result that firm value and leverage are positively related follows from the fact that these two endogenous variables move in the same direction with changes in the exogenous factors (Hirshleifer and Thakor (1989), Harris and Raviv (1990a), Stulz (1990)). Therefore, leverage increasing (decreasing) changes in capital structure caused by a change in one of these exogenous factors will be accompanied by stock price increases (decreases).

II. Asymmetric Information

The introduction into economics of the explicit modeling of private information has made possible a number of approaches to explaining capital structure. In these theories, firm managers or insiders are assumed to possess private information about the characteristics of the firm's return stream or investment opportunities. In one set of approaches, choice of the firm's capital structure signals to outside investors the information of insiders. This stream of research began with the work of Ross (1977) and Leland and Pyle (1977). In another, capital structure is designed to mitigate inefficiencies in the firm's investment decisions that are caused by the information asymmetry. This branch of the literature starts with Myers and Majluf (1984) and Myers (1984). We survey the various approaches in the following subsections.

A. Interaction of Investment and Capital Structure

In their pioneering work, Myers and Majluf (1984) showed that, if investors are less well-informed than current firm insiders about the value of the firm's assets, then equity may be mispriced by the market. If firms are required to finance new projects by issuing equity, underpricing may be so severe that new investors capture more than the NPV of the new project, resulting in a net loss to existing shareholders. In this case the project will be rejected even if its NPV is positive. This underinvestment can be avoided if the firm can finance the new project using a security that is not so severely undervalued by the market. For example, internal funds and/or riskless debt involve no undervaluation, and, therefore, will be preferred to equity by firms in this situation. Even (not too) risky debt will be preferred to equity. Myers (1984) refers to this as a "pecking order" theory of financing, i.e., that capital structure will be driven by firms' desire to finance new investments, first internally, then with low-risk debt, and finally with equity only as a last resort.[11]

---

[11] Strictly speaking, Myers and Majluf show only that debt whose value is not sensitive to the private information is preferred to equity (e.g. riskless debt). Moreover, if such debt is available, the theory implies that equity never be issued by firms in the situation of extreme information asymmetry they model. Consequently, the "pecking order" theory requires an exogenous debt constraint in the Myers and Majluf model. Note also that there can be a pooling equilibrium in which all firms issue securities, because the project's NPV exceeds the worst underpricing. This equilibrium would not have the properties of the separating equilibrium mentioned in the text.

To understand why firms may pass up positive NPV projects, suppose there are only two types of firms. The current assets of the firm are worth either H or $L < H$, depending on type. Initially, the firm's type is known only to the firm's managers whose objective is to maximize the true value of the current shareholders' claim.[12] Outside investors believe the firm is of type H with probability p and type L with probability $1 - p$. Both types of firm have access to a new project that requires an investment of I and has NPV of v (I and v can be assumed to be common knowledge). The firm must decide whether to accept the project. If the project is accepted, the investment I must be financed by issuing equity to new shareholders. Consider the following candidate equilibrium. A type H firm rejects the project and issues no equity while a type L firm accepts the project and issues equity worth I. Investors believe that issuance of equity signals that the firm is of type L. To verify that this is an equilibrium, first notice that investor beliefs are rational. Second, given these beliefs, the equity issued by type L firms is fairly priced by the market, i.e., current shareholders give up a fraction $\beta = I/(L + v + I)$ of the firm to new shareholders. Their payoff from taking the project and issuing equity is $(1 - \beta)(L + v + I) = L + v$. Consequently, the current shareholders of type L firms capture the NPV of v in the new project by issuing equity. They would not prefer to imitate type H firms since this would require passing up the project along with its positive NPV with no compensating gain in valuation of the existing assets, i.e., their payoff would be L. Third, if a type H firm passes up the project, the payoff to current shareholders is simply H. On the other hand, if a type H firm imitates a type L firm by issuing equity, this equity will be priced by the market as if the firm were type L. In this case, the current shareholders' payoff is $(1 - \beta)(H + v + I)$. The underpricing of the new equity can be so severe that current shareholders of the type H firm give up claims to the existing assets as well as the entire NPV of the new project. They are thus worse off by taking the project. This will happen when the above expression is less than H, or $(H - L)\beta > v$. Consequently, for parameters satisfying this inequality, in equilibrium, only type L firms will accept the positive NPV project. The left hand side of the inequality is the value transferred to the new equity holders who acquire the fraction β of the firm at the bargain price of L instead of the true value H. The inequality then states that underinvestment occurs if this transfer exceeds the NPV of the project.

What are the empirical implications of Myers' "pecking order" theory? Probably the most important implication is that, upon announcement of an equity issue, the market value of the firm's existing shares will fall. Prior to the announcement, the firm's market value (of current shares) is $pH + (1 -$

---

[12] This objective function assumes that outside investors will discover the true value of the firm's existing assets soon after the decision to invest is made and that current shareholders will not sell their stakes before this occurs. Dybvig and Zender (1989) point out that optimal contracts with managers could completely resolve the underinvestment problem rendering capital structure irrelevant. The papers surveyed in this section thus implicitly assume that such contracts are ruled out.

$p)(L + v)$, reflecting prior beliefs about firm type and the equilibrium behavior of the firm. Upon announcement of an equity issue, investors realize that the firm is of type L, so firm value becomes $L + v$. For parameter values satisfying the above inequality, $pH + (1 - p)(L + v) > L + v$, i.e., announcement of the equity issue results in a fall in the price of current shares. Moreover, financing via internal funds or riskless debt (or any security whose value is independent of the private information) will not convey information and will not result in any stock price reaction. A second implication is that new projects will tend to be financed mainly from internal sources or the proceeds of low-risk debt issues.[13] Third, Korajczyk, et al. (1990b,c) argue that the underinvestment problem is least severe after information releases such as annual reports and earnings announcements. Therefore equity issues will tend to cluster after such releases and the stock price drop will be negatively related to the time between the release and the issue announcement.[14] Finally, suppose firms with comparatively little tangible assets relative to firm value are more subject to information asymmetries. For such firms, then, the underinvestment problem will occur more often than for similar firms with less severe information asymmetries. These firms can be expected to accumulate more debt over time, other things equal.

A number of authors have extended the basic Myers-Majluf idea. Krasker (1986) allows firms to choose the size of the new investment project and the accompanying equity issue. He confirms the results of Myers and Majluf in this context and also shows that the larger the stock issue the worse the signal and the fall in the firm's stock price.

Narayanan (1988) and Heinkel and Zechner (1990) obtain results similar to Myers and Majluf using a slightly different approach. They show that when the information asymmetry concerns only the value of the new project, there can be overinvestment, i.e., some negative NPV projects will be taken. The reason is that full separation of firms by project NPV is impossible when the only observable signal is whether the project is taken. The equilibrium involves pooling of firms with projects of various NPV with the equity issued by all such firms being priced at the average value. Firms whose projects have low NPV will benefit from selling overpriced equity. This may more than compensate for a negative project NPV. The result is a negative cut-off NPV such that all firms with project NPV above the cut-off accept the project. In Narayanan's model, because (risky) debt is less overpriced than equity, the cut-off level is higher when projects are financed by debt issues.

[13] For example, Bradford (1987) shows that if managers are allowed to purchase the new equity issued by firms in the situation described by Myers and Majluf (1984), then the underinvestment problem is mitigated.

[14] Lucas and McDonald (1990) consider a model in which Myers-Majluf type informational asymmetries are temporary and firms can delay the adoption of projects. They show that firms with private information that current earnings are low will not delay projects, while firms whose current earnings are high will delay until this information becomes public. The result is that, on average, equity is issued after a period of abnormally high returns to the firm and to the market. They also obtain the result that, on average, stock price drops in response to stock issues.

In Heinkel and Zechner, existing debt makes investment less attractive (as in Myers (1977)) and increases the cut-off level. Thus new (Narayanan) or existing (Heinkel and Zechner) debt reduces the overinvestment problem relative to all equity financing. The models imply that when a firm accepts a new project, the firm's stock price will increase since the market discovers that the firm's new project's NPV is above the cut-off level. Narayanan shows that when firms are allowed to issue either debt or equity, all firms either issue debt or reject the project. In this sense, his results are consistent with the "pecking order" theory. Since project acceptance is associated with issuing debt, debt issues are good news, i.e., result in an increase in the firm's stock price. This implication is the opposite of Myers and Majluf (1984). Debt is not a signal in Heinkel and Zechner since it is issued before firms have private information. Also, internal funds can substitute for debt in Heinkel and Zechner. Note that it is crucial to the results of both Narayanan and Heinkel-Zechner that acceptance or rejection of the project is the signal. If investors could observe only whether the firm issues securities, firms with negative NPV projects could imitate good firms by issuing the same security but investing the proceeds in Treasury bills.

Brennan and Kraus (1987), Noe (1988), and Constantinides and Grundy (1989) cast doubt on the "pecking order" theory. These papers enrich the set of financing choices that a firm may make when faced with the situation modeled by Myers and Majluf (1984).[15] They conclude that firms do not necessarily have a preference for issuing straight debt over equity and that the underinvestment problem can be resolved through signaling with the richer set of financing options.

Brennan and Kraus offer an example similar to those in Myers and Majluf. There are two types of firms, say L and H, as above. Here, each type of firm has debt outstanding initially. In equilibrium, firm type H issues enough equity to finance the new project *and* retire its outstanding debt at face value. Firm type L issues only enough equity to finance the new project. Investors infer the firm type correctly. The debt of type H firms is risk free in this example. Therefore, type H firms obtain a "fair" deal on both their equity issue and debt repurchase. Type H firms do not imitate type L firms because by so doing the type H firm's equity would be underpriced. Type L firms do not imitate type H firms because repurchase of their debt at full face value entails an overpayment (i.e., for type L firms, the debt is risky). The cost of this overpayment for the debt exceeds the benefits available from selling overpriced equity. Thus, in equilibrium, both types of firms issue equity and accept the positive NPV project. Obviously, the underinvestment result of Myers and Majluf does not obtain in this example. Moreover, firms are allowed to issue debt but do not. This is inconsistent with the "pecking order" theory. Finally, issuing equity in the Brennan and Kraus model is a

---

[15] Brennan-Kraus and Constantinides-Grundy use a method similar to one first introduced by Heinkel (1982) to obtain costless signaling (see Section II.B).

negative signal, but simultaneously issuing equity and using *part* of the proceeds to repurchase debt is a positive signal.

Constantinides and Grundy (1989) allow firms to issue any type of security and to repurchase existing equity. Another variation from the basic Myers-Majluf setup is that managers are assumed to have an equity stake in the firm whose true value they maximize. Constantinides and Grundy show that there is a fully separating equilibrium (even with a continuum of firm types) in which all types of firm take the positive NPV investment financed by an issue of a security that is neither straight debt nor equity. The new security is issued in an amount sufficient to finance the new investment and repurchase some of the firm's existing equity. This issued security is locally convex in firm value at the true value and locally concave for at least some firm value below the true value (see their (1989) Theorem 3). Constantinides and Grundy interpret these characteristics as being those of convertible debt. The basic idea is that the repurchase of equity makes it costly for firms to overstate their true value while the issuance of a security that is sensitive to firm value makes it costly to understate true value. Separation is attained by the design and size of the new issue so that, at the true value of the firm, these effects balance at the margin. In this model, the underinvestment problem is costlessly resolved. Although firms may issue some form of debt, the model does not support the "pecking order" rule. That is, there is no overriding reason to finance using internal funds or riskless debt.

Noe (1988) allows firms to issue either debt or equity. He presents an example with three firm types, say L, M, and H. In equilibrium all types accept the positive NPV project, but types L and H issue debt while type M issues equity. Investors revise their beliefs about firm type using Bayes' rule (e.g., they correctly identify type M). Either security issued by type L would be overpriced as a result of being confused either with type M or type H. Debt is less sensitive to firm type than equity, but, since firm type H is much better than firm type M in this example, L's debt is more overpriced than its equity. Consequently, type L chooses to "imitate" type H. Debt issued by type M is actually risk free, but, if it is confused with debt of type L, will be perceived to be risky by investors. Consequently, if type M issues debt, the debt will be underpriced. Therefore, type M prefers to issue fairly priced equity. Either security issued by type H would be underpriced. In the example, firm type H's debt is less underpriced both because it is less sensitive to firm quality and because the probability that a firm is of type L (the only type whose debt is risky) is low. Consequently, type H prefers to "imitate" type L and issue debt. Notice that all three types accept the project, that one type actually prefers to issue equity, and that the equity issuing firm is not the lowest quality.[16]

---

[16] Nachman and Noe (1989) consider a similar situation in which firms have private information about the value of a new investment. They assume, however, that firms can issue any monotone increasing security in a broad class. They show, under certain assumptions on the ordering of firm types, that the only equilibrium is one in which all firms issue debt.

Brennan and Kraus, Constantinides and Grundy, and Noe demonstrate that allowing firms a wider range of financing choices can invalidate the Myers-Majluf results in some cases. Whether the type of examples identified in these papers are more important empirically than those of Myers-Majluf is an open question. We note, however, that Noe shows that the average quality of firms issuing debt is higher in equilibrium than that of firms issuing equity. Therefore, like Myers-Majluf, Noe's model predicts a negative stock market response to an announcement of an equity issue. Noe also predicts a positive market response to an announcement of a debt issue. Moreover, when Constantinides and Grundy further extend the model to allow different firm types to have different optimal investment levels and assume that investment is observable, they show that firms can fully separate using investment and the size of a straight bond issue (with some share repurchase) as signals. Thus, in this situation straight debt is a preferred financing tool, although the reason here is that it helps to signal a firm's true type while in Myers-Majluf, debt is a device to avoid signaling. Also in this variant of the model, the market reaction to a stock repurchase financed by debt is more favorable the larger is the transaction.

B. Signaling with Proportion of Debt

In the previous subsection, capital structure emerged as part of the solution to problems of over- and underinvestment. We turn now to models in which investment is fixed and capital structure serves as a signal of private insider information.

The seminal contribution in this area is that of Ross (1977). In Ross' model, managers know the true distribution of firm returns, but investors do not. Firm return distributions are ordered by first order stochastic dominance. Managers benefit if the firm's securities are more highly valued by the market but are penalized if the firm goes bankrupt. Investors take larger debt levels as a signal of higher quality.[17] Since lower quality firms have higher marginal expected bankruptcy costs for any debt level, managers of low quality firms do not imitate higher quality firms by issuing more debt.

The following is a simple formal model. Suppose that the date-one returns $\tilde{x}$ of a firm of type t are distributed uniformly on $[0, t]$. The manager is privately informed about t. He chooses the face value of debt D to maximize a weighted average of the market value of the firm at date zero and the expected value at date one, net of a penalty L for bankruptcy.[18] We denote by

---

[17] An equivalent approach is to assume that managers can commit to paying dividends and suffer a penalty if the promised dividend is not paid. Ravid and Sarig (1989) consider a combination of debt and dividend commitment. They show that both dividends and debt level increase with firm quality.

[18] This objective function reflects the implicit assumptions that the manager's welfare is increasing in the current and future stock price and decreases in the event of bankruptcy. This "bankruptcy penalty" could result from loss of reputation or search costs of finding a new position. The penalty is not a bankruptcy cost since it effects only the manager's welfare and not firm value.

$V_0(D)$ the value assigned to the firm at date zero by the market if the debt level is D. The manager's objective function is then

$$(1 - \gamma)V_0(D) + \gamma(t/2 - LD/t).$$

The parameter γ is a weight. The expected payoff at date one, given the manager's information is simply $t/2$. He evaluates the bankruptcy probability as D/t. If investors infer that $t = a(D)$ when the manager issues debt of face value D, then

$$V_0(D) = a(D)/2.$$

Substituting this into the objective function and taking the derivative with respect to D gives the first order condition. In equilibrium, investors correctly infer t from D, i.e., if $D(t)$ is the manager's optimal choice of debt level as a function of the firm type t, then $a(D(t)) \equiv t$. Using this in the first order condition and solving the resulting differential equation gives

$$D(t) = ct^2/L + b,$$

where c and b are constants.

The main empirical result is that firm value (or profitability) and the debt-equity ratio are positively related.[19] It is also easily seen from the above formula that increases in the bankruptcy penalty, other things equal, decrease the debt level and the probability of bankruptcy. Ross also shows that this probability is increasing in firm type t. Thus firm value, debt level, and bankruptcy probability are all positively related in this model.

Heinkel (1982) considers a model similar to Ross but does not assume that firm returns are ordered by first order stochastic dominance. Instead, the return distribution is assumed to be such that "higher" quality firms have higher overall value but lower quality bonds (lower market value for given face value), hence higher equity value. This allows firms to separate costlessly when insiders maximize the value of their residual claim subject to raising a given amount of external capital.[20] The reason is that any firm attempting to convince the market that it is a type other than its true type will gain from overvaluation of one security and lose from undervaluation of the other. In equilibrium, the amounts issued of the two securities for each type firm are such that the gains and losses balance at the margin. High value firms issue more debt. To imitate a high value firm, a lower value firm must issue more underpriced debt and reduce the amount of overpriced equity. Similarly, to imitate a low value firm, a higher value firm must issue

---

[19] This can be seen by calculating the value of the debt and equity as functions of $D(t)$ and t, taking the ratio, and showing that this ratio is increasing in t (see Ross (1977, p.37)). As will be seen below, many other models also imply a positive relation between firm profitability and leverage. Interestingly, Chang (1987), using an agency model, obtains the opposite results. Since Chang derives optimal securities, his paper is considered in our companion survey, Harris and Raviv (1990b).

[20] See also Franke (1987) for a similar financial signaling model with costless separation of firms.

less overpriced debt and more underpriced equity. Since higher quality firms have higher total value, the result that they issue more debt is consistent with Ross' result.[21]

Another model that uses debt as a signal is that of Poitevin (1989) which involves potential competition between an incumbent firm and an entrant. The entrant's marginal costs are privately known by the entrant.[22] In equilibrium, low cost entrants signal this fact by issuing debt while the incumbent and high cost entrants issue only equity. The cost to a firm of issuing debt is that it makes the firm vulnerable to predation by the other firm, possibly resulting in bankruptcy of the debt-financed firm. The benefit of debt is that the financial market places a higher value on the debt financed firm since it believes such a firm to be low cost. High cost entrants will not issue debt since the resulting probability of bankruptcy due to predation by the incumbent renders the cost of misleading the capital market too high (incumbents prey equally on all debt-financed firms, even if thought to be low cost). The main result, like the other models in this subsection, is that issuance of debt is good news to the financial market. Since predation is used only to drive one's rival into bankruptcy, there will be predation only against debt-financed firms.

C. Models Based on Managerial Risk Aversion

Several studies exploit managerial risk aversion to obtain a signaling equilibrium in which capital structure is determined. The basic idea is that increases in firm leverage allow managers to retain a larger fraction of the (risky) equity. The larger equity share reduces managerial welfare due to risk aversion, but the decrease is smaller for managers of higher quality projects. Thus managers of higher quality firms can signal this fact by having more debt in equilibrium.[23]

A simple formal model based on Leland and Pyle (1977) is as follows. Consider an entrepreneur whose project returns $\tilde{x} = \mu + \tilde{\epsilon}$ with $E\tilde{\epsilon} = 0$ and

---

[21] Another signaling model that obtains this result is John (1987).

[22] Glazer and Israel (1990) also consider a model in which capital structure is used to signal costs of production. Unlike in Poitevin, in Glazer and Israel, an incumbent monopolist signals his cost to prevent entry. The incumbent's manager is assumed to be compensated based on the terminal value of equity, *not* including any dividends. Glazer and Israel assume that the proceeds of any debt issued are paid out in dividends. Therefore, leverage increases are costly for the manager. In equilibrium, potential entrants interpret more debt as indicative that the incumbent has lower marginal production costs. It is optimal for managers of low cost incumbents to issue more debt since for them the benefit of preventing entry exceeds the cost of debt. Managers of high cost incumbents will not imitate since for them the value of entry prevention is lower. Note, however, that signaling could work equally well using dividends financed by retained earnings or preferred stock instead of by debt. The authors recognize this point and do not claim that their results constitute a theory of capital structure. Gertner, et al. (1988) also consider a model in which firms use capital structure as a signal in the output market (as well as in the capital market). Their main result is that whether the equilibrium will involve pooling or separation depends on what is best for the informed firm.

[23] In addition to the papers discussed below, see Blazenko (1987).

who must raise I from external sources. The entrepreneur observes expected return μ, but investors do not. He chooses the fraction of the equity he retains α and the face value of default-free debt D to maximize his expected utility of end-of-period wealth $Eu(\tilde{W})$ where:[24]

$$\tilde{W} = \alpha(\tilde{x} - D) + (1 - \alpha)(V(\alpha) - D) + D = \alpha\tilde{x} + (1 - \alpha)V(\alpha),$$

subject to the constraint that I of external funds must be raised.

$$(1 - \alpha)[V(\alpha) - D] + D = I.$$

Here $V(\alpha)$ is the market's assessment of the value of the firm given that the entrepreneur retains the fraction α of the equity. We have also assumed that there is no investment required ($K = 0$ in Leland and Pyle's notation) since this does not affect the results. Although the debt level D does not affect the entrepreneur's objective directly, his choice of α implies a debt level through the external-funds constraint.[25] It is clear from the formula for $\tilde{W}$ that increases in the entrepreneur's share α increase the riskiness of his portfolio (since $V(\alpha)$ is riskless cash) but also increase the amount he obtains for the share sold to outsiders through signaling (since V is increasing in α, in equilibrium).

The first order condition for α is obtained by differentiating $Eu(\tilde{W})$ with respect to α, substituting the equilibrium condition that $V(\alpha(\mu)) = \mu$ (where $\alpha(\mu)$ is the entrepreneur's optimal ownership share if his expected return is μ), and setting the result equal to zero. It can be shown from this condition that the entrepreneur's equilibrium ownership share α increases with firm quality. To translate this into a capital structure theory, we must calculate the effect on the debt level D of changes in firm quality using the external-funds constraint. Increases in μ result in increases in α as just shown; however, the increase in α has two opposing effects on D. The increased ownership of the entrepreneur, other things equal, would require that more funds be raised by debt. Firm value V is, however, larger for larger α, so that equity holders may pay more for the smaller fraction of the firm they receive. Consequently, D may not need to increase to finance the increased ownership share of the entrepreneur. Leland and Pyle (1977) derive some conditions on the parameters of an example that guarantee that debt increases with α. Under these conditions, firms with larger debt also have a larger fraction of the equity owned by insiders and are of higher quality.[26]

---

[24] This expression reflects the assumption that the amount raised externally, $(1 - \alpha)[V(\alpha) - D] + D$, is invested in a riskless asset with zero return.

[25] In fact, the debt level determined in the Leland and Pyle model is the total debt issued by the corporation and the entrepreneur on personal account. The results can be interpreted as a theory of corporate capital structure only if personal debt is costly.

[26] Darrough and Stoughton (1986) incorporate moral hazard into the Leland and Pyle formulation. The manager is assumed to choose an effort level after securities are issued. The marginal product of effort μ and the standard deviation of returns σ are known only to the entrepreneur, but investors know that $\sigma = \mu^2$. In this model, the fraction of equity retained by the entrepreneur is both a signal of μ and σ and an incentive device. The entrepreneur retains a smaller fraction the more risky are the returns. There are no specific results linking debt level or capital structure to observable characteristics of the firm.

D. Summary of Section II

The main predictions of asymmetric information theories concern stock price reactions to issuance and exchange of securities, the amount of leverage, and whether firms observe a pecking order for security issues.

Stock Price Effects of Security Issues

- Debt: Myers and Majluf (1984) and Krasker (1986) predict the absence of price effects upon issuance of (riskless) debt. Noe (1988) and Narayanan (1988) predict a positive price effect of a (risky) debt issue.
- Equity: Myers and Majluf (1984), Krasker (1986), Noe (1988), Korajczyk, et al. (1990c), and Lucas and McDonald (1990) predict a negative price effect of an equity issue. This price drop will be larger the larger is the informational asymmetry and the larger is the equity issue. Moreover, Lucas and McDonald (1990) show that, on average, equity issues will be preceded by abnormal stock price increases.

Stock Price Effects of Exchange Offers

- Debt Increasing Offers: Constantinides and Grundy (1989) predict a positive stock price reaction that is larger the larger the exchange.
- Equity Increasing Offers: Brennan and Kraus (1987) predict a positive stock price reaction.

Is There a Pecking Order?

- Yes: Myers and Majluf (1984), Krasker (1986), and Narayanan (1988).
- No: Brennan and Kraus (1987), Noe (1988), Constantinides and Grundy (1989) dispute the pecking order result in models similar to that of Myers and Majluf. Other signaling models, such as Ross (1977), Leland and Pyle (1977), and Heinkel (1982) do not obtain a pecking order result.

Leverage

Myers and Majluf (1984) implies that leverage increases with the extent of the informational asymmetry. Ross (1977), Leland and Pyle (1977), Heinkel (1982), Blazenko (1987), John (1987), Poitevin (1989), and Ravid and Sarig (1989) all derive a positive correlation between leverage and value in a cross section of otherwise similar firms. Ross (1977) also predicts a positive correlation between leverage or value and bankruptcy probability, while Leland and Pyle (1977) predict a positive correlation between value and equity ownership of insiders.

III. Models Based on Product/Input Market Interactions

Models of capital structure that use features of the theory of industrial organization have begun to appear in the literature. These models can be classified into two categories. One class of approaches exploits the relationship between a firm's capital structure and its *strategy* when competing in the product market. A second class of approaches addresses the relationship between a firm's capital structure and the *characteristics* of its product or inputs. These two literatures are surveyed in the next two subsections.

A. Debt Influences Strategic Interaction Among Competitors

Until recently, the industrial organization literature has assumed that in choosing its competitive strategy the firm's objective is to maximize total profits. The finance literature, on the other hand, has focused on maximization of equity value while generally ignoring product market strategy. The new literature linking capital structure and product market strategy adopts the finance view that managers generally have incentives to maximize equity value as opposed to profits or total value. In these papers, leverage changes the payoffs to equity and thus affects the equilibrium product market strategies.

One of the initial papers in this line of research was Brander and Lewis (1986).[27] They use the basic idea of Jensen and Meckling (1976) (see Section I) that increases in leverage induce equity holders to pursue riskier strategies. In the Brander and Lewis model, oligopolists increase risk by a more aggressive output policy. Thus, to commit to pursuing a more aggressive strategy in a subsequent Cournot game, firms choose positive debt levels.

To see how this process works in somewhat more detail, consider the following formal model based on Brander and Lewis. There are two firms, $i = 1, 2$. The two firms first commit simultaneously to a debt level D_i, then choose simultaneously an output level q_i. Profits to firm i are given by $R^i(q_i, q_j, z_i)$ where z_1 and z_2 are independent and identically distributed shocks to the firms' profits. We assume that firm i's profits are decreasing in the other firm's output and increasing in the random shock z_i. Also, firm i's marginal profit $(\partial R^i / \partial q_i)$ is increasing in the random shock z_i and decreasing in the other firm's output.

These assumptions are fairly standard in Cournot-equilibrium models except for the assumption that marginal profit increases with the random component.[28] This assumption states that the marginal "product" (profit) of output is large in "good" states (when z is large). If the marginal product of output is high, the firm will optimally choose higher output than if it is low. But in this model the firm must choose output before its marginal product is known. Since levered equity holders receive payoffs only in good states (because of limited liability), however, they ignore the possibility that the marginal product of output is low. Consequently, leverage creates an incentive to increase output. Moreover, in Cournot oligopoly models, firms have an incentive to commit to producing large outputs since this causes their rivals

---

[27] Two other treatments that are contemporaneous with Brander and Lewis (1986) are Allen (1985) and Maksimovic (1986). For a similar treatment, see Maksimovic (1989).

[28] Brander and Lewis consider both this case and the case in which the marginal profit is decreasing with z. They consider the increasing case to be the most important empirically, since, in the other case, firms will be unlevered in equilibrium.

to produce less. Leverage thus provides a device that allows firms to commit to producing more in the Cournot oligopoly. Therefore, in equilibrium, both firms will choose a positive debt level. Notice that the firms are worse off in this equilibrium than they would be in an all-equity Cournot equilibrium since, with leverage, firms produce more than the Cournot output.[29]

When oligopolies persist over time, tacit collusion is possible through the use of punishment strategies triggered when a rival deviates from the collusive output level. It is well known (see Green and Porter (1984)) that the monopoly solution can be achieved in an infinitely repeated Cournot oligopoly by a subgame perfect equilibrium in which each firm reverts to the Cournot output forever in the period after any firm deviates from its share of the monopoly output. The condition that is required for this result is that the present value of monopoly profits exceeds the value of deviating for one period, then obtaining Cournot profits forever. If we denote monopoly profits per period by π_m, Cournot profits per period by π_c, the one-period profit from deviating by π_d, and the discount rate by r, the condition required for supporting the monopoly solution is

$$\pi_m + \pi_m/r > \pi_d + \pi_c/r.$$

Maksimovic (1988) points out that if managers are assumed to maximize the value of equity (as opposed to the value of the firm) this condition must be modified. In particular, suppose the firm has issued debt that promises to pay b per period forever, where $b \geq \pi_c$ (otherwise, the debt has no effect since it will be paid even if the firm reverts to the Cournot equilibrium). Now, if the firm deviates, equity holders receive $\pi_d - b$ for one period, then nothing thereafter since the assets will be transferred to bondholders (who will then follow the Cournot strategy forever). The condition for supporting the monopoly solution is therefore

$$\pi_m - b + (\pi_m - b)/r > \pi_d - b \quad \text{or} \quad b < \pi_m + (\pi_m - \pi_d)r.$$

Maksimovic interprets this as a debt capacity, i.e., the maximum amount of leverage that firms in such industries can support without destroying the possibility of tacit collusion.

By modeling profits explicitly in terms of demand and cost functions and number of firms, Maksimovic is able to derive comparative static results on debt capacity as a function of industry and firm characteristics. He shows that debt capacity increases with the elasticity of demand and decreases with the discount rate. Assuming some advantage for debt (e.g. taxes), so that the firm's actual debt will be at capacity, makes these implications potentially testable.[30]

---

[29] Glazer (1989) shows that when long run considerations are taken into account in a Brander and Lewis type model, firms have an incentive to issue long term debt which helps in enforcing a form of tacit collusion.

[30] Maksimovic (1990) extends this analysis to the case in which firms are privately informed about their own productivity.

B. Debt Influences Interaction with Customers and/or Suppliers

The second industrial-organization-based approach to capital structure determination is to identify product (input) or product market (input market) characteristics that interact in a significant way with the debt level. The examples included here are customers' need for a particular product or service, the need for workers to invest in firm-specific human capital, product quality, and the bargaining power of workers or other suppliers.

Titman (1984) observes that liquidation of a firm may impose costs on its customers (or suppliers) such as inability to obtain the product, parts, and/or service.[31] These costs are transferred to the stockholders in the form of lower prices for the firm's product. Consequently, the stockholders would like to commit to liquidate only in those states in which the net gains to liquidation exceed the costs imposed on customers. Unfortunately, when the firm's investors make the liquidation decision, they ignore these costs. Titman shows that capital structure can be used to commit the shareholders to an optimal liquidation policy. Specifically, capital structure is arranged so that stockholders never wish to liquidate, bondholders always wish to liquidate when the firm is in bankruptcy, and the firm will default only when the net gain to liquidation exceeds the cost to customers. It is shown that firms for which this effect is more important, e.g., computer and automobile companies, will have less debt, other things equal, than firms for which this effect is less important, e.g., hotels and restaurants. In general, for unique and/or durable products, the cost imposed on customers when a producer goes out of business is higher than for nondurable products or those made by more than one producer.

Maksimovic and Titman (Forthcoming) show that producers of nonunique and nondurable goods may also be subject to a similar effect. Consider a firm that can produce goods of high or low quality in any period, and suppose that consumers cannot distinguish quality until after consuming the good. Even though high quality costs more to produce, it may be worthwhile for the firm to produce high quality if it can establish a reputation for being a high quality producer. If, however, this reputation is lost (at least to stockholders) when the firm goes bankrupt, then the incentive to produce high quality is diminished by debt. Consequently, one would expect firms that can easily switch from high to low quality output but whose customers cannot distinguish quality without purchasing the good, to have less debt, other things equal.

Another advantage of debt is that debt strengthens the bargaining position of equity holders in dealing with input suppliers. Sarig (1988) argues that bondholders bear a large share of the costs of bargaining failure but get only a small share of the gains to successful bargaining. That is, bondholders insure stockholders to some extent against failure of negotiations with sup-

---

[31] Allen (1985) also focuses on bankruptcy costs emanating from the product market. He points out that firms in financial distress may postpone investments, thus giving an advantage to their competitors. See also John and Senbet (1988).

pliers. Increases in leverage increase the extent of this insurance and therefore increase the equity holders'. threat point in negotiating with suppliers. As a result, debt can increase firm value. This implies that a firm should have more debt the greater is the bargaining power and/or the market alternatives of its suppliers. Thus, Sarig predicts that highly unionized firms and/or firms that employ workers with highly transferable skills will have more debt, *ceteris paribus*.

C. Summary of Section III

Capital structure models based on product/input market interactions are in their infancy. These theories have explored the relationship between capital structure and either product market strategy or characteristics of products/inputs. The strategic variables considered are product price and quantity. These strategies are determined to affect the behavior of rivals, and capital structure in turn affects the equilibrium strategies and payoffs. Models involving product or input characteristics have focused on the effect of capital structure on the future availability of products, parts and service, product quality, and the bargaining game between management and input suppliers.

The models show that oligopolists will tend to have more debt than monopolists or firms in competitive industries (Brander and Lewis (1986)), and that the debt will tend to be long term (Glazer (1989)). If, however, tacit collusion is important, debt is limited, and debt capacity increases with the elasticity of demand (Maksimovic (1988)). Firms that produce products that are unique or require service and/or parts and firms for which a reputation for producing high quality products is important may be expected to have less debt, other things equal (Titman (1984) and Maksimovic and Titman (Forthcoming)). Finally, highly unionized firms and firms whose workers have easily transferable skills should have more debt (Sarig (1988)).

Models of capital structure based on industrial organization considerations have the potential to provide interesting results. For example, models similar to the ones surveyed above could delineate more specifically the relationship between capital structure and observable industry characteristics such as demand and supply conditions and extent of competition. In addition, it would be useful to explore the impact of capital structure on the choice of strategic variables other than price and quantity. These could include advertising, research and development expenditure, plant capacity, location, and product characteristics. Such research could help in explaining inter-industry variations in capital structure.

IV. Theories Driven by Corporate Control Considerations

Following the growing importance of takeover activities in the 1980's, the finance literature began to examine the linkage between the market for corporate control and capital structure. These papers exploit the fact that common stock carries voting rights while debt does not. In this section, we discuss three contributions. In Harris and Raviv (1988) and Stulz (1988), capital structure affects the outcome of takeover contests through its effect on the distribution of votes, especially the fraction owned by the manager. In Israel (Forthcoming), capital structure affects the distribution of cash flows between voting (equity) and nonvoting (debt) claimants.

The first models to exploit the differential voting rights of debt and equity are those of Harris and Raviv (1988) and Stulz (1988). These two models generate a relationship between the fraction of the equity owned by a firm's manager and the value of outside equity (equity held by noncontestants). This relationship follows from the dependence of firm value on whether the firm is taken over and, if so, how much is paid by the successful bidder. The manager's equity ownership is determined in part by the firm's capital structure. Thus, capital structure affects the value of the firm, the probability of takeover, and the price effects of takeover. In what follows, we explain the models in more detail and compare their implications.

Harris and Raviv (1988) focus on the ability of an incumbent firm manager to manipulate the method and probability of success of a takeover attempt by changing the fraction of the equity he owns. Since the incumbent and the rival have different abilities to manage the firm, the value of the firm depends on the outcome of the takeover contest. The manager's ownership share determines one of three possible outcomes: the rival takes over for sure, the incumbent remains in control for sure, or the outcome is determined by the votes of passive investors, and this results in the election of the better candidate. The optimal ownership share is determined by the incumbent manager who trades off capital gains on his stake against the loss of any personal benefits derived from being in control. Since the manager's ownership share is determined indirectly by the firm's capital structure, this tradeoff results in a theory of capital structure.

The following is a simplified version of the Harris and Raviv model. An incumbent entrepreneur/manager I owns an initial fraction α_0 of an all-equity-financed firm. The remaining equity is held by passive investors who are not contenders for control. The incumbent obtains benefits of control of expected value B as long as he controls the firm. These benefits can be thought of as private control benefits or as the value of cash flows that he can expropriate from the firm if he is in control. The value of the cash flows (not including B) generated by the firm depends on the ability of the manager. There are two possible ability levels, 1 and 2, and the corresponding values of the cash flows are denoted Y_1 and Y_2, with $Y_1 > Y_2$.

In addition to the incumbent and passive investors, there is also a rival for control of the firm, R. If the rival takes over, he also obtains benefits of control. The abilities of the incumbent and rival are unobservable by all parties, but it is common knowledge that one is of higher ability than the other. That is, everyone knows that, with probability p, the incumbent has ability 1 and, with probability $1 - p$, the rival has ability 1. The other has ability 2. Thus the value of the firm's cash flows if the incumbent controls is

Y_I, and if the rival controls it is Y_R, where

$$Y_I = pY_1 + (1 - p)Y_2 \text{ and } Y_R = (1 - p)Y_1 + pY_2.$$

When the rival appears, the incumbent first chooses a new fraction α of the equity of the firm (this change in ownership is the result of a change in capital structure; see below). The rival then acquires equity from the passive investors. The takeover contest is decided by a simple majority vote (ties go to the incumbent) where the two contestants each vote for themselves, and the fraction π of the passive investors vote for the incumbent (the rest vote for the rival).[32]

Depending on the choices of equity ownership by the incumbent and rival, the takeover contest can have one of three possible outcomes. First, the incumbent's stake may be so small that, even if the rival is of lower ability, he still succeeds in taking over. Harris and Raviv (1988) refer to this case as that of a *successful* tender offer. The value of the cash flows in this case is Y_R. Second, the incumbent's stake may be so large that even if he is of lower ability, he still remains in control. This is referred to as the case of an *unsuccessful* tender offer, and the value of the cash flows in this case is Y_I. Finally, for intermediate values of α, the incumbent will win if and only if he is of higher ability. This case is called a *proxy fight*, since the identity of the winner is uncertain until the vote is actually taken. Note, however, that in this case, the best candidate wins for sure, and hence the value of the cash flows is Y_1. The value of the firm's cash flows $Y(\alpha)$ is determined by the incumbent's stake α through its effect on which of the above three cases prevails. Since Y_1 is larger than either Y_I or Y_R if the objective were to maximize the value of the cash flow to outside investors, then α in the proxy fight range would be optimal. This would result in a model more similar to that of Stulz (1988) as will be seen below.

The objective in choosing the incumbent's share α is to maximize his expected payoff. This payoff is the value of his equity stake plus the value of his control benefits if he remains in control. The value of the incumbent's equity stake is $\alpha_0 Y(\alpha)$, where α_0 is his *initial* equity stake, since any transactions in which he engages to change his stake have zero net present value. Therefore, the incumbent's payoff $V(\alpha)$ is $\alpha_0 Y_R$ if there is a successful tender offer (benefits of control are lost), $\alpha_0 Y_I + B$ if there is an unsuccessful tender offer (benefits retained for sure), and $\alpha_0 Y_1 + pB$ if there is a proxy fight (benefits retained with probability p). The optimal ownership share for the incumbent maximizes $V(\alpha)$. The tradeoffs are apparent from the description of V. In particular, as α is increased, the probability that the incumbent retains control and its benefits increases. On the other hand, if α is increased too much, the value of the firm and the manager's stake are reduced.

In Harris and Raviv, α is determined indirectly through the firm's capital structure. In particular, the incumbent is assumed to have a fixed amount of wealth represented by his initial stake α_0. He can increase his stake by

---

[32] In the Harris and Raviv paper, π is derived from a model of passive investors' information.

having the firm repurchase equity from the passive investors, financing the repurchase by issuing debt. Debt decreases the value of the equity allowing him to purchase a larger fraction with his given wealth. Maximizing the manager's payoff is actually accomplished by choosing the debt level that determines the optimal share α. Since Harris and Raviv assume that the expected benefits of control B decrease with the debt level, within any of the three cases described above, it is optimal to choose the lowest debt level consistent with that case.[33]

It follows from the above arguments that if the case of successful tender offer is optimal, the firm will have no debt. It is also shown that generally, proxy fights require some debt, and guaranteeing that the tender offer is unsuccessful requires even more debt. Thus, takeover targets will increase their debt levels on average and targets of unsuccessful tender offers will issue more debt on average than targets of successful tender offers or proxy fights. Also, firms that increase leverage either have unsuccessful tender offers or proxy fights. In the former case, firm value remains at Y_I on average, while in the latter it increases to Y_1. Thus, on average, debt issues are accompanied by stock price increases.

Finally, note that the fraction of passive investors who vote for the incumbent is determined by the information that these passive investors receive regarding the relative abilities of the two candidates. A larger fraction will vote for the incumbent if the passive investors' prior probability that he is more able, p, increases. Consequently, less debt is required to effect a proxy fight if the incumbent is more likely to be of higher ability. Since winning a proxy fight is positively related to the probability of being more able, the incumbent's winning is also associated with less debt. Therefore, in a sample of firms experiencing proxy fights, one would expect to observe less leverage among firms in which the incumbent remains in control.[34]

Stulz (1988) also focuses on the ability of shareholders to affect the nature of a takeover attempt by changing the incumbent's ownership share. In particular, as the incumbent's share α increases, the premium offered in a tender offer increases, but the probability that the takeover occurs and the shareholders actually receive the premium is reduced. Stulz discusses how the ownership share of the incumbent is affected by capital structure (as well as other variables).

The basic idea of Stulz's model can be presented simply as follows. As in Harris and Raviv (1988), there is an incumbent manager of a firm, a potential rival, and a large number of passive investors. The incumbent owns the fraction α of the shares and obtains private benefits of control. Stulz assumes the incumbent will not tender his shares in any takeover attempt.

[33] Expected benefits may decrease with the debt level because the benefits are lost in bankruptcy, higher debt results in more monitoring by creditors, and/or less free cash flow allows the manager less discretion.

[34] The model also has a number of other testable implications regarding stock price changes of takeover targets classified by the type of takeover attempt (proxy fight or tender offer) and the outcome (successful or unsuccessful).

The rival can obtain a random benefit of control B from taking over. Initially, B is unknown to all parties. The value of the benefit becomes known to the rival before he must decide what premium to offer shareholders. To acquire control, the rival must purchase 50% of the shares. These shares are purchased from the passive investors. This reflects the assumption that the passive investors vote for the incumbent in any takeover contest. The passive investors are assumed to have heterogeneous reservation prices for selling their shares. In particular, let $s(P)$ be the fraction of passive investors who tender if the total premium paid by the rival (above the value under the incumbent) is P. The supply function s is assumed to be increasing in P. Then the minimum price that the rival must offer to purchase 50% of the votes, $P^*(\alpha)$, satisfies the condition

$$s\big(P^*(\alpha)\big)(1 - \alpha) = 1/2.$$

Since s is increasing in P, this condition implies that the offer premium P^* is increasing in the incumbent's share α. Intuitively, the larger the incumbent's stake, the larger the fraction of the passive investors' shares that must be acquired by the rival, hence the more he must pay. The rival will bid P^* if and only if his benefit B exceeds P^*. Therefore, the probability that the passive investors actually obtain the premium P^* is

$$Pr\big(B \ge P^*(\alpha)\big) \equiv \pi\big[P^*(\alpha)\big].$$

Since P^* increases with α and π is a decreasing function, the probability of a takeover declines with α. The expected gain to the passive investors is

$$Y(\alpha) = P^*(\alpha)\pi\big[P^*(\alpha)\big].$$

The incumbent's share α is chosen to maximize Y. As mentioned above, increases in α increase the takeover premium given success but decrease the probability of success.

As in Harris and Raviv, α can be increased by increasing the firm's leverage.[35] Therefore, Stulz obtains the result that takeover targets have an optimal debt level that maximizes the value of outside investors' shares. Targets of hostile takeovers will have more debt than firms that are not targets. Since becoming a takeover target is good news, one would expect exchanges of debt for equity that accompany such an event to be associated with stock price increases. Moreover, the probability of a takeover is negatively related to the target's debt/equity ratio, and the takeover premium is positively related to this ratio.

A similar approach was taken by Israel (Forthcoming). In his model, as in Stulz (1988), increases in debt also increase the gain to target shareholders if a takeover occurs but lower the probability of this event. The reason that increases in debt increase the gain to target shareholders is different from

---

[35] Stulz also considers a number of other methods for changing α such as ESOP's, voting trusts, supermajority rules, and differential voting rights. Results derived from these considerations are not directly relevant to the topic at hand.

that in Stulz (1988), however. Israel observes that debt commands a contrac-
tually fixed share of any gains from takeover. Target and acquiring shareholders bargain only over that portion of the gains that is not previously
committed to debtholders. The more debt, the less gain is left for target and
acquiring shareholders to split and the smaller is the portion of the gain
captured by acquiring shareholders. Moreover, target shareholders can capture the gains accruing to target debtholders when the debt is issued. Thus,
they capture all of the gain not going to acquiring shareholders. Since debt
reduces the gain captured by acquiring shareholders, the payoff to target
shareholders, given that a takeover occurs, is increased by increased debt
levels. The optimal debt level is determined by balancing this effect against
the reduced probability of takeover resulting from the reduced share of the
gain that accrues to acquiring stockholders.

The essence of Israel's (Forthcoming) model is the following. Suppose that
a takeover can generate a random total gain G in firm value, but a takeover
will cost T. Further, suppose the firm has issued risky debt of face value D,
and, in the event of a takeover, this debt increases in value by $\delta(D, G)$. If the
takeover occurs, the acquiring and target shareholders can then split the
remaining net gain $G - \delta - T$. Assume that target shareholders obtain the
fixed fraction $1 - \gamma$ of this net gain and acquiring shareholders capture the
remaining fraction γ (γ can be thought of as measuring the acquirer's
bargaining power). Thus, a takeover will occur if and only if $\gamma(G - \delta - T) > 0$
or $G - \delta(D, G) \geq T$, and the probability of a takeover is the probability of
this event, denoted $\pi(D, T)$. In addition, when issuing the debt, target
shareholders also capture the expected gain to debtholders. Consequently,
target shareholders' total expected payoff is

$$Y(D) = E\big[\{(1 - \gamma)[\tilde{G} - \delta(D, \tilde{G}) - T]$$
$$+ \delta(D, \tilde{G})\} \mid \tilde{G} - \delta(D, \tilde{G}) > T\big] \pi(D, T)$$
$$= E\big[\{(1 - \gamma)[\tilde{G} - T] + \gamma\delta(D, \tilde{G})\} \mid \tilde{G} - \delta(D, \tilde{G}) > T\big] \pi(D, T).$$

As can be seen from this last expression, target shareholders capture the
fraction $1 - \gamma$ of the net total gains to takeover plus an additional fraction γ
of the gain to target debtholders. The optimal debt level is obtained by
maximizing $Y(D)$. This involves trading off the increase in amount extracted
from the acquirer represented by the term in braces against the decrease in
the probability that takeover occurs, π.[36]

Israel (Forthcoming) obtains several interesting comparative statics results. First, an increase in the costs of mounting a takeover contest T results
in a decrease in leverage but an increase in the appreciation of target equity
if a takeover occurs. Second, if the distribution of potential takeover gains

---

[36] In a related paper, Israel (1989) notes that increases in leverage reduce the capital loss
suffered by an incumbent manager if he resists a value-increasing takeover. As a result, the
manager can extract a larger share of the surplus for the firm's shareholders. Debt is limited by
the amount of the surplus to be extracted.

shifts to the right, debt level increases. Such a shift could result from a *decrease* in the ability of the incumbent manager. Third, the optimal debt level increases, and the probability of takeover and the gain to target equity in the event of a takeover decrease with the rival's bargaining power γ.

A. Summary of Section IV

The papers discussed in this section provide a theory of capital structure related to takeover contests. The major results are as follows. First, all three papers conclude that takeover targets will increase their debt levels on average, and this will be accompanied by a positive stock price reaction. Second, all three show that leverage is negatively related on average to whether the tender offer succeeds. Third, Harris and Raviv (1988) also show that targets of unsuccessful tender offers will have more debt on average than targets of proxy fights. They also show that among firms involved in proxy fights, leverage is lower on average when the incumbent remains in control. Fourth, with regard to the relationship between fraction of the takeover premium captured by the target's equity and the amount of debt, Stulz (1988) and Israel (Forthcoming) obtain opposite results. In Stulz, the premium paid to target shareholders increases with increases in the target's debt level. In Israel, as the bargaining power of the target shareholders decreases, the target optimally issues more debt, and the fraction of the takeover premium captured by the target equity falls. Fifth, Israel shows that targets that are more costly to take over have less debt but capture a larger premium if a takeover occurs. Sixth, Israel predicts that firms that have greater potential takeover gains will have more debt.[37]

Two important observations should be noted here. First, the theories surveyed in this section should be viewed as theories of short-term changes in capital structure taken in response to imminent takeover threats, since the optimal capital structure derived in these models can be implemented in response to hostile takeover activity. As a result, theories based on corporate control considerations have nothing to say about the long run capital structure of firms. Second, these papers take as given the characteristics of the securities issued by firms. In particular, both the cash flow aspects and the assignment of voting rights and other control-related features are treated as exogenous.

V. Summary of Results

The purpose of this section is to present the collected lessons of the literature surveyed. These lessons are presented in three subsections. In the first, we discuss the theoretical predictions of the models surveyed above. In the

---

[37] Similar results are undoubtedly available from Stulz's model although he does not derive them. One can view B in Stulz's model as takeover benefits net of takeover costs. Then any increase in potential benefits or decrease in costs is simply a rightward shift of the distribution of B.

second, we briefly summarize the available empirical evidence. In the third, we compare the theoretical predictions with the evidence. Much of the material in this section is synthesized in tables. These tables are as follows:

- Table II: Summary of Theoretical Results
- Table III: Industry Leverage Rankings
- Table IV: Determinants of Leverage
- Table V: Comparison of Theoretical and Empirical Results
- Table VI: Other Empirical Results
- Table VII: Summary of Results by Model Type

A. Summary of Theoretical Results

Those theoretical results that are potentially testable are summarized in Table II, consisting of four panels. Panel A contains implications regarding the relationship between leverage and exogenous factors that are not the result of decisions by agents in the model, e.g., profitability, characteristics of the product market, etc. Panel B contains implications regarding the relationship between leverage and endogenous factors that are the result of decisions by agents in the model. In this case, both leverage and the other factor are jointly determined by some third, exogenous factor. Typically, in these cases the endogenous factors are more readily observable than the exogenous driving factor. In Panel C, we list results relating the firm's stock price response to announcements of capital structure changes. Panel D contains other results that do not fit into the above three groups.[38] In each panel, the first column contains the theoretical prediction; the second column indicates the type(s) of model(s) from which the result was derived and corresponds to the various sections of the survey; the third column provides the specific references for the result.

The table makes it clear that the literature provides a substantial number of implications. The other striking feature is that there are very few cases in which two or more theories have opposite implications (these are indicated by a shaded background). Such conflicts can provide sharp tests capable of rejecting one or more theories in favor of another. The only instances of conflicting results are: i) Chang (1987) predicts a negative relationship of leverage and firm profitability while several studies predict a positive relationship (see Panel A); ii) Myers and Majluf (1984) predicts a negative relationship between leverage and free cash flow while Jensen (1986) and Stulz (1990) predict a positive relationship (see Panel A); iii) Stulz (1988) predicts a positive relationship between leverage and the takeover premium captured by a target while Israel (Forthcoming) predicts the opposite relationship (see Panel B); iv) Myers and Majluf (1984) and related papers predict the absence of a stock price reaction to a debt issue announcement while numerous papers predict a positive reaction (see Panel C); and v) several papers argue against the pecking order theory of Myers and Majluf (1984)

---

[38] Other theoretical results not directly relating to capital structure are not included in this summary even though they may be potentially testable.

Table II

Summary of Theoretical Results

The table shows, for each theoretical result, the type of model from which the result was derived and the specific papers that obtain the result. Model types also refer to sections in the paper. The shaded cells (separated by dashed line) indicate results that are in conflict.

Panel A. Association Between Leverage and Exogenous Factors

Leverage increases with:	Model	References
Extent of information asymmetry	Asymmetric Info.	Myers & Majluf (1984)
Increases in profitability	Asymmetric Info.	Ross (1977), Leland & Pyle (1977), Heinkel (1982), Blazenko (1987), John (1987), Poitevin (1989), Ravid & Sarig (1989)
Decreases in profitability	Agency	Chang (1987)
Extent of *strategic* interaction in the product market	Product/Input Markets	Brander & Lewis (1986)
Elasticity of demand for the product	Product/Input Markets	Maksimovic (1988)
Extent to which product is not unique and does not require specialized service	Product/Input Markets	Titman (1984)
Extent to which reputation for product quality is unimportant	Product/Input Markets	Maksimovic & Titman (Forthcoming)
Extent to which workers are unionized or have transferable skills	Product/Input Markets	Sarig (1988)
Extent to which the firm is a takeover target or lack of anti-takeover measures	Control	Harris & Raviv (1988), Stulz (1988), Israel (Forthcoming)
	Agency	Stulz (1990), Hirshleifer & Thakor (1989)
Potential gains to takeover and reductions in their costs	Control	Israel (Forthcoming)
Fraction of cash flow that is unobservable	Agency	Chang (1987)
Lack of growth opportunities, extent of regulation	Agency	Jensen & Meckling (1976), Stulz (1990)

Table II—(Continued)

Panel A. Association Between Leverage and Exogenous Factors

Leverage Increeases with:	Model	References
Increases in free cash flow	Agency	Jensen (1986), Stulz (1990)
Decreases in free cash flow	Asymmetric Info.	Myers & Majluf (1984)
Increases in liquidation value	Agency	Williamson (1988), Harris & Raviv (1990a)
Decreases in investigation costs	Agency	Harris & Raviv (1990a)
Increases in the importance of managerial reputation	Agency	Hirshleifer & Thakor (1989)

Panel B. Association Between Leverage and Endogenous Factors

Result	Model	References
Leverage is positively correlated with firm value	Agency	Harris & Raviv (1990a), Stulz (1990), Hirshleifer & Thakor (1989)
	Asymmetric Info.	Ross (1977), Noe (1988), Narayanan (1988), Poitevin (1989)
	Control	Harris & Raviv (1988), Stulz (1988), Israel (Forthcoming)
Leverage is positively correlated with default probability	Agency Asymmetric Info.	Harris & Raviv (1990c), Ross (1977)
Leverage is positively correlated with the extent of managerial equity ownership	Asymmetric Info. Control	Leland & Pyle (1977) Harris & Raviv (1988), Stulz (1988)
Leverage is positively correlated with target premium	Control	Stulz (1988)
Leverage is negatively correlated with target premium	Control	Israel (Forthcoming)
Leverage is negatively correlated with probability of successful takeover	Control	Stulz (1988)

154

Table II—*(Continued)*

Panel B. Association Between Leverage and Endogenous Factors

Results	Model	References
Leverage is negatively correlated with the interest coverage ratio and the probability of reorganization following default	Agency	Harris & Raviv (1990a)
Targets of an unsuccessful tender offer have more debt than targets of proxy fights or successful tender offer	Control	Harris & Raviv (1988)
Targets of successful proxy fights have more debt than targets of unsuccessful proxy fights	Control	Harris & Raviv (1988)
Targets of proxy fights have more debt than targets of successful tender offers	Control	Harris & Raviv (1988)

Panel C. Announcement of Security Issues

Stock Price	Model	References
Increases on announcement of debt issues, debt-for-equity exchanges or stock repurchases	Agency	Harris & Raviv (1990a), Stulz (1990), Hirshleifer & Thakor (1989)
	Asymmetric Info.	Ross (1977), Noe (1988), Narayanan (1988), Poitevin (1989)
	Control	Harris & Raviv (1988), Stulz (1988), Israel (Forthcoming)
Isn't affected by announcement of debt issue	Asymmetric Info.	Myers & Majluf (1984), Krasker (1986), Korajczyk, et al. (1990c)
Decreases on announcement of equity issue	Agency	Harris & Raviv (1990a), Stulz (1990), Hirshleifer & Thakor (1989).
	Asymmetric Info.	Ross (1977), Myers & Majluf (1984), Krasker (1986), Korajczyk, et al. (1990c), Noe (1988), Narayanan (1988), Poitevin (1989), Lucas & McDonald (1990)
	Control	Harris & Raviv (1988), Stulz (1988), Israel (Forthcoming)

Table II —*(Continued)*

Panel C. Announcement of Security Issues

Stock Price	Model	References
Decreases more the larger is the informational asymmetry	Asymmetric Info.	Myers & Majluf (1984), Krasker (1986), Korajczyk, et al. (1990c)
Decreases more the larger is the size of the issue	Asymmetric Info.	Krasker (1986)
Increases if some proceeds of equity issue used to repurchase debt	Asymmetric Info.	Brennan & Kraus (1987)
Increases on announcement of issue of convertible debt in exchange for equity	Asymmetric Info.	Constantinides & Grundy (1989)

Panel D. Other Results

Result	Model	References
There is a pecking order: firms prefer internal finance, then issuing securities in order of increasing sensitivity to firm performance	Asymmetric Info.	Myers & Majluf (1984), Krasker (1986), Narayanan (1988)
There is no pecking order	Asymmetric Info.	Brennan & Kraus (1987), Noe (1988), Constantinides & Grundy (1989)
Firms tend to issue equity following abnormal price appreciation	Asymmetric Info.	Lucas & McDonald (1990)
Firms tend to issue equity when information asymmetry is smallest	Asymmetric Info.	Myers & Majluf (1984), Korajczyk, et al. (1990c)
Bonds can be expected to have covenants prohibiting "asset substitution"	Agency	Jensen & Meckling (1976)
Firms with longer track records have lower default probabilities	Agency	Diamond (1989)

and others (see Panel D). Since conflicting implications are rare, the large majority of the studies surveyed must therefore be considered as complements, i.e., any or all of the effects traced by these theories could be present simultaneously. The relative significance of these effects is an empirical issue.

B. Summary of Empirical Evidence

The evidence fits into four categories. The first group contains evidence of general capital structure trends. The second group, event studies, generally measures the impact on stock value of an announcement of a capital structure change. The third group relates firm/industry characteristics to financial structure. The fourth group measures the relationship between capital structure and factors associated with corporate control. We discuss these four classes of empirical studies in the next subsections.

Before turning to this discussion, a word of caution is in order. The interpretation of the results must be tempered by an awareness of the difficulties involved in measuring both leverage and the explanatory variables of interest. In measuring leverage, one can include or exclude accounts payable, accounts receivable, cash, and other short-term debt. Some studies measure leverage as a ratio of book value of debt to book value of equity, others as book value of debt to market value of equity, still others as debt to market value of equity plus book value of debt. With regard to the explanatory variables, proxies are often difficult to interpret. For example, several studies measure growth opportunities as the ratio of market value of the firm to book value of assets. While firms with large growth opportunities should have large values of this ratio, other firms whose assets have appreciated significantly since purchase but which do not have large growth opportunities will also have large values of this ratio. In addition to measurement problems, there are the usual problems with interpreting statistical results. In what follows, we take the results reported at face value and compare results of various studies largely ignoring differences in measurement technique.

B.1. General Trends

Firms raise funds for new investment both externally, through security issues, and internally from retained earnings. Internal sources, which add to total firm equity, have historically constituted a large but fairly steadily declining fraction of these funds. For example, undistributed profits accounts for about 22% of total sources of funds for nonfarm, nonfinancial corporate business in 1986. By comparison, the same figure averaged about 49% over the period 1946–1966 (see Masulis (1988, Table 1-1, p. 3)).

The second major trend in financial structure has been the secular increase in leverage. Taggart (1985) reports secular trends in leverage using a variety of different measurements. He concludes that leverage has increased steadily since World War II but that current debt levels may not be high relative to those of the prewar period.

B.2. Event Studies

Event studies have documented the stock price reaction to announcements of security offerings, exchanges and repurchases.[39] In some cases, the studies also document the reaction of earnings or earnings forecasts to the events. Generally, equity-increasing transactions result in stock price decreases while leverage-increasing transactions result in stock price increases. Earnings and earnings forecasts react consistently with the stock price reactions.

With regard to security issues,[40]

- abnormal returns associated with announcements of common stocks are the most negative (about − 3% according to Smith (1986)),
- abnormal returns associated with convertible bonds or convertible preferred stock are more negative than those associated with the respective nonconvertible security,
- abnormal returns associated with straight debt or preferred stock are not statistically significantly different from zero,[41]
- abnormal returns associated with securities issued by utilities are less negative than those associated with the same securities issued by industrial firms.

Marsh (1982) finds that firms are more likely to issue long-term debt to the extent that their current long-term debt is below their target as measured by the average debt level of the previous 10 years. He also finds that market conditions play a highly significant role in determining the probability that a firm will issue debt. Specifically, firms are more likely to issue debt (equity) when they expect other firms to issue debt (equity) and are more likely to issue equity to the extent that the previous year's share return exceeds that of the market portfolio. Korajczyk, et al. (1990a) also document that a firm's stock price experiences significant abnormal rises on average prior to its issuing equity. In addition, Korajczyk, et al. (1990b) find that equity issues are clustered after earnings announcements and the extent of the price drop at the announcement increases insignificantly with time since the last earnings announcement. Korajczyk, et al. (1990a) examine the cross-sectional properties of the price rise and track debt ratios and Tobin's q around the time of equity issues. They find that debt ratios do not increase prior to equity issues, "suggesting that strained debt capacity is not the main reason for equity issues." Tobin's q (the ratio of market to book value of assets) is observed to rise prior to an equity issue and fall following the issue. This suggests that equity is issued to finance new investments.

---

[39] Much of the literature is surveyed in Smith (1986). Masulis (1988) provides a more recent and comprehensive survey.

[40] See Asquith and Mullins (1986), Dann and Mikkelson (1984), Eckbo (1986), Linn and Pinegar (1988), Masulis and Korwar (1986), Mikkelson and Partch (1986), and Schipper and Smith (1986).

[41] Kim and Stulz (1988), however, found a significantly positive effect associated with Eurobond issues.

With regard to exchange offers, Masulis (1983) reports:[42]

- debt issued in exchange for common stock results in a 14% abnormal stock return.
- preferred stock issued in exchange for common stock results in a 8.3% abnormal stock return,
- debt issued in exchange for preferred stock results in a 2.2% abnormal stock return,
- common stock issued in exchange for preferred stock results in a −2.6% abnormal stock return,
- common stock issued in exchange for debt results in a −9.9% abnormal stock return,
- preferred stock issued in exchange for debt results in a −7.7% abnormal stock return.

Further evidence on exchanges is offered by Lys and Sivaramakrishnan (1988), Cornett and Travlos (1989), and Israel, et al. (Forthcoming). Cornett and Travlos confirm Masulis' (1980, 1983) results that leverage increasing (decreasing) exchanges of securities are accompanied by positive (negative) abnormal common stock returns. They further document that abnormal price drops following leverage decreasing capital structure exchanges are positively related to unexpected earnings decreases. Finally, they observe that abnormal price increases following leverage increasing capital structure exchanges are positively related to changes in managerial stock holdings. Lys and Sivaramakrishnan (1988) and Israel, et al. (Forthcoming) consider the effect of capital structure exchanges on the revisions of financial analysts' forecasts. In a study of leverage decreasing exchanges, they find that analysts revise their forecasts of net operating income downward and that these revisions are positively correlated with the size of the stock price reaction to the exchange announcement.

Stock repurchases via tender offers result in sharp stock price increases. Masulis (1980) reports a 21% abnormal stock return, Dann (1981) finds a 15.4% abnormal stock return, and Vermaelen (1981) documents a 13.3% abnormal stock return. Consistent with this evidence, Dann, et al. (1989) document positive earnings surprises subsequent to tender offer stock repurchases (but not before).

B.3. Firm and Industry Characteristics

The most basic stylized facts concerning industry characteristics and capital structure are that firms within an industry are more similar than those in different industries and that industries tend to retain their relative leverage ratio rankings over time (Bowen, et al. (1982), Bradley et al. (1984)). Leverage ratios of specific industries have been documented by Bowen, et al. (1982), Bradley, et al. (1984), Long and Malitz (1985), and Kester (1986). Their results are in broad agreement and show that Drugs, Instruments,

---

[42] See also Masulis (1980), Eckbo (1986), Mikkelson and Partch (1986), Pinegar and Lease (1986), and Cornett and Travlos (1989).

Electronics, and Food have consistently low leverage while Paper, Textile Mill Products, Steel, Airlines, and Cement have consistently high leverage. Moreover, regulated industries (Telephone, Electric and Gas Utilities and Airlines) are among the most highly levered firms according to the study by Bradley, et al. (1984). The evidence on industry leverage ratios is summarized in Table III.

Several studies shed light on the specific characteristics of firms and industries that determine leverage ratios (Bradley, et al. (1984), Castanias (1983), Long and Malitz (1985), Kester (1986), Marsh (1982), and Titman and Wessels (1988)). These studies generally agree that leverage increases with fixed assets, nondebt tax shields, growth opportunities, and firm size and decreases with volatility, advertising expenditures, research and development expenditures, bankruptcy probability, profitability and uniqueness of the product. These results are summarized in Table IV. In addition to the evidence cited in Table IV, Castanias (1983) also finds a negative correlation between leverage and default probability.

B.4. Corporate Control Considerations

Finally, since capital structure is used as an antitakeover device (DeAngelo and DeAngelo (1985), Dann and DeAngelo (1988), and Amihud, et al. (1990)),

Table III
Industry Leverage Rankings

Rankings of industries by leverage ratio are reported based on four studies: Bradley, et al. (1984, Table 1) [denoted BJK], Bowen, et al. (1982, Exhibit 1) [BDH], Long and Malitz (1985, Table 3) [LM], and Kester (1986, Exhibit 2). We have listed industries from lowest to highest based on average debt-to-value ratio over the period 1962–1981 using Bradley, et al. The classification into "Low," "Medium," and "High," is our own and is somewhat arbitrary. The rankings in Bowen, et al. are an average of rankings over the period 1951–1969 based on long-term plus short-term debt divided by total assets. For Long and Malitz, "Low" ("High") means that the industry was one of the five lowest (highest) in leverage ratio (book value of long-term funded debt divided by total funded capital) out of a sample of 39 firms. The rankings for Kester are based on the average of net debt divided by market value of equity for a sample of 344 Japanese and 452 U.S. companies in 27 industries over the period April, 1982 through March, 1983.

Industry	BJK	BDH	LM	Kester
Drugs	Low[a]		Low	Low
Cosmetics	Low		Low	Medium[b]
Instruments	Low		Low[c]	Low[d]
Metal Mining	Low			
Publishing	Low			
Electronics	Low		Low[e]	Low
Machinery	Low			Medium[f]
Food	Low			Low[g]
Petroleum Exploration	Medium			
Construction	Medium			
Petroleum Refining	Medium	Low[h]	High	High
Metal Working	Medium			
Chemicals	Medium	Medium		High

Table III—*(Continued)*

Industry	BJK	BDH	LM	Kester
Apparel	Medium			Medium
Lumber	Medium			
Motor Vehicle Parts	Medium	Medium[i]	Low[j]	Medium
Paper	Medium		High	High
Textile Mill Products	High	Medium	High	High
Rubber	High			Medium
Retail Department Stores	High	Medium		
Retail Grocery Stores	High	Medium		
Trucking	High			
Steel	High	Low	High	High
Telephone	High			
Electric and Gas Utilities	High			
Airlines	High	High		
Cement			High	High
Glass				High

[a] Drugs (SIC code 2830) and Cosmetics (SIC code 2840) are combined.

[b] Soaps and Detergents (SIC code 2841) part of Cosmetics (SIC code 2840) only.

[c] Photographic Equipment (SIC code 3861) part of Instruments (SIC code 3800) only.

[d] Photographic Equipment (SIC code 3861) part of Instruments (SIC code 3800) only.

[e] Radio and TV Receiving (SIC code 3651) part of Electronics (SIC code 3600) only.

[f] Construction Machinery, Agricultural Machinery, and Machine Tools (SIC codes 3530, 3520, 3540).

[g] Confectionery and Alcoholic Beverages (SIC codes 2065, 2082, 2085) part of Food (SIC code 2000) only.

[h] Oil-Integrated Domestic (SIC code 2912) part of Petroleum Refining (SIC code 2900) only.

[i] BDH split Motor Vehicle Parts (SIC code 3700) into Auto Parts and Accessories (SIC code 3714) and Aerospace (SIC code 3721). In their study, the former ranks consistently at or near the lowest leverage ratio while the latter ranks near the highest.

[j] Aircraft (SIC code 3721) part of Motor Vehicle Parts (SIC code 3700) only.

several studies of the market for corporate control have produced evidence about capital structure. First, leverage is positively correlated with the extent of managerial equity ownership (Kim and Sorensen (1986), Agrawal and Mandelker (1987), Amihud et al. (1990)).[43] Second, Dann and DeAngelo (1988) find that hostile bidders rarely prevail in the face of capital restructuring. Indeed, Palepu (1986) finds that leverage is negatively correlated with the probability of being successfully taken over. Third, stock price decreases following dual class recapitalization and other defensive strategies (Partch (1987), Dann and DeAngelo (1988), and Jarrell and Poulsen (1988)). Fourth, claims with superior voting power command higher prices than similar claims with inferior voting power (Levy (1983), Lease, et al. (1984), DeAngelo and DeAngelo (1985)). Fifth, high free cash flow is associated with higher probability of going private and larger premiums paid to stockholders upon going private (Lehn and Poulsen (1989)). Sixth, the distribution of equity

---

[43] Friend and Hasbrouck (1988) and Friend and Lang (1988) find evidence to the contrary, although in the former the sign is insignificant.

Table IV
Determinants of Leverage

The sign of the change in leverage as a result of an increase in the given characteristic is shown for each of six studies. Blank entry indicates that the specific study did not include the given characteristic. The studies are Bradley, et al. (1984) [denoted BJK], Chaplinsky and Niehaus (1990) [CN], Friend and Hasbrouck (1988), and Friend and Lang (1988) [FH/L], Gonedes, et al. (1988) [GLC], Long and Malitz (1985) [LM], Kester (1986) [Kest.], Kim and Sorensen (1986) [KS], Marsh (1982) [Mar.], and Titman and Wessels (1988) [TW]. Comparisons suffer from the fact that these studies used different measures of the firm characteristics, different time periods, different leverage measures, and different methodologies.

Characteristic	BJK	CN	FH/L	GLC	LM	Kest.	KS	Mar.[a]	TW
Volatility	−		−	·		−*	+		−*
Bankruptcy Probability							−		
Fixed Assets			+	+	+			+	+*
Non-Debt Tax Shields	+	+					−		−*
Advertising	−[b]			−					
R & D Expenditures	−			−					
Profitability			−	−*	+*	−			−
Growth Opportunities		−*				+	−		−*
Size		−*	+*			−*	−*	+	−*
Free Cash Flow	−								
Uniqueness[c]									−

[a] Marsh measures the probability of issuing debt conditional on issuing securities and on firm characteristics. The sign indicates the direction of change of this probability given a change in the indicated characteristic.

[b] Advertising and R & D expenditures are combined.

[c] This refers to the uniqueness of the product and is included specifically to test the model of Titman (1984).

*Indicates that the result was either not statistically significantly different from zero at conventional significance levels or that the result was weak in a nonstatistical sense.

ownership seems to play a role in both managerial behavior and capital structure. In particular, Agrawal and Mandelker (1987) find that when managers own a larger share of the equity they tend to choose higher variance targets. Also, Friend and Lang (1988) and Gonedes, et al. (1988) find that leverage is lower in firms with dispersed outside ownership.

C. Comparison of Theoretical Predictions and Empirical Evidence

This subsection integrates the information described in the previous two subsections. Table V matches the empirical evidence with the theoretical results in Table II. Table V is organized exactly as Table II except that columns two and three of Table II are replaced by the evidence. Specifically, for each theoretical result we list the relevant empirical studies divided into two groups: those consistent with the prediction (indicated by "Yes") and those inconsistent with it (indicated by "No").

Table V

Comparison of Theoretical and Empirical Results

The table lists, for each theoretical result in Table II, those empirical studies whose findings are either consistent (after the word "Yes;") or inconsistent (after "No;") with the theoretical result. Blank cells indicate the lack of empirical evidence.

Panel A. Association Between Leverage and Exogenous Factors

Leverage increases with:	Empirical Evidence
Extent of information asymmetry	
Increases in profitability	Yes: Long & Malitz (1985)* No: Kester (1986), Friend & Hasbrouck (1988), Friend & Lang (1988), Gonedes, et al. (1988), Titman & Wessels (1988)
Extent of *strategic* interaction in the product market	Yes: Titman & Wessels (1988)
Elasticity of demand for the product	
Extent to which product is not unique and does not require specialized service	
Extent to which reputation for product quality is unimportant	
Extent to which workers are unionized or have transferrable skills	
Extent to which the firm is a takeover target or lack of anti-takeover measures	
Potential gains to takeover and reductions in their costs	
Fraction of cash flow that is unobservable	
Lack of growth opportunities	Yes: Kim & Sorensen (1986), Titman & Wessels (1988),* Chaplinsky & Niehaus (1990)* No: Kester (1986)
Extent of regulation	Yes: Bowen, et al. (1982), Bradley, et al. (1984)
Increases in free cash flow	No: Chaplinsky & Niehaus (1990)

Table V —*(Continued)*

Panel A. Association Between Leverage and Exogenous Factors

Leverage increases with:	Empirical Evidence
Increases in liquidation value	Yes: Bradley, et al. (1984), Long & Malitz (1985), Friend & Hasbrouck (1988) Friend & Lang (1988), Gonedes, et al. (1988), Titman & Wessels (1988),* Chaplinsky & Niehaus (1990) No: Kim & Sorensen (1986), Titman & Wessels (1988)*
Decreases in investigation costs	
Increases in the importance of managerial reputation	

Panel B. Association Between Leverage and Endogenous Factors

Result	Empirical Evidence
Leverage is positively correlated with firm value	Yes: Lys & Sivaramakrishnan (1988), Cornett & Travlos (1989), Dann, et al. (1989), Israel, et al. (Forthcoming)
Leverage is positively correlated with default probability	No: Castanias (1983)
Leverage is positively correlated with the extent of managerial equity ownership	Yes: Kim & Sorensen (1986), Agrawal & Mandelker (1987), Amihud, et al. (1990) No: Friend & Hasbrouck (1988),* Friend & Lang (1988)
Leverage is positively correlated with target premium	
Leverage is negatively correlated with probability of successful takeover	Yes: Palepu (1986)
Leverage is negatively correlated with the interest coverage ratio and the probability of reorganization following default	

Table V – *(Continued)*

Panel B. Association Between Leverage and Endogenous Factors	
Result	Empirical Evidence
Targets of an unsuccessful tender offer have more debt than targets of proxy fights or successful tender offers	
Targets of successful proxy fights have more debt than targets of unsuccessful proxy fights	
Targets of proxy fights have more debt than targets of successful tender offers	

Panel C. Announcement of Security Issues	
Stock price:	Empirical Evidence
Increases on announcement of debt issue	Yes: Kim & Stulz (1988) No: Dann & Mikkelson (1984),* Eckbo (1986),* Mikkelson & Partch (1986)*
Increases on announcement of debt for equity exchange	Yes: Masulis (1980, 1983), Cornett & Travlos (1989)
Increases on announcement of stock repurchase	Yes: Masulis (1980), Dann (1981), Vermaelen (1981), Dann, et al. (1989)
Decreases on announcement of equity issue	Yes: Asquith & Mullins (1986), Masulis & Korwar (1986), Mikkelson & Partch (1986), Schipper and Smith (1986)
Decreases on announcement of equity for debt exchange	Yes: Masulis (1980, 1983), Eckbo (1986), Mikkelson & Partch (1986), Cornett & Travlos (1989)
Decreases more the larger is the informational asymmetry	Yes: Korajczyk, et al. (1990b)*
Decreases more the larger is the size of the issue	Yes: Asquith & Mullins (1986)

Table V –*(Continued)*

Panel C. Announcement of Security Issues

Increases if some proceeds of equity issue used to repurchase debt

Increases on announcement of issue of convertible debt in exchange for equity

Panel D. Other Results

Result	Empirical Evidence
There is a pecking order: firms prefer internal finance, then issuing securities in order of increasing sensitivity to firm performance	Yes: Chaplinsky & Niehaus (1990), Amihud, et al. (1990) No: Korajczyk, et al. (1990a)
Firms tend to issue equity following abnormal price appreciation	Yes: Marsh (1982), Korajczyk, et al. (1990a)
Firms tend to issue equity when information asymmetry is smallest	Yes: Korajczyk, et al. (1990b)
Low returns optimally entail change of control or ownership	
Bonds can be expected to have covenants prohibiting "asset substitution"	Yes: Smith & Warner (1979)
Firms with longer track records have lower default probabilities	

* = weak or statistically insignificant relationship.

The evidence cited in Table V is either direct evidence about the particular result or, in some cases, represents an interpretation of the actual independent variable used in the study. In particular, the following interpretations are embedded in Table V.

- Extent of regulation: telephone, electric and gas utilities, and airlines are both highly regulated and highly levered as indicated in Table III.
- Liquidation value: fixed assets and nondebt tax shields are generally regarded as proxies for the tangibility or liquidation value of assets. On the other hand, research and development and advertising expenditures can be interpreted as measuring the extent to which assets are intangible. See Table IV.
- Firm value: in Panel B, the studies cited document increases in earnings or earnings forecasts following leverage increases.
- Pecking order: the fact that leverage decreases with internal funds is interpreted as evidence that firms prefer to use internal financing before issuing debt (Chaplinsky and Niehaus (1990)). Also, Amihud, et al. (1990) find that, in acquisitions, managers prefer to finance with cash or debt rather than equity, at least when they have a large equity stake. Finally, Korajczyk, et al. (1990a) interpret the fact that debt ratios do not increase prior to equity issues used to finance investment as evidence that "strained debt capacity is not the main reason for equity issues."

Other evidence from Table III (industry leverage ratio rankings) may conceivably bear on the predictions of the theory. For example, one might argue that the airline industry is marked by a high degree of strategic interaction across firms. If so, the fact that airlines are highly levered is consistent with the results of Brander and Lewis (1986). Similarly, if reputation for product quality is especially important in the drug industry, the fact that drug firms have low leverage is consistent with the results of Maksimovic and Titman (Forthcoming). Also, to the extent that trucking is highly unionized, the high leverage found in this industry supports the model of Sarig (1988). Obviously, such inferences depend on detailed knowledge of the industries involved—knowledge we do not possess.

In addition to Table V, which matches the empirical evidence with the theoretical results, we also present, in Table VI, those empirical findings that do not bear on any specific theoretical prediction. Some of these lend support to the assumptions of certain models. Others provide evidence to be explained.

Finally, in Table VII, we organize the information in Table V to present the theoretical results and the evidence by model type. In Panels A through D we list, in turn, the implications of agency models (Panel A), asymmetric information models (Panel B), product/input market models (Panel C), and corporate control models (Panel D). The results are ordered, in each panel, so that those with evidence are listed first, followed by those for which there is no available evidence. Table VII is useful for determining whether any model or class of models has been rejected by the evidence and what additional evidence would be useful for testing the models.

Table VI
Other Empirical Results
This table lists empirical evidence not directly related to any theoretical result.

Empirical Result	Source
The extent of external financing has increased over time	Masulis (1988)
Total leverage has increased steadily since World War II	Taggart (1985)
Capital structure is used to protect control	DeAngelo & DeAngelo (1985), Dann & DeAngelo (1988), Amihud, et al. (1990)
Hostile bidders rarely prevail in face of capital restructuring	Dann & DeAngelo (1988)
Dual class recapitalization and other defensive strategies result in stock price decrease	Partch (1987),* Dann & DeAngelo (1988), Jarrell & Poulsen (1988)
Stock price increases with voting power	Levy (1983), Lease, et al. (1984), DeAngelo & DeAngelo (1985)
High free cash flow is associated with higher probability of going private and higher premiums	Lehn & Poulsen (1989)
Firms more likely to issue debt if current debt level is below target	Marsh (1982)
Leverage decreases with return volatility	Bradley; et al. (1984), Kester (1986),* Friend & Hasbrouck (1988), Friend & Lang (1988), Titman & Wessels (1988)*
Leverage increases with increases in operating risk	Kim & Sorensen (1986)
Leverage decreases with increases in firm size	Yes: Kester (1986),* Kim & Sorensen (1986),* Titman & Wessels (1988)* No: Friend & Hasbrouck (1988),* Friend & Lang (1988)*
High inside ownership is associated with return variance increasing investments	Agrawal & Mandelker (1987)
Leverage decreases with increases in dispersion outside ownership	Friend & Lang (1988), of Gonedes, et al. (1988)

* = weak or statistically insignificant relationship.

VI. Conclusions

The theories surveyed here have identified a great many *potential* determinants of capital structure (in addition to taxes). These can be most easily seen in Table II, Panels A and D. Since the theories are, for the most part, complementary, which of these factors is important in various contexts remains a largely unanswered empirical question.

Although many potential factors emerge from the theory, a fairly small number of "general principles" is evident. The literature that takes debt and

Table VII
Summary of Results by Model Type

The table shows, for each model type, the main results [with sources in brackets] and the empirical studies whose findings are either consistent (after the word "Yes:") or inconsistent (after "No:") with the theoretical result.

Panel A. Agency Models

Theoretical Result [source]	Empirical Evidence
Stock price increases on announcement of debt issues, debt-for-equity exchanges, or stock repurchases and decreases on announcement of equity issues or equity-for-debt exchanges [Harris & Raviv (1990a), Stulz (1990), Hirshleifer & Thakor (1989)]	**Debt Issues** Yes: Kim & Stulz (1988) No: Dann & Mikkelson (1984),* Eckbo (1986),* Mikkelson & Partch (1986)* **Debt-for-Equity Exchanges** Yes: Masulis (1980, 1983), Cornett & Travlos (1989) **Stock Repurchases** Yes: Masulis (1980), Dann (1981), Vermaelen (1981), Dann, et al. (1989) **Equity Issues** Yes: Asquith & Mullins (1986), Masulis & Korwar (1986), Mikkelson & Partch (1986), Schipper and Smith (1986) **Equity-for-Debt Exchanges** Yes: Masulis (1980, 1983), Eckbo (1986), Mikkelson & Partch (1986, Cornett & Travlos (1989)
Leverage is positively correlated with firm value [Harris & Raviv (1990a), Stulz (1990), Hirshleifer & Thakor (1989)]	Yes: Lys & Sivaramakrishnan (1988), Cornett & Travlos (1989), Dann, et al. (1989), Israel, et al. (1990)
Leverage is positively correlated with default probability [Harris & Raviv (1990a)]	No: Castanias (1983)
Leverage increases with lack of growth opportunities [Jensen & Meckling (1976), Stulz (1990)]	Yes: Kim & Sorensen (1986), Titman & Wessels (1988),* Chaplinsky & Niehaus (1990)* No: Kester (1986)

Table VII—*(Continued)*

Panel A. Agency Models

Theoretical Result [source]	Empirical Evidence
Leverage increases with decreases in profitability [Chang (1987)]	Yes: Kester (1986), Friend & Hasbrouck (1988), Friend & Lang (1988), Gonedes, et al. (1988),* Titman & Wessels (1988) No: Long & Malitz (1985)*
Leverage increases with extent of regulation [Jensen & Meckling (1976), Stulz (1990)]	Yes: Bowen, et al. (1982), Bradley, et al. (1984)
Leverage increases with increases in free cash flow [Jensen (1986), Stulz (1990)]	No: Chaplinsky & Niehaus (1990)
Leverage increases with increases in liquidation value [Williamson (1988), Harris & Raviv (1990a)]	Yes: Bradley, et al. (1984), Long & Malitz (1985), Friend & Hasbrouck (1988), Friend & Lang (1988), Gonedes, et al. (1988), Titman & Wessels (1988),* Chaplinsky & Niehaus (1990) No: Kim & Sorensen (1986), Titman & Wessels (1988)*
Bonds can be expected to have covenants prohibiting "asset substitution" [Jensen & Meckling (1976)]	Yes: Smith & Warner (1979)
Leverage is negatively correlated with the interest coverage ratio and the probability of reorganization following default [Harris & Raviv (1990a)]	
Leverage increases with fraction of cash flow that is unobservable [Chang (1987)]	
Leverage increases with extent to which the firm is a takeover target or lack of anti-takeover measures [Stulz (1990), Hirshleifer & Thakor (1989)]	
Firms with longer track records have lower default probabilities [Diamond (1989)]	
Leverage increases with decreases in investigation costs [Harris & Raviv (1990a)]	

Table VII – *(Continued)*

Panel A. Agency Models

Theoretical Result [source]	Empirical Evidence
Leverage increases with increases in the importance of managerial reputation [Hirshleifer & Thakor (1989)]	

Panel B. Asymmetric Information Models

Theoretical result [source]	Empirical Evidence
Stock price increases on announcement of debt issues, debt-for-equity exchanges, or stock repurchases and decreases on announcement of equity-for-debt exchanges [Ross (1977), Noe (1988), Narayanan (1988), Poitevin (1989)]	Debt Issues Yes: Kim & Stulz (1988) No: Dann & Mikkelson (1984),* Eckbo (1986),* Mikkelson & Partch (1986)* Debt-for-Equity Exchanges Yes: Masulis (1980, 1983), Cornett & Travlos (1989) Equity-for-Debt Exchanges Yes: Masulis (1980, 1983), Eckbo (1986), Mikkelson & Partch 91986), Cornett & Travlos (1989) Stock Repurchases Yes: Masulis (1980), Dann (1981), Vermaelen (1981), Dann, et al. (1989)
Stock price is unaffected by debt issues [Myers & Majluf (1984), Krasker (1986), Korajczyk, et al. (1990c)]	See previous cell
Leverage increases with increases in profitability [Ross (1977), Leland & Pyle (1977), Heinkel (1982), Blazenko (1987), John (1987), Poitevin (1989)]	Yes: Long & Malitz (1985)* No: Kester (1986), Friend & Hasbrouck (1988), Friend & Lang (1988), Gonedes, et al. (1988),* Titman & Wessels (1988)
Leverage increases with decreases in free cash flow [Myers & Majluf (1984)]	Yes: Chaplinsky & Niehaus (1990)

Table VII—*(Continued)*

Panel B. Asymmetric Information Models

Theoretical Result [source]	Empirical Evidence
Stock price decreases on an announcement of equity issue [Ross (1977), Myers & Majluf (1984), Krasker (1986), Korajczyk, et al. (1990c), Noe (1988), Narayanan (1988), Poitevin (1989), Lucas & McDonald (1990)]	Yes: Asquith & Mullins (1986), Masulis & Korwar (1986), Mikkelson & Partch (1986), Schipper and Smith (1986)
There is a pecking order: firms prefer internal finance, then issuing securities in order of increasing sensitivity to firm performance [Myers & Majluf (1984), Krasker (1986), Narayanan (1988)]	Yes: Chaplinsky & Niehaus (1990), Amihud, et al. (1990) No: Korajczyk, et al. (1990a)
Leverage is positively correlated with firm value [Ross (1977), Noe (1988), Narayanan (1988), Poitevin (1989)]	Yes: Lys & Sivaramakrishnan (1988), Cornett & Travlos (1989), Dann, et al. (1989), Israel, et al. (Forthcoming)
Leverage is positively correlated with default probability [Ross (1977)]	No: Castanias (1983)
Leverage is positively correlated with the extent of managerial equity ownership [Leland & Pyle (1977)]	Yes: Kim & Sorensen (1986), Agrawal & Mandelker (1987), Amihud, et al. (1990) No: Friend & Hasbrouck (1988),* Friend & Lang (1988)
Firms tend to issue equity following abnormal price appreciation [Lucas & McDonald (1990)]	Yes: Marsh (1982), Korajczyk, et al. (1990a)
Firms tend to issue equity when information asymmetry is smallest [Myers & Majluf (1984), Korajczyk, et al. (1990c)]	Yes: Korajczyk, et al. (1990a)
Stock price decreases more the larger is the informational asymmetry [Myers & Majluf (1984), Krasker (1986), Korajczyk, et al. (1990c)]	Yes: Korajczyk, et al. (1990b)*
Leverage increases with extent of information asymmetry [Myers & Majluf (1984)]	

Table VII—*(Continued)*

Panel B. Asymmetric Information Models

Theoretical result [source]	Empirical Evidence
Stock price decreases more the larger is the size of the issue [Krasker (1986)]	Yes: Asquith & Mullins (1986)
Stock price increases if some proceeds of equity issue used to repurchase debt [Brennan & Kraus (1987)]	
Stock price increases on announcement of issue of convertible debt in exchange for equity [Constantinides & Grundy (1989)]	

Panel C. Product/Input Market Models

Theoretical Result [source]	Empirical Evidence
Leverage increases with extent to which product is not unique and does not require specialized service [Titman (1984)]	Yes: Titman & Wessels (1988)
Leverage increases with extent of *strategic* interaction in the product market [Brander & Lewis (1986)]	
Leverage increases with elasticity of demand for the product [Maksimovic (1988)]	
Leverage increases with extent to which reputation for product quality is unimportant [Maksimovic & Titman (Forthcoming)]	
Leverage increases with extent to which workers are unionized or have transferable skills [Sarig (1988)]	

173

Table VII—*(Continued)*

Panel D. Corporate Control Models

Theoretical Result [source]	Empirical Evidence
Stock price increases on announcement of debt issues, debt-for-equity exchanges, or stock repurchases and decreases on announcement of equity issues or equity-for-debt exchanges [Harris & Raviv (1988), Stulz (1988), Israel (Forthcoming)]	**Debt Issues** Yes: Kim & Stulz (1988) No: Dann & Mikkelson (1984),* Eckbo (1986),* Mikkelson & Partch (1986)* **Debt-for-Equity Exchanges** Yes: Masulis (1980, 1983), Cornett & Travlos (1989) **Stock Repurchases** Yes: Masulis (1980), Dann (1981), Vermaelen (1981), Dann, et al. (1989) **Equity Issues** Yes: Asquith & Mullins (1986), Masulis & Korwar (1986), Mikkelson & Partch (1986), Schipper and Smith (1986) **Equity-for-Debt Exchanges** Yes: Masulis (1980, 1983), Eckbo (1986), Mikkelson & Partch (1986), Cornett & Travlos (1989)
Leverage is positively correlated with firm value [Harris & Raviv (1988), Stulz (1988), Israel (Forthcoming)]	Yes: Lys & Sivaramakrishnan (1988), Cornett & Travlos (1989), Dann, et al. (1989), Israel, et al. (Forthcoming)
Leverage is positively correlated with the extent of managerial equity ownership [Harris & Raviv (1988), Stulz (1988)]	Yes: Kim & Sorensen (1986), Agrawal & Mandelker (1987), Amihud, et al. (1990) No: Friend & Hasbrouck (1988),* Friend & Lang (1988)
Leverage is negatively correlated with probability of successful takeover [Stulz (1988)]	Yes: Palepu (1986)

Table VII—*(Continued)*

Panel D. Corporate Control Models

Theoretical Result [source]	Empirical Evidence
Leverage increases with potential gains to takeover and reductions in their costs [Israel (Forthcoming)]	
Leverage is positively correlated with target premium [Stulz (1988)]	
Leverage increases with extent to which the firm is a takeover target or lack of anti-takeover measures [Harris & Raviv 1988), Stulz (1988), Israel (Forthcoming)]	
Leverage is negatively correlated with target premium [Israel (Forthcoming)]	
Targets of an unsuccessful tender offer have more debt than targets of proxy fights or successful tender offers [Harris & Raviv (1988)]	
Targets of successful proxy fights have more debt than targets of unsuccessful proxy fights [Harris & Raviv (1988)]	
Targets of proxy fights have more debt than targets of successful tender offers [Harris & Raviv (1988)]	

* = weak or statistically insignificant relationship.

equity as given is based on four important properties of the debt contract:

- Bankruptcy, i.e., debt provides for a costly takeover of the firm by debtholders under certain conditions. This fact is exploited in Ross (1977), Grossman and.Hart (1982), Titman (1984), Jensen (1986), Harris and Raviv (1988, 1990a), Maksimovic and Titman (Forthcoming), Poitevin (1989), Stulz (1990), and others.
- Cash flow to levered equity is a convex function of returns to the firm. This fact leads to the asset substitution effect which is central in Jensen and Meckling (1976), Brander and Lewis (1986), Sarig (1988), Diamond (1989), and others.
- Leverage increases the manager's equity ownership share. This effect works in two ways: it forces manager's payoffs to be more sensitive to firm performance, and, since debt is nonvoting, it concentrates voting power. These properties are exploited in Jensen and Meckling (1976), Leland and Pyle (1977), Harris and Raviv (1988), Stulz (1988), and others.
- The value of debt is relatively insensitive to firm performance. Thus, debt is priced more accurately than equity in situations involving asymmetric information. This fact is used by Myers and Majluf (1984) among others.

Since the survey shows that theory has identified numerous potential determinants, it is not surprising that the models have a wealth of different implications (very few opposing, however) (see Table II). Models within a given type (e.g., agency), however, have many common predictions (see Table VII). Moreover, models of almost all types share the prediction that stock price will increase on announcement of leverage-increasing capital structure changes (see Table II, Panel B). This is probably because the models were designed to produce this prediction, since this effect is so well documented by event studies. Although the event studies have generally been interpreted as evidence that announcements of security offerings, exchanges, and repurchases contain new information about the firm's future cash flows, i.e., as evidence for signaling models, in fact they support at least three of the four types of models.

From Tables V and VII it is clear that the empirical evidence thus far accumulated is broadly consistent with the theory. It is perhaps unfortunate that there seem to be no significant empirical anomalies to guide further theoretical work. Indeed, it would be difficult to reject any models based on the available evidence.[44] Note, however, that many of the theoretical impli-

---

[44] Inspection of Table VII produces only the following candidates: the signaling models listed in Panel B, line 3 (see also line 8); the free cash flow models listed in Panel A, line 7 and Harris and Raviv (1990a) (Panel A, line 3). In each case, the empirical studies were not designed specifically to test the model and hence generally do not meet the *ceteris paribus* conditions demanded by the theory.

cations have not yet been tested (as evidenced by the empty cells in Tables V and VII).

While recommendations for further work are always tentative, it seems clear that certain areas are underexplored. In our view, models which relate capital structure to products and inputs are the most promising.[45] This area is still in its infancy and is short on implications relating capital structure to industrial organization variables such as demand and cost parameters, strategic variables, etc. On the other hand, it seems to us that models exploiting asymmetric information have been investigated to the point where diminishing returns have set in. It is unlikely that further effort in this area will lead to significant new insights. With regard to empirical work, Table V (or VII) provides a list of theoretical predictions that have not been tested. Of course, testing these results (or any of the others) is complicated by the wealth of *ceteris paribus* conditions each requires. Nevertheless, it is essential that empirical work be directed specifically at sorting out which effects are important in various contexts.

REFERENCES

Agrawal, Anup and Gershon Mandelker, 1987, Managerial incentives and corporate investment and financing decisions, *Journal of Finance* 42, 823–837.

Allen, Franklin, 1985, Capital structure and imperfect competition in product markets, Working paper, The Wharton School, University of Pennsylvania.

———, 1990, The changing nature of debt and equity: A financial perspective, in Richard W. Kopcke and Eric S. Rosengren eds.: *Are the Distinctions Between Debt and Equity Disappearing?*, (Federal Reserve Bank of Boston, Boston), Conference Series No. 33, 12–38.

Amihud, Yakov, Baruch Lev, and Nickolaos G. Travlos, 1990, Corporate control and the choice of investment financing: The case of corporate acquisitions, *Journal of Finance* 45, 603–616.

Asquith, Paul and David W. Mullins, Jr., 1986, Equity issues and offering dilution, *Journal of Financial Economics* 15, 61–89.

Barnea, Amir, Robert Haugen, and Lemma Senbet, 1985, *Agency Problems and Financial Contracting*, Prentice-Hall, Englewood Cliffs, NJ.

Bergman, Yaacov Z. and Jeffrey L. Callen, Opportunistic underinvestment in debt renegotiations and capital structure, *Journal of Financial Economics*, Forthcoming.

Berkovitch, Elazar and E. Han Kim, 1990, Financial contracting and leverage induced over- and under-investment incentives, *Journal of Finance* 45, 765–794.

Bhattacharya, Sudipto, 1988, Corporate finance and the legacy of Miller and Modigliani, *Journal of Economic Perspectives* 2, 135–148.

Blazenko, George, 1987, Managerial preference, asymmetric information, and financial structure, *Journal of Finance* 42, 839–862.

Bowen, Robert M., Lane A. Daly, and Charles C. Huber, Jr., 1982, Evidence on the existence and determinants of inter-industry differences in leverage, *Financial Management* 11, 10–20.

Bradford, William, 1987, The issue decision of manager-owners under information asymmetry, *Journal of Finance* 42, 1245–1260.

Bradley, Michael, Gregg Jarrell, and E. Han Kim, 1984, On the existence of an optimal capital structure: Theory and evidence, *Journal of Finance* 39, 857–878.

Brander, James A. and Tracy R. Lewis, 1986, Oligopoly and financial structure: The limited

---

[45] Most promising of those areas surveyed here; we also believe that security design is an important underexplored topic — see our companion survey Harris and Raviv (1990b).

liability effect, *American Economic Review* 76, 956-970.

—— and Michel Poitevin, 1989, Managerial compensation and the agency costs of debt finance, Working paper, University of British Columbia.

Brennan, Michael and Alan Kraus, 1987, Efficient financing under asymmetric information, *Journal of Finance* 42, 1225-1243.

Castanias, Richard, 1983, Bankruptcy risk and optimal capital structure, *Journal of Finance* 38, 1617-1635.

Chang, Chun, 1987, Capital structure as optimal contracts, Working paper, Carlson School of Management, University of Minnesota.

Chaplinsky, Susan and Greg Niehaus, 1990, The determinants of inside ownership and leverage, Working paper, University of Michigan.

Constantinides, George M. and Bruce D. Grundy, 1989, Optimal investment with stock repurchase and financing as signals, *The Review of Financial Studies* 2, 445-466.

Cornett, Marcia and Nickolaos Travlos, 1989, Information effects associated with debt-for-equity and equity-for-debt exchange offers, *Journal of Finance* 44, 451-468.

Dann, Larry Y., 1981, Common stock repurchases: An analysis of returns to bondholders and stockholders, *Journal of Financial Economics* 9, 113-138.

—— and Wayne H. Mikkelson, 1984, Convertible debt issuance, capital structure change and financing-related information: Some new evidence, *Journal of Financial Economics* 13, 157-186.

—— and Harry DeAngelo, 1988, Corporate financial policy and corporate control: A study of defensive adjustments in asset and ownership structure, *Journal of Financial Economics* 20, 87-127.

——, Ronald Masulis, and David Mayers, 1989, Repurchase tender offers and earnings information, Working paper, University of Oregon.

Darrough, Masako and Neal Stoughton, 1986, Moral hazard and adverse selection: The question of financial structure, *Journal of Finance* 41, 501-513.

DeAngelo, Harry and Linda DeAngelo, 1985, Managerial ownership of voting rights: A study of public corporations with dual classes of common stock, *Journal of Financial Economics* 14, 33-69.

Diamond, Douglas W., 1989, Reputation acquisition in debt markets, *Journal of Political Economy* 97, 828-862.

Dybvig, Philip and Jaime Zender, 1989, Capital structure and dividend irrelevance with asymmetric information, Working paper, Yale School of Organization and Management.

Eckbo, B. Espen, 1986, Valuation effects of corporate debt offerings, *Journal of Financial Economics* 15, 119-151.

Fama, Eugene F. and Merton H. Miller, 1972, *The Theory of Finance*, (Holt, Rinehart, and Winston, New York).

Franke, Günter, 1987, Costless signalling in financial markets, *Journal of Finance* 42, 809-822.

Friend, Irwin and Joel Hasbrouck, 1988, Determinants of capital structure, in Andy Chen ed.: *Research in Finance, Volume 7*, (JAI Press Inc., New York), pp. 1-19.

—— and Larry Lang, 1988, An empirical test of the impact of managerial self-interest on corporate capital structure, *Journal of Finance* 43, 271-281.

Gertner, Robert, Robert Gibbons, and David Scharfstein, 1988, Simultaneous signalling to the capital and product markets, *Rand Journal of Economics* 19, 173-190.

Glazer, Jacob, 1989, Live and let live: Collusion among oligopolists with long-term debt, Working paper, Boston University.

—— and Ronen Israel, 1990, Managerial incentives and financial signaling in product market competition, *International Journal of Industrial Economics* 8, 271-280.

Gonedes, Nicholas J., Larry Lang, and Mathias Chikaonda, 1988, Empirical results on managerial incentives and capital structure, Working paper, The Wharton School, University of Pennsylvania.

Green, Edward J. and Robert H. Porter, 1984, Noncooperative collusion under imperfect price information, *Econometrica* 52, 87-100.

Green, Richard C., 1984, Investment incentives, debt, and warrants, *Journal of Financial Economics* 13, 115-136.

Grossman, Sanford J. and Oliver Hart, 1982, Corporate financial structure and managerial incentives, in J. McCall, ed.: *The Economics of Information and Uncertainty*, University of Chicago Press, Chicago.

Harris, Milton and Artur Raviv, 1988, Corporate control contests and capital structure, *Journal of Financial Economics* 20, 55-86.

―― and Artur Raviv, 1990a, Capital structure and the informational role of debt, *Journal of Finance* 45, 321-349.

―― and Artur Raviv, 1990b, Financial contracting theory, Working paper #82, Kellogg School, Northwestern University.

Hart, Oliver and John Moore, 1990, A theory of corporate financial structure based on the seniority of claims, Working paper #560, MIT.

Haugen, Robert and Lemma Senbet, 1987, On the resolution of agency problems by complex financial instruments: A reply, *Journal of Finance* 42, 1091-1095.

Heinkel, Robert, 1982, A theory of capital structure relevance under imperfect information, *Journal of Finance* 37, 1141-1150.

―― and Josef Zechner, 1990, The role of debt and preferred stock as a solution to adverse investment incentives, *Journal of Financial and Quantitative Analysis* 25, 1-24.

Hirshleifer, David and Anjan V. Thakor, 1989, Managerial reputation, project choice and debt, Working paper #14-89, Anderson Graduate School of Management at UCLA.

Israel, Ronen, 1989, Capital and ownership structure, and the market for corporate control, Working paper, University of Michigan.

――, Capital structure and the market for corporate control: The defensive role of debt financing, *Journal of Finance*, Forthcoming.

――, Aharon R. Ofer, and Daniel Siegel, The information content of equity for debt swaps: An investigation of analysts' forecasts of firm cash flows, *Journal of Financial Economics*, Forthcoming.

Jarrell, Gregg and Annette Poulsen, 1988, Dual-class recapitalizations as antitakeover mechanisms: The recent evidence, *Journal of Financial Economics* 20, 129-152.

Jensen, Michael C., 1986, Agency costs of free cash flow, corporate finance and takeovers, *American Economic Review* 76, 323-339.

――, 1989, Eclipse of the public corporation, *Harvard Business Review* 61-74.

―― and William Meckling, 1976, Theory of the firm: Managerial behavior, agency costs, and capital structure, *Journal of Financial Economics* 3, 305-360.

John, Kose, 1987, Risk-shifting incentives and signalling through corporate capital structure, *Journal of Finance* 42, 623-641.

―― and David C. Nachman, 1985, Risky debt, investment incentives, and reputation in a sequential equilibrium, *Journal of Finance* 40, 863-880.

―― and Lemma W. Senbet, 1988, Limited liability, corporate leverage, and public policy, Working paper, Stern School of Business, New York University.

Kester, Carl W., 1986, Capital and ownership structure: A comparison of United States and Japanese manufacturing corporations, *Financial Management*, 5-16.

Kim, Moshe and Vojislav Maksimovic, Technology, debt and the exploitation of growth options, *Journal of Banking and Finance*, Forthcoming.

Kim, Wi Saeng and Eric H. Sorensen, 1986, Evidence on the impact of the agency costs of debt in corporate debt policy, *Journal of Financial and Quantitative Analysis* 21, 131-144.

Kim, Yong Cheol and René M. Stulz, 1988, The Eurobond market and corporate financial policy: A test of the clientele hypothesis, *Journal of Financial Economics* 22, 189-205.

Korajczyk, Robert A., Deborah Lucas, and Robert L. McDonald, 1990a, Understanding stock price behavior around the time of equity issues, in R. Glenn Hubbard, ed.: *Asymmetric Information, Corporate Finance, and Investment*, (University of Chicago Press, Chicago), pp.257-277.

――, Deborah Lucas, and Robert McDonald, 1990b, The effect of information releases on the pricing and timing of equity issues, Working paper #83, Kellogg School, Northwestern University.

――, Deborah Lucas, and Robert McDonald, 1990c, Equity issues with time-varying asymmetric information, Working paper #84, Kellogg School, Northwestern University.

Krasker, William, 1986, Stock price movements in response to stock issues under asymmetric information, *Journal of Finance* 41, 93-105.

Lease, Ronald C., John J. McConnell, and Wayne H. Mikkelson, 1984, The market value of differential voting rights in closely held corporations, *Journal of Business* 57, 443-467.

Lehn, Kenneth and Annette Poulsen, 1989, Free cash flow and stockholder gains in going private transactions, *Journal of Finance* 44, 771-787.

Leland, Hayne and David Pyle, 1977, Information asymmetrics, financial structure, and financial intermediation, *Journal of Finance* 32, 371-388.

Levy, Haim, 1983, Economic evaluation of voting power of common stock, *Journal of Finance* 38, 79-93.

Linn, Scott C. and J. Michael Pinegar, 1988, The effect of issuing preferred stock on common and preferred stockholder wealth, *Journal of Financial Economics* 22, 155-184.

Long, Michael and Ileen Malitz, 1985, The investment-financing nexus: Some empirical evidence, *Midland Corporate Finance Journal* 3, 53-59.

Lucas, Deborah and Robert McDonald, 1990, Equity issues and stock price dynamics, *Journal of Finance* 45, 1019-1043.

Lys, Thomas and Konduru Sivaramakrishnan, 1988, Earnings expectations and capital restructuring: The case of equity-for-debt swaps, *Journal of Accounting Research* 26, 273-299.

Maksimovic, Vojislav, 1986, *Optimal Capital Structure in Oligopolies*, Doctoral dissertation, Harvard University.

——, 1988, Capital structure in repeated oligopolies, *Rand Journal of Economics* 19, 389-407.

——, 1989, Optimal financial structure and value dissipation in imperfect product markets, Working paper, University of British Columbia.

——, 1990, Oligopoly, price wars and bankruptcy, Working paper, University of British Columbia.

—— and Sheridan Titman, Financial policy and a firm's reputation for product quality, *Review of Financial Studies*, Forthcoming.

Marsh, Paul, 1982, The choice between equity and debt: An empirical study, *Journal of Finance* 37, 121-144.

Masulis, Ronald W., 1980, The effects of capital structure change on security prices: A study of exchange offers, *Journal of Financial Economics* 8, 139-178.

——, 1983, The impact of capital structure change on firm value: Some estimates, *Journal of Finance*, 38, 107-126.

——, 1988, *The Debt/Equity Choice*, (Ballinger Publishing Company, New York).

—— and Ashok N. Korwar, 1986, Seasoned equity offerings: An empirical investigation, *Journal of Financial Economics* 15, 91-118.

Mikkelson, Wayne H. and M. Megan Partch, 1986, Valuation effects of security offerings and the issuance process, *Journal of Financial Economics* 15, 31-60.

Miller, Merton H., 1988, The Modigliani-Miller propositions after thirty years, *Journal of Economic Perspectives* 2, 99-120.

Modigliani, Franco, 1988, MM—past, present, and future, *Journal of Economic Perspectives* 2, 149-158.

—— and Merton H. Miller, 1958, The cost of capital, corporation finance, and the theory of investment, *American Economic Review* 48, 261-297.

Myers, Stewart C., 1977, Determinants of corporate borrowing, *Journal of Financial Economics* 5, 147-175.

——, 1984, The capital structure puzzle, *Journal of Finance* 39, 575-592.

—— and Nicholas S. Majluf, 1984, Corporate financing and investment decisions when firms have information that investors do not have, *Journal of Financial Economics* 13, 187-221.

Nachman, David C. and Thomas H. Noe, 1989, Design of securities under asymmetric information, Working paper, Georgia Institute of Technology.

Narayanan, M. P., 1987, On the resolution of agency problems by complex financial instruments: A comment, *Journal of Finance* 42, 1083-1090.

——, 1988, Debt versus equity under asymmetric information, *Journal of Financial and Quantitative Analysis* 23, 39-51.

Noe, Thomas, 1988, Capital structure and signaling game equilibria, *Review of Financial Studies* 1, 331-356.

Palepu, Krishna G., 1986, Predicting takeover targets: A methodological and empirical analysis, *Journal of Accounting and Economics* 3-37.

Partch, Megan, 1987, The creation of a class of limited voting common stock and shareholder wealth, *Journal of Financial Economics* 18, 313-339.

Pinegar, J. Michael and Ronald C. Lease, 1986, The impact of preferred-for-common exchange offers on firm value, *Journal of Finance* 41, 795-814.

Poitevin, Michel, 1989, Financial signalling and the "deep-pocket" argument, *Rand Journal of Economics* 20, 26-40.

Ravid, S. Abraham, 1988, On interactions of production and financial decisions, *Financial Management* 8, 87-99.

—— and Oded H. Sarig, 1989, Financial signalling by precommitting to cash outflows, Working paper, Rutgers, The State University of New Jersey.

Ross, Stephen, 1977, The determination of financial structure: The incentive signalling approach, *Bell Journal of Economics* 8, 23-40.

——, 1988, Comment on the Modigliani-Miller propositions, *Journal of Economic Perspectives* 2, 127-134.

——, 1989, Institutional markets, financial marketing, and financial innovation, *Journal of Finance* 44, 541-556.

Sarig, Oded H., 1988, Bargaining with a corporation and the capital structure of the bargaining firm, Working paper, Tel Aviv University.

Schipper, Katherine and Abbie Smith, 1986, A comparison of equity carve-outs and seasoned equity offerings: Share price effects and corporate restructuring, *Journal of Financial Economics* 15, 153-186.

Smith, Jr., Clifford, 1986, Investment banking and the capital acquisition process, *Journal of Financial Economics* 15, 3-29.

Smith, Clifford and Jerold Warner, 1979, On financial contracting, *Journal of Financial Economics* 7, 117-161.

Stiglitz, Joseph E., 1988, Why financial structure matters, *Journal of Economic Perspectives* 2, 121-126.

Stulz, René, 1988, Managerial control of voting rights: Financing policies and the market for corporate control, *Journal of Financial Economics* 20, 25-54.

——, 1990, Managerial discretion and optimal financing policies, *Journal of Financial Economics* 26, 3-27.

—— and Herb Johnson, 1985, An analysis of secured debt, *Journal of Financial Economics* 14, 501-521.

Taggart, Jr., Robert A., 1985, Secular patterns in the financing of U.S. Corporations, in B. Friedman, ed.: *Corporate Capital Structures in the United States* (University of Chicago Press), pp.13-80.

Titman, Sheridan, 1984, The effect of capital structure on a firm's liquidation decision, *Journal of Financial Economics* 13, 137-151.

—— and Roberto Wessels, 1988, The determinants of capital structure choice, *Journal of Finance* 43, 1-19.

Vermaelen, Theo, 1981, Common stock repurchases and market signalling: An empirical study, *Journal of Financial Economics* 9, 139-183.

Williamson, Oliver, 1988, Corporate finance and corporate governance, *Journal of Finance* 43, 567-591.

Appendix B

On the Existence of an Optimal Capital Structure: Theory and Evidence

Source: M. Bradley, G. A. Jarrell, and E. H. Kim, "On The Existence of an Optimal Capital Structure: Theory and Evidence," *Journal of Finance* (July 1984), pp. 857–878. Reprinted with permission.

MICHAEL BRADLEY, GREGG A. JARRELL, and E. HAN KIM*

ONE OF THE MOST contentious issues in the theory of finance during the past quarter century has been the theory of capital structure. The geneses of this controversy were the seminal contributions by Modigliani and Miller [18, 19]. The general academic view by the mid-1970s, although not a consensus, was that the optimal capital structure involves balancing the tax advantage of debt against the present value of bankruptcy costs. No sooner did this general view become prevalent in the profession than Miller [16] presented a new challenge by showing that under certain conditions the tax advantage of debt financing at the firm level is exactly offset by the tax disadvantage of debt at the personal level. Since then there has developed a burgeoning theoretical literature attempting to reconcile Miller's model with the balancing theory of optimal capital structure [e.g., DeAngelo and Masulis [5], Kim [12], and Modigliani [17]. The general result of this work is that if there are significant "leverage-related" costs, such as bankruptcy costs, agency costs of debt, and loss of non-debt tax shields, and if the income from equity is untaxed, then the marginal bondholder's tax rate will be less than the corporate rate and there will be a positive net tax advantage to corporate debt financing. The firm's optimal capital structure will involve the trade off between the tax advantage of debt and various leverage-related costs. The upshot of these extensions of Miller's model is the recognition that the existence of an optimal capital structure is essentially an empirical issue as to whether or not the various leverage-related costs are economically significant enough to influence the costs of corporate borrowing.

The Miller model and its theoretical extensions have inspired several time-series studies which provide evidence on the existence of leverage-related costs. Trczinka [28] reports that from examining differences in average yields between taxable corporate bonds and tax-exempt municipal bonds, one cannot reject the Miller hypothesis that the marginal bondholder's tax rate is not different from the corporate tax rate. However, Trczinka is careful to point out that this finding does not necessarily imply that there is no tax advantage of corporate debt if the personal tax rate on equity is positive. Indeed, Buser and Hess [1], using a longer time series of data and more sophisticated econometric techniques, estimate that the average effective personal tax rate on equity is statistically positive and is not of a trivial magnitude. More importantly, they document evidence that is consistent with the existence of significant leverage-related costs in the economy.

* The University of Michigan, Lexecon Inc., and The University of Michigan, respectively. This research was supported by summer research grants from the University of Michigan Graduate School of Business Administration.

Their results show that leverage-related costs and the tax rate on equity have important impacts on the relation between taxable and tax-exempt yields. These findings of Buser and Hess are further buttressed by Trzcinka and Kamma [29] who find that the marginal bondholder's tax rate is significantly less than the corporate rate. They conclude that the extensions of Miller's model with positive leverage-related costs describe the data better than the original Miller model.

In this study we take a more direct approach to the issue of an optimal capital structure. In contrast to the above studies that are based on time-series analyses of macrodata, we use cross-sectional, firm-specific data to test for the existence of an optimal capital structure.[1] Thus, the evidence provided in this study may be viewed as a complementary to the above time-series evidence.[2]

Section I develops a theoretical model that synthesizes the recent advances in the theory of optimal capital structure. Section II presents testable implications of the theory by using comparative statics and a simulation of the model. The simulation shows that firm leverage ratios will be negatively related to the volatility of firm earnings if the costs of *financial distress* (bankruptcy costs and agency costs of debt) are non-trivial.

In Section III we examine the cross-sectional variations in firm leverage ratios to see if they are related to 1) the through-time volatility of firm earnings, 2) the relative amount of non-debt tax shields (depreciation and tax credits), and 3) the intensity of research and development and advertising expenditures. We focus on a 20-year average debt-to-value measure, to minimize the effects of transient variations through time because of business cycles or lagged adjustments by firms towards their "target" leverage ratios. We find that the "permanent" or average firm leverage ratios are strongly related to industry classification, and that this relation remains strong even after we exclude regulated firms. More important, we find firm leverage ratios are related inversely to earnings volatility. These results are consistent with the theory of optimal capital structure.

I. A Model of Optimal Capital Structure

In this section we develop a single period model that synthesizes the current state of the art in the theory of optimal capital structure. The model captures the essence of the tax-advantage-and-bankruptcy-costs trade off models of Kraus and Litzenberger [14], Scott [24], Kim [11], and Titman [27], the agency costs of debt arguments of Jensen and Meckling [10] and Myers [20], the potential loss of non-debt tax shields in non-default states in DeAngelo and Masulis [5],

[1] Other recent empirical studies of optimal capital structure that are based on cross-sectional, firm-specific data include [6], [7], [15], [3], [2], and [26]. In contrast to the consensus among the authors who have examined the differential yields between taxable and tax-exempt bonds, these authors reach quite different conclusions on the existence of an optimal capital structure. This lack of consensus reflects the fact that these authors use different methodologies and samples.

[2] Another empirical implication of Miller's model is that shareholders will sort themselves into leverage clienteles depending upon their tax rates relative to the corporate tax rate. Kim, Lewellen, and McConnell [13] develop this implication of Miller's model and provide some preliminary evidence. Harris, Roenfeldt, and Cooley [9] provide further evidence on the existence of shareholder leverage clienteles.

the differential personal tax rates between income from stocks and bonds in Miller [16], and the extensions of Miller's model by DeAngelo and Masulis [5], Kim [12], and Modigliani [17].

To develop a model that represents the current state of the art in the theory of optimal capital structure. we make the following assumptions.

1. Investors are risk-neutral.
2. Investors face a progressive tax rate on returns from bonds, t_{pb}, while the firm faces a constant statutory marginal tax rate, t_c.
3. Corporate and personal taxes are based on end-of-period wealth; consequently, debt payments (interest and principle) are fully deductable in calculating the firm's end-of-period tax bill, and are fully taxable at the level of the individual bondholder.
4. Equity returns (dividends and capital gains) are taxed at a constant rate, t_{ps}.
5. There exist non-debt tax shields, such as accelerated depreciation and investment tax credits. that reduce the firm's end-of-period tax liability.
6. Negative tax bills (unused tax credits) are not transferrable (saleable) either through time or across firms.
7. The firm will incur various costs associated with financial distress should it fail to meet, in full, the end-of-period payment promised to its bondholders.
8. The firm's end-of-period value before taxes and debt payments, $\tilde{X}$, is a random variable. If the firm fails to meet the debt obligation to its bondholders, $\tilde{Y}$, the costs associated with financial distress will reduce the value of the firm by a constant fraction k.

Assumption 1, that of risk neutrality, eliminates the need to model the general equilibrium issue of the trade-off between the tax status and the risk/expected return characteristic of debt and equity securities (e.g., Kim [12] and Modigliani [17]). In this context, risk-neutrality is equivalent to assuming that investors form either all-equity or all-debt portfolios depending on their tax rates.

Assumptions 2 through 4 describe the tax environment of the model. Assumption 2 originates with Miller [16], while Assumption 3, that of wealth tax, has been used by a number of authors to capture the spirit of a perpetuity analysis in a single period framework (e.g., [14], [5], and [12]). Assumption 4 relaxes the undesirable assumption of a zero tax rate on income from stocks that has been commonly used by previous authors.

Assumptions 5 and 6 are made to incorporate the effects of non-debt tax shields on the corporate leverage decision. Assumption 6 prohibits firms from carrying tax credits backward or forward, or from selling them via a leasing agreement or through a merger. While this assumption is admittedly too restrictive, the purpose is to capture DeAngelo and Masulis' [5] argument that the possibility of losing non-debt tax shields in non-default states creates a substitution effect between the level of non-debt tax shields and the tax benefits of corporate leverage.

Finally, Assumptions 7 and 8 allow for the existence of costs associated with risky debt that are incurred when the firm encounters difficulty in meeting its end-of-period obligation to its debtholders. In the agency costs framework of Jensen and Meckling [10] and Myers [20], these costs include the costs of renegotiating the firm's debt contracts and the opportunity costs of non-optimal production/investment decisions that arise when the firm is in financial distress. In the bankruptcy cost framework of Kraus and Litzenberger [14], Scott [24], Kim [11], and Titman [27], these costs represent the direct and indirect costs of bankruptcy. Since both the agency costs of debt and bankruptcy costs become economically significant only when the firm is in financial distress we use the term "costs of *financial distress*" in a generic sense to include both bankruptcy and agency costs of debt. The costs of financial distress are assumed to be a constant fraction k of $\tilde{X}$, the firm's end-of-period value before taxes, in the event of financial distress, and zero otherwise.

Under the above assumptions of the model, the uncertain end-of-period pre-tax returns to the firm's stockholders and bondholders can be written as follows:

$$
\tilde{Y}_s = \begin{cases} (\tilde{X} - \hat{Y})(1 - t_c) + \phi, & \tilde{X} \geq \hat{Y} + \phi/t_c \\ \tilde{X} - \hat{Y}, & \hat{Y} \leq \tilde{X} < \hat{Y} + \phi/t_c \\ 0, & \tilde{X} < \hat{Y} \end{cases} \tag{1}
$$

$$
\tilde{Y}_b = \begin{cases} \hat{Y}, & \tilde{X} \geq \hat{Y} \\ \tilde{X}(1 - k), & 0 \leq \tilde{X} < \hat{Y} \\ 0, & \tilde{X} < 0, \end{cases} \tag{2}
$$

where

$\tilde{Y}_s, \tilde{Y}_b$ = the gross end-of-period returns to stockholders and bondholders, respectively,

$\hat{Y}$ = the total end-of-period promised payment to bondholders,

ϕ = the total *after-tax* value of the non-debt shields if they are fully utilized at the end-of-period,

k = costs of financial distress per dollar of end-of-period value of the firm.

Equation (1) shows that if pre-tax earnings are large enough for the firm to fully utilize the non-debt tax shield (ϕ/t_c), then the gross end-of-period return to stockholders is $(\tilde{X} - \hat{Y} - \phi/t_c)(1 - t_c) + \phi/t_c = (\tilde{X} - \hat{Y})(1 - t_c) + \phi$. If the firm's pre-tax earnings are such that $\tilde{X} - \hat{Y} - \phi/t_c < 0$, the firm will pay no tax and Assumption 6 implies that the end-of-period return to stockholders is $\tilde{X} - \hat{Y}$. The end-of-period pre-tax return to bondholders in Equation (2) follows from Assumption 8 and the fact that bondholders have limited liability in the event that the firm's end-of-period value $\tilde{X}$ is negative.

Invoking Assumption 1, that of risk neutrality, Equations (1) and (2) provide the following beginning-of-period market value of the firm's stocks (S) and bonds (B):

$$
S = E(\tilde{Y}_s)/E(\tilde{r}_s) = \frac{1 - t_{ps}}{r_o} \cdot \left[\int_{\hat{Y}+\phi/t_c}^{\infty} [(\tilde{X} - \hat{Y})(1 - t_c) + \phi] f(\tilde{X}) \, d\tilde{X} \right.
$$

$$
\left. + \int_{\hat{Y}}^{\hat{Y}+\phi/t_c} (\tilde{X} - \hat{Y}) f(\tilde{X}) \, d\tilde{X} \right] \tag{3}
$$

$$
B = E(\tilde{Y}_b)/E(\tilde{r}_b) = \frac{1 - t_{pb}}{r_o} \left[\int_{\hat{Y}}^{\infty} \hat{Y} f(\tilde{X}) \, d\tilde{X} + \int_{0}^{\hat{Y}} \tilde{X}(1 - k) f(\tilde{X}) \, d\tilde{X} \right], \tag{4}
$$

where

S, B = the market value of the firm's stocks and bonds, respectively,
$E(\tilde{r}_s), E(\tilde{r}_b)$ = one plus the, expected pre-tax rate of return from stocks and bonds, respectively,
r_o = one plus the rate of return on default-free, tax-exempt bonds,
$f(\tilde{X})$ = probability density of $\tilde{X}$.

Adding Equations (3) and (4) yields the market value of the firm (V):

$$V = \frac{1}{r_o}\left[(1 - t_{pb}) \int_0^{\hat{Y}} \tilde{X}(1 - k)f(\tilde{X})\, d\tilde{X} \right.$$

$$+ \int_{\hat{Y}}^{\hat{Y}-c/t_c} [(\tilde{X} - \hat{Y})(1 - t_{ps}) + \hat{Y}(1 - t_{pb})]f(\tilde{X})\, d\tilde{X}$$

$$\left. + \int_{\hat{Y}-o/t_c}^{\infty} [(1 - t_{ps})\{(\tilde{X} - \hat{Y})(1 - t_c) + \phi\} + (1 - t_{pb})\hat{Y}]f(\tilde{X})\, d\tilde{X} \right] \quad (5)$$

Equation (5) shows that the value of the firm is equal to the present value of the sum of three expected values (integrals). The first integral represents the situation in which X is positive but insufficient to meet its debt obligation. Under this condition, the payment to the firm's bondholders is $\tilde{X}$ less total costs of financial distress, $k\tilde{X}$. Consistent with the assumption of a wealth tax, the payment to the firm's bondholders, net of costs of financial distress, is subject to the personal tax rate t_{pb}. The second integral represents the states of world in which the firm's end-of-period pre-tax value, $\tilde{X}$, is greater than its debt obligation ($\hat{Y}$) but less than the maximum level of earnings that would result in a zero end-of-period corporate tax bill ($\hat{Y} + \phi/t_c$). In these states, the firm has no corporate tax bill; however, the payments to bondholders and stockholders are subject to the personal tax rates. Finally, the third integral defines the after-tax cash flows to the firm's securityholders if earnings are sufficient to pay bondholders and to generate a positive corporate tax liability.

The firm's optimal leverage decision involves setting $\hat{Y}$, the end-of-period payment promised to bondholders, such that the market value of the firm is maximized. Differentiating (5) with respect to $\hat{Y}$ yields the first order condition of Equation (6), where $V_{\hat{Y}}$ is the partial derivative $\partial V/\partial \hat{Y}$.

$$V_{\hat{Y}} = \frac{(1 - t_{pb})}{r_o}\left\{ [1 - F(\hat{Y})]\left[1 - \frac{(1 - t_c)(1 - t_{ps})}{1 - t_{pb}}\right]\right.$$

$$\left. - \frac{(1 - t_{ps})t_c}{1 - t_{pb}} [F(\hat{Y} + \phi/t_c) - F(\hat{Y})] - k\hat{Y}f(\hat{Y})\right\}. \quad (6)$$

where $F(\cdot)$ is the cumulative probability density function of $\tilde{X}$.

To explain the implications of Equation (6), we use it to illustrate the existing theories of capital structure. The Miller irrelevancy model [16] assumes no tax on income from stocks and no leverage-related costs, i.e., $t_{ps} = k = \phi = 0$, which reduce (6) to:

$$V_{\hat{Y}} = \{[1 - F(\hat{Y})]t_c - [1 - F(\hat{Y})]t_{pb}\}/r_o \quad (7)$$

The first term in Equation (7) is the marginal expected tax benefit of debt, while the second term is the marginal tax premium firms expect to pay bondholders. When debt is risky, the marginal expected tax benefit of debt is the corporate tax rate (t_c) times the probability that the firm will keep its promise to the bondholders $[1 - F(\hat{Y})]$. Equation (7) shows that firms will issue debt up to the point where the marginal tax premium they expect to pay bondholders, $[1 - F(\hat{Y})]t_{pb}$, is equal to the marginal expected tax benefit of debt, $[1 - F(\hat{Y})]t_c$. Firms in the economy will continue to issue debt until, due to the progressivity of the personal tax schedule, t_{pb} equals t_c. Thus, in equilibrium the *net* tax advantage of debt is zero.

Alternatively, DeAngelo and Masulis [5] and Kim [12], while retaining the assumption of no personal tax on income from stocks $(t_{ps} = 0)$, allow for positive leverage-related costs. In this case, (6) becomes

$$V_{\hat{Y}} = \{[1 - F(\hat{Y})](t_c - t_{pb}) - t_c[F(\hat{Y} + \phi/t_c)$$
$$- F(\hat{Y})] - (1 - t_{pb})k\hat{Y}f(\hat{Y})]/r_o \quad (8)$$

Equation (8) now shows that firms will stop issuing debt when

$$t_c - t_{pb} = \{t_c[F(\hat{Y} + \phi/t_c) - F(\hat{Y})] + (1 - t_{pb})k\hat{Y}f(\hat{Y})\}/[1 - F(\hat{Y})]. \quad (9)$$

Note that as long as either ϕ or k is positive, the RHS of Equation (9) is unambiguously positive and hence t_c is greater than t_{pb}. That is, firms will stop issuing debt while the marginal bondholder's t_{pb} is less than t_c. Thus, in equilibrium the first term in Equation (8) is positive, which means that the net tax advantage of debt is positive. The second and third terms define the marginal cost of debt. The second term represents the increase in the probability of wasting interest tax shields in states where the nondebt tax shields are greater than taxable earnings. The third term represents the marginal increase in expected costs of financial distress. Thus, the firm's leverage decision involves a tradeoff between the expected net tax advantage of debt and expected leverage-related costs.

Finally, if we allow for a positive personal tax rate on income from stocks $(t_{ps} > 0)$, Equation (6) shows that the tax terms become more complicated; however, the essence of the results obtained by DeAngelo and Masulis and Kim does not change. The first term in (6) represents the marginal net tax advantage of debt, while the second and third terms represent marginal expected leverage-related costs. The optimal leverage involves balancing the net tax advantage of debt against leverage-related costs.

To show that the net tax advantage of debt is positive with a positive t_{ps}, consider both the demand and supply of corporate debt and equity. In a risk neutral world, investors are indifferent between holding stocks and bonds as long as the expected after-tax returns are the same:

$$E(\tilde{r}_s)(1 - t_{ps}) = E(\tilde{r}_b)(1 - t_{pb}). \quad (10)$$

On the corporate side, firms are indifferent between issuing stocks and bonds as long as the marginal expected after-tax cost of issuing debt is the same as the marginal expected cost of issuing equity:

$$[E(\tilde{r}_b) + l](1 - t_c) + \psi = E(\tilde{r}_s), \tag{11}$$

where l is the marginal expected costs of financial distress that firms pay in the form of higher promised interest rates and ψ is the interest tax shields that are expected to be wasted due to states where non-debt tax shields are greater than taxable earnings. Since in equilibrium demand must equal supply, we substitute Equation (10) into Equation (11) and rearrange terms to obtain the equilibrium condition:

$$(1 - t_c)(1 - t_{ps})/(1 - t_{pb}) = [E(\tilde{r}_b) - \psi(1 - t_{ps})/(1 - t_{pb})]/[E(\tilde{r}_b) + l]. \tag{12}$$

Note that if either ψ or l is positive, the LHS of Equation (12) must be less than one and hence the first term in Equation (6), the net tax advantage of debt financing, must be positive.

II. Comparative Statics and Simulation of the Model

The comparative statics of the leverage relevancy model can be shown by differentiating the optimality condition (6) with respect to each of the relevant exogenous variables. Differentiating $V_{\hat{Y}}$ in (6) with respect to k, ϕ, t_{pb}, and t_{ps} yields the following cross-partial derivatives:

$$V_{\hat{Y}k} = -(1 - t_{pb})\hat{Y}f(\hat{Y})/r_o < 0 \tag{13}$$

$$V_{\hat{Y}o} = -(1 - t_{ps})f(\hat{Y} + \phi/t_c)/r_o < 0 \tag{14}$$

$$V_{\hat{Y}t_{ps}} = \{[1 - F(\hat{Y})] - t_c[1 - F(\hat{Y} + \phi/t_c)]\}/r_o$$
$$> (1 - t_c)[1 - F(\hat{Y})]/r_o > 0 \tag{15}$$

$$V_{\hat{Y}t_{pb}} = \{k\hat{Y}f(\hat{Y}) - [1 - F(\hat{Y})]\}/r_o. \tag{16}$$

The cross-partial derivatives in Equations (13) and (14) are unambiguously negative. An increase in either the cost of financial distress or in non-debt tax shields will lead to a reduction in the optimal level of debt.

The cross-partial derivative in Equation (15) is unambiguously positive. An increase in the personal tax rate on equity increases the stockholder's after-personal-tax value of corporate interest tax shields and hence increases the optimal level of corporate debt. Finally, the cross-partial derivative in Equation (16) is unambiguously negative at the firm's optimal capital structure.[3] An

---

[3] Substituting the optimality condition (6) into Equation (16) yields the cross-partial at the optimal capital structure:

$$V_{\hat{Y} \cdot t_{pb}} = -\left\{[1 - F(\hat{Y}^*)]\frac{(1 - t_c)(1 - t_{ps})}{(1 - t_{pb})} + \frac{(1 - t_{ps})t_c}{1 - t_{pb}}\right.$$
$$\left. \cdot [F(\hat{Y}^* + \phi/t_c) - F(\hat{Y}^*)]\right\} \bigg/ r_o < 0, \tag{17}$$

where $\hat{Y}^*$ is the optimal level of debt.

increase in the marginal bondholder's tax rate decreases the optimal level of debt because it increases the tax premium component of corporate bond yields.

A factor that does not appear explicitly in the leverage optimality condition (6) but is important to the theory of optimal capital structure is the variability of the firm's end-of-period value. Intuitively, the greater the variability of the firm's value, the greater the probability of incurring costs of financial distress at the end of the period and the greater the probability of wasting interest tax shields. However, this intuitively appealing argument is not an unambiguous implication of the model. To demonstrate this ambiguity, we differentiate (6) with respect to σ, the standard deviation of the distribution of the firm's end-of-period value, assuming that $\tilde{X}$ is normally distributed.

$$
V_{\hat{Y}_\sigma} = \left\{ t_c(1 - t_{ps})f(\hat{Y} + \phi/t_c)\left(\frac{\hat{Y} + \phi/t_c - \bar{X}}{\sigma}\right) - (t_{pb} - t_{ps})f(\hat{Y})\left(\frac{\hat{Y} - \bar{X}}{\sigma}\right) \right.
$$
$$
\left. - (1 - t_{pb})k\hat{Y}f(\hat{Y})\left[\left(\frac{\hat{Y} - \bar{X}}{\sigma}\right)^2 - 1\right] \middle/ \sigma \right\} \middle/ r_o \gtreqless 0, \quad (18)
$$

where $\bar{X}$ is the mean of $\tilde{X}$. The ambiguity of the sign of this cross-partial derivative, when the underlying distribution is normal, has been pointed out by Scott [24] and Castanias [3]. Equation (18) indicates that the sign of $V_{\hat{Y}_\sigma}$ is determined in part by the magnitudes of $\hat{Y}$ and $\hat{Y} + \phi/t_c$ relative to $\bar{X}$, and by the magnitudes of k and ϕ relative to other variables.[4]

In order to establish the empirically relevant sign of the cross-partial derivative $V_{\hat{Y}_\sigma}$, we perform a simulation of the firm's leverage decision based on the first-order condition (6). In this simulation we assume a normal distribution for $\tilde{X}$ and specific values for the relevant variables and compute the optimal level of debt $\hat{Y}^*$, which is the value that sets $V_{\hat{Y}}$ in (6) equal to zero. Then, we compute the market value of the firm's stock at $\hat{Y}^*$ using Equation (3).

The optimal debt ratio, d, is defined as $\hat{Y}^*/(S + \hat{Y}^*)$. Note that in this definition, debt is measured by the end-of-period payment promised to the bondholders, instead of by the market value of bonds, while equity is measured by the market value of stock. The purpose here is to be consistent with our empirical proxy for the debt ratio in the cross-sectional tests, which is the book value of debt divided by the sum of the market value of equity and the book value of debt. The book value of debt is more representative of the promised payment to debtholders than is the market value of debt.

After obtaining the optimal debt ratio for a set of specific variables, the simulation changes the assumed values of σ, ϕ, and k systematically and shows how the relation between the optimal debt ratio and σ changes under different values for ϕ and k. The results from this sensitivity analysis provide the basis for interpreting the empirical results in the next section.

The numerical values assumed for the simulation are as follows: $\bar{X} = 100$, $\sigma =$ (5 through 100) in units of 5, $\phi =$ (0 through 40) in units of 10, and $k =$ (0

---

[4] It is possible for the cross-partial to be positive, because beyond a certain level of $\hat{Y}$, an increase in σ will decrease the probability that $\tilde{X}$ will be less than $\hat{Y}$ and/or $\hat{Y} + \phi/t_c$, which will in turn lead the firm to increase its $\hat{Y}$.

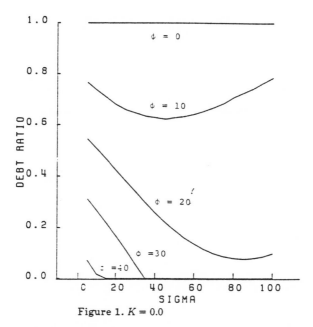

Figure 1. $K = 0.0$

through 1) in units of 0.2. The initial set of marginal tax rates assumed are: t_{pb} = t_c = 45%, and t_{ps} = 12%.[5] Figures 1 through 6 depict the results of the simulation of the firm's optimal leverage decision. The vertical axis measures the optimal debt ratio. The horizontal axis measures different levels of σ. Each line in the figures depicts the functional relation between the optimal debt ratio and the variability of the firm's value, for different levels of k and ϕ. There is a separate figure for each value of k, ranging from zero (Figure 1) to one (Figure 6). In each figure, five different levels of non-debt tax shields (ϕ from 0 to 40) generate five curves relating leverage to sigma.

As predicted by the comparative statics in (13) and (14), Figures 1 through 6 show that, for any given level of σ, an increase either in the cost of financial distress (k) or in non-debt tax shields (ϕ) leads to a reduction in the optimal debt ratio.

Also as predicted by the cross-partial in (18), the simulation results confirm that the effect of an increase in σ on the optimal debt ratio is ambiguous. Further, the functional relation between the optimal debt ratio and σ changes as we vary

[5] This set of tax rates is consistent with the recent empirical estimates provided by Buser and Hess [1] and by Trczinka [28]. Based on one-year T-bill rates and one-year prime, high grade municipal yields over the period of 1950 through 1982, Buser and Hess estimate the average marginal bondholder's tax rate to be 42.5%. Also during the same period they estimate that the average effective personal tax rates on equity and marginal corporate tax rates are 12% and 45%, respectively. Trczinka's estimate of the marginal bondholder's tax rate is based on monthly averages of yields of various grades and maturities during the period of 1970 through 1979. He concludes that he cannot reject the hypothesis that t_{pb} is equal to t_c of 48% but provides no estimate for the personal tax rate on income from stocks.

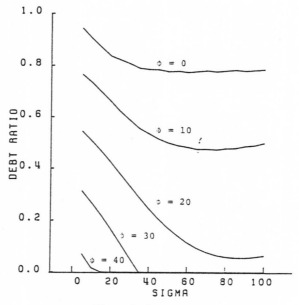

Figure 2. $K = 0.2$

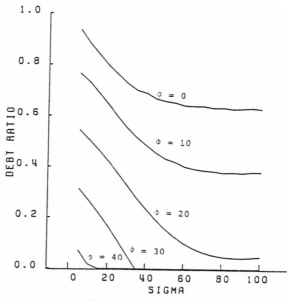

Figure 3. $K = 0.4$

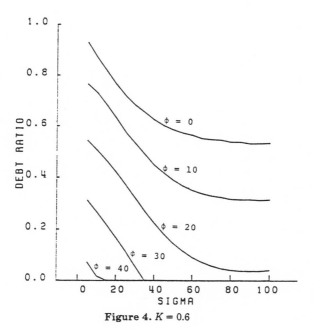

Figure 4. $K = 0.6$

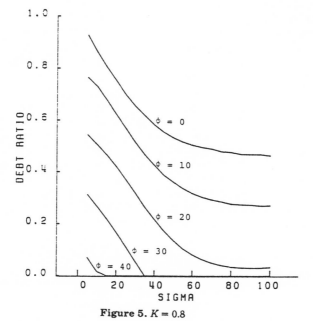

Figure 5. $K = 0.8$

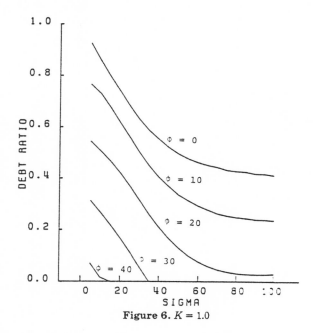

Figure 6. $K = 1.0$

the assumed values of ϕ and k. When both k and ϕ are zero. Figure 1 shows that the optimal debt ratio is always equal to one. This is because a firm that has zero leverage-related costs sees only the positive tax advantage of debt, leading to one hundred percent debt financing. Figure 1 also shows that if k is zero, a positive ϕ alone does not ensure an inverse relation between the optimal debt ratio and sigma. For example, when $k = 0$ and $\phi = 10$, Figure 1 shows that the relation between the debt ratio and σ is U-shaped.

When both k and ϕ are positive, however, Figures 2 through 6 show that, in general, the optimal debt ratio decreases with an increase in σ.[6] This inverse relation between the debt ratio and earnings variability is consistent with the notion that the greater the variability of the earnings. the greater the present value of leverage-related costs and hence the lower the optimal level of debt.

In summary, the comparative statics and the simulation of the model provide the following testable implications:

    (1) The debt ratio is inversely related to the costs of financial distress, which include bankruptcy costs and the agency costs of debt.

    (2) The debt ratio is inversely related to the level of non-debt tax shields.

---

[6] Although the above simulation results are relatively insensitive to small changes in the assumed values of the tax rates, when t_c is significantly higher than t_{pb} the inverse relation between the debt ratio and σ becomes less pronounced, especially at low levels of k. For example, at $t_c = 48\%$, $t_{pb} = 33\%$, and $t_{ps} = 0\%$, the inverse relation holds only when k approaches something like forty cents on a dollar or more. At $t_c = 48\%$, $t_{pb} = 33\%$, and $t_{ps} = 9\%$, the inverse relation requires k to be sixty cents on the dollar or more. In either case, the magnitude of ϕ has little influence on the relation between the debt ratio and σ. In sum, when t_{pb} is substantially less than t_c, the inverse relation requires significant costs of financial distress, but does not require high levels of non-debt tax shields.

(3) The debt ratio is inversely related to the variability of firm value, if the costs of financial distress are significant.

III. Empirical Tests and Results

The theory highlights three firm-specific factors that influence the firm's optimal capital structure: the variability of firm value, the level of non-debt tax shields, and the magnitude of the costs of financial distress. These three factors could quite plausibly also exhibit important industry commonalities. This may account for the empirical evidence that firm leverage ratios are industry related, although this result is contradicted by some studies. Schwartz and Aronson [22] and Scott [23] in particular report persistent differences across industries and strong intra-industry similarities in firm leverage ratios. However, the contrary findings by Remmers, et. al. [21], Ferri and Jones [6], and Chaplinsky [2] justify another investigation of this important empirical question. We first re-examine the cross-sectional relation between 20-year average firm leverage ratios and industrial classification with a sample of 851 firms covering 25 two-digit SIC industries. We then regress firm leverage ratios on empirical proxy variables for the three firm-specific factors in an effort to test the more direct implications of the theory of optimal capital structure.

A. Analysis of Variance of Firm Leverage Ratios by Industrial Classification

Table I reports the mean debt to value ratios of 25 industries, which covers 851 firms. Firm leverage is estimated by the ratio of the mean level of long-term debt (book value) during 1962–1981 to the mean level of long-term debt plus market value of equity over the same time period. These data are taken from the Annual COMPUSTAT file. The mean industry leverage ratios are ranked in ascending order to highlight the disparity of this variable across industries. The mean industry leverage ratios range from a low of 9.1% (drugs and cosmetics) to a high of 58.3% (airlines).

To test the statistical significance of the observed differences in the mean leverage ratios across industries, we perform a standard Analysis of Variance (ANOVA) using industry dummy variables. The fifth column in Table I reports the coefficients (t-statistics) of the 24 industry dummy variables included in the cross-sectional regression on firm leverage. (The paper industry is the omitted variable because its mean leverage ratio is closest to the sample mean.) The R^2 statistic reported in Table I shows that almost 54% of the cross-sectional variance in firm leverage ratios can be explained by industrial classification. There is more variation in mean leverage ratios across industries than there is in firm leverage ratios within industries.[7]

---

[7] As a check on the appropriateness of our industry classification and firm leverage measures, we ran a simple linear regression of the log of one plus our debt to equity measure to the log of the betas of the equity of the firms in our sample. We found that our leverage measure and equity betas are negatively related. However, if we include the matrix of industry dummy variables in this regression, the relation between leverage and equity beta turns significantly positive, as predicted and empirically verified by Hamada [8]. This suggests that our industry classification is capable of proxying for "business risk" across industries and our leverage measure is capable of explaining the effect of leverage on the risk of the firm's equity.

Table I

Mean and Dummy Variable Coefficient of the Debt to Value Ratios[A] for 25 Industries, Ranked in Ascending Order of Mean Debt to Value Ratios.

Sic	Industry	Nobs	Mean (Standard Deviation) Debt to Value	Dummy Variable Coefficients (t-statistics) All Firms	Non-Regulated
2830, 40	Drugs and Cosmetics	31	.0907 (.095)	−.199 (−5.64)	−.148 (−3.21)
3800	Instruments	27	.1119 (.086)	−.173 (−4.88)	−.126 (−2.69)
1000	Metal Mining	23	.1347 (.099)	−.155 (−4.09)	−.104 (−2.15)
2700	Publishing	16	.1552 (.169)	−.134 (−3.21)	−.083 (−1.61)
3600	Electronics	77	.1579 (.121)	−.132 (−4.34)	−.080 (−1.91)
3500	Machinery	80	.1957 (.114)	−.094 (−3.11)	−.043 (−1.02)
2000	Food	50	.2056 (.128)	−.084 (−2.60)	−.033 (−0.75)
1300	Petroleum Exploration	24	.2258 (.151)	−.064 (−1.70)	−0.13 (−0.26)
15, 16, 1700	Construction	12	.2384 (.151)	−.051 (−1.12)	B
2900	Petroleum Refining	31	.2436 (.121)	−.046 (−1.30)	.005 (0.11)
3400	Metal Working	33	.2502 (.139)	−.039 (−1.13)	.012 (0.26)
2800	Chemicals	47	.2544 (.135)	−.035 (−1.08)	.060 (0.36)
2300	Apparel	18	.2603 (.123)	−.029 (−0.72)	.022 (0.43)
2400	Lumber	7	.2605 (.182)	−.029 (−0.52)	.022 (0.34)
3700	Motor Vehicle Parts	52	.2714 (.138)	−.015 (−0.56)	.033 (0.76)
2600	Paper	24	.2895 (.114)	B	.051 (1.07)
2200	Textile Mill Products	21	.3257 (.133)	.036 (0.93)	.087 (1.78)
3000	Rubber	26	.3262 (.167)	.037 (1.00)	.088 (1.86)
5300	Retail Dept. Stores	20	.3433 (.150)	.054 (1.37)	.105 (2.12)
5400	Retail Grocery Stores	16	.3460 (.187)	.056 (1.35)	.108 (2.08)
4200	Trucking	10	.3730 (.209)	.083 (1.71)	
3300	Steel	45	.3819 (.195)	.092 (2.82)	.143 (3.26)
4800	Telephone	10	.5150 (.097)	.226 (4.62)	
4900	Elec. & Gas Utilities	135	.5309 (.081)	.241 (8.40)	
4500	Airlines	16	.5825 (.171)	.293 (7.00)	
	TOTAL	851	.2913 (.188)		
	R-SQRD			.536	.248
	F-STATISTIC			39.71	10.85

[A] Firm Debt to Value Ratio is calculated as the 20-year (1962–1981) sum of annual book value of long-term debt divided by the sum of long-term debt and the market value of equity.
[B] Omitted industry.

Table I contains several industries that were highly regulated by governmental agencies over the sample period of 1962 through 1981, and there appears to be a systematic relation between regulation and financial leverage. Regulated firms such as telephone, electric and gas utilities, and airlines are consistently among the most highly levered firms, which raises the possibility that differences between regulated and unregulated firm leverage ratios (for whatever reasons) are primarily responsible for the overall ANOVA results. Thus, we rerun the ANOVA of firm leverage excluding firms in the regulated industries.

The sixth column in Table I reports the coefficient (t-statistics) of the dummy variables of the ANOVA for non-regulated firms. While both the R^2 and F-statistics fall with the exclusion of the regulated industries, industry classification *still* accounts for almost 25% of the cross-sectional variation in firm leverage. In sum, a regulatory effect is evident in the data, but there still exist significant differences in the mean leverage ratios of firms across non-regulated industries.[8]

B. Empirical Proxies

Although our confirmation of a systematic relation between the debt ratio and industry classification is consistent with the prediction of the theory of optimal capital structure, it is also consistent with what Miller [16] calls "neutral mutations." To provide a more direct test of the theory, we now seek empirical proxies for the three determinants of optimal capital structure: the variability in firm value, the level of non-debt tax shields, and the costs of financial distress.

Following Chaplinsky [2] we measure variability in firm value with the standard deviation of the first difference in annual earnings, scaled by the average value of the firm's total assets over the period. As Chaplinsky points out, this kind of volatility measure has been used by others and it does not suffer from the statistical problems associated with alternative measures of firm volatility.[9] The earnings series is obtained from the Annual COMPUSTAT Tape (1962–1981) and is before deduction of interest, depreciation and taxes (the sum of data items 13 and 61 on the file).

Non-debt tax shield is measured by the sum of annual depreciation charges and investment tax credits divided by the sum of annual earnings before depreciation, interest, and taxes. Since we do not know the marginal tax rate of the firms in our sample, we do not account for the fact that depreciation is a deduction while the ITC is a tax credit.

In addition to depreciation and tax credits, there are other non-debt tax shields available to firms. Since investments in research and development and advertising capital can be expensed (100% depreciated) in the year they are incurred, firms engaged heavily in these activities are expected to issue less debt, ceteris paribus.[10] More important, Myers (1977) argues advertising and R&D create assets that may be viewed as options, which will be exercised or not depending on the firm's financial well-being. The future value of these kinds of assets are subject to more managerial discretion, which suggests that the associated agency costs are higher compared with other kinds of assets. Whether one emphasizes

---

[8] Chaplinsky [2] also uses the ANOVA to examine the relation between debt ratios and industry classification. Although she finds a significant industry effect for the entire sample of firms including regulated firms, the industry effect becomes much weaker without regulated firms. This difference between her results and ours may be due to the fact that her measure of leverage is based on the book value of debt to the book value of total assets whereas our measure of leverage incorporates the market value of equity. A measure of leverage based on the book value of equity is not consistent with the specification of the theory, and hence is likely to produce weaker results.

[9] We scale our volatility measure by book value of assets (as opposed to the market value) to avoid a spurious correlation between our measure of leverage and the market value of the firm. The simple correlation between our measure of leverage and the book value of total assets is 0.022. For a discussion of why the standard deviation of the first difference in earnings is the appropriate proxy for firm volatility, see Chaplinsky [2].

[10] Of course, advertising and R&D expenditures are not the only capital investments that can be expensed in the year they are incurred. For example, investments in firm-specific human capital are expensed in the year they are incurred but generate benefits to the firm over several years.

Table II

Summary Statistics, Correlation Matrix and Analysis of Variance on Industrial Classification of Firm Volatility[A], Non-Debt Tax Shields[B] and Advertising and Research and Development Expenses[C].

	Volatility	Non-Debt Tax Shields	Advertising and R & D
Correlation Coefficients			
Volatility		0.05	−0.05
Non-Debt Tax Shields			−0.25
Anova Results			
R-SQRD	.337	.357	.562
F-Statistic	16.91	18.47	43.75
Summary Statistics			
Mean	.053	.263	.020
Standard Deviation	.038	.113	.030
Minimum	.008	.020	.000
Maximum	.332	.914	.221

[A] Firm Volatility is calculated as the standard deviation of the first difference in annual earnings before interest, depreciation and taxes over the period 1962–1981 divided by the average value of total assets over the same time period.

[B] The level of firm Non-Debt Tax Shields is calculated as the ratio of the 20-year (1962–1981) sum of annual depreciation plus investment tax credits divided by the sum of annual earnings before interest, depreciation and taxes over the same period.

[C] The level of firm Advertising plus Research and Development expenses is given by the 10-year (1971–1982) sum of annual advertising, plus research and development expenses divided by the sum of annual net sales over the same period.

the agency costs of discretionary assets or their role as a non-debt tax shield, we expect the intensity of advertising and R&D expenses to be inversely related to firm leverage ratios. Our empirical measure of this variable is the sum of annual advertising and R&D expenses divided by the sum of annual net sales.[11]

Table II reports summary statistics of our three empirical proxies of the determinants of corporate leverage. The first two rows of the table report the correlation coefficients between each pair of these variables. The second two rows report the results of an analysis of variance of each variable on industrial classification, again using the dummy variable technique. The bottom four rows report summary statistics.

The R^2 and F-statistics reported in Table II show that industry classifications are important determinants of our empirical proxies. Approximately 34% of the cross-sectional variation in firm volatility; 36% of non-debt tax shields, and 56% of advertising and R&D expenditures can be explained by industry variables. Therefore, each variable is a legitimate candidate for explaining the within industry similarities of firm leverage ratios documented in Table I.

[11] Due to limitations of the COMPUSTAT files regarding the reporting of these data, these sums are calculated only over the last 10-year interval of our sample period (1972–1981).

Table III

Ordinary Least Squares Regression Results of Firm Debt to Value Ratio[A] on Firm Volatility[B], Non-Debt Tax Shields[C] and Advertising plus Research and Development Expenses[D], with and without Industry Dummy Variables for All and Non-Regulated Firms.

	All Firms		Non-Regulated Firms	
Firms	821		655	
Industries	25		21	
	Without Industry Dummy Variables	With Industry Dummy Variables	Without Industry Dummy Variables	With Industry Dummy Variables
Constant	.330 (19.96)	.225 (7.30)	.202 (11.24)	.191 (4.77)
Firm Volatility	−1.73 (−12.33)	−0.645 (−4.66)	−0.806 (−5.85)	−0.579 (−3.94)
Non-Debt Tax Shields	.370 (7.61)	.308 (6.51)	.423 (8.51)	.316 (6.12)
Advertising and R & D Expense	−2.42 (−13.13)	−0.98 (−4.43)	−1.34 (−7.53)	−0.956 (−4.13)
R-SQRD	.342	.586	.236	.337
F-Statistic	141.73	41.63	67.11	13.92

[A] Firm Debt to Value Ratio is calculated as 20-year (1962–1981) sum of annual book value of long-term debt divided by the sum of long-term debt and the market value of equity.

[B] Firm Volatility is calculated as the standard deviation of the first difference in annual earnings before interest, depreciation and taxes over the period 1962–1981 divided by the average value of total assets over the same time period.

[C] The level of firm Non-Debt Tax Shields is calculated as the ratio of the 20-year (1962–1981) sum of annual depreciation plus investment tax credits divided by the sum of annual earnings before interest, depreciation and taxes over the same period.

[D] The level of firm Advertising plus Research and Development expenses is given by the 10-year (1971–1982) sum of annual advertising, plus research and development expenses divided by the sum of annual net sales over the same period.

C. Cross-Sectional Tests and Results

Table III reports the results of the cross-sectional regressions of firm leverage ratios on their hypothesized determinants. The table is divided into two major sections. The left hand side shows the regressions over all 821 firms in the sample.[12] The right hand side shows the regressions over the 655 unregulated firms, which excludes firms in the trucking, telephone, electric and gas utility, and airline industries.

The data reported in the first column of Table III indicate that our measure of firm volatility is significant and negatively related to firm leverage ratios

[12] The difference between this number and the 851 in Table I is due to missing data on the COMPUSTAT file.

across the 821 firms in the sample. The *t*-statistic is −12.33. The data also show that the level of advertising and R&D expense is related negatively to firm leverage (*t* = − 13.13). These results are consistent with the implications of our theoretical model.

In contrast to firm volatility and to advertising and R&D expenditures, the sign of the coefficient on non-debt tax shields is perverse. The model predicts that non-debt tax shields, being substitutes for the tax benefits from debt financing, should be related inversely to firm leverage. The significant *positive* relation between leverage and the level of non-tax shields (*t* = 7.61) is in contradiction to this prediction.[13]

The lack of negative relation between non-debt tax shields and leverage ratios raises doubts as to the validity of DeAngelo and Masulis' argument that non-debt tax shields are substitutes for interest tax shields. The results suggest that firms that invest heavily in tangible assets, and thus generate relatively high levels of depreciation and tax credits, tend to have higher financial leverage. This is consistent with Scott's [25] "secured debt" hypothesis, which states that, ceteris paribus, firms can borrow at lower interest rates if their debt is secured with tangible assets.[14]

To examine the extent to which the independent variables reflect industry factors, we add a matrix of industry dummy variables to the regression model and re-estimate the coefficients on firm volatility, non-debt tax shields, and advertising and R&D expenses. The results of this expanded regression over all firms are reported in the second column of Table III. While the addition of the industry dummy variables reduces the magnitude and significance of the coefficients of the independent variables, firm leverage ratios remain inversely related to firm volatility and to advertising and R&D expenses, and directly related to the level of non-debt tax shields.

The second half of Table III reports the results of our cross-sectional analysis of non-regulated firms. These data show that the results based on the full sample are not driven by a regulatory effect. Even across just the non-regulated firms, leverage is related negatively to firm volatility and to advertising and R&D expenses, and it is related positively to the level of non-debt tax shields. These results hold up when industry dummy variables are included in the regression.[15]

As a final test of the relation between firm leverage and our independent

---

[13] The negative relation between leverage and advertising and R&D expenditures and the positive relation between leverage and non-debt tax shields are also reported by Titman [26].

[14] This explanation implies that our cross-sectional regression is misspecified, because it omits an important independent variable, a proxy for secured debt. The positive correlation between the missing variable and the included variable measuring non-debt tax shield is the suspected reason for the seemingly perverse positive relation. This also raises the possibility that correlation between missing variable and the other included variables is causing us to misinterpret their coefficients as well.

[15] Chaplinsky [2] also finds a negative relation between leverage and firm volatility; however, her *t*-statistics are substantially less than those reported in Table III. This difference may be due to the fact that her measure of leverage is based on the book value of total assets whereas our measure incorporates the market value of equity. As mentioned earlier, a measure of leverage based on the book value of equity is not consistent with the specification of the theory and hence is likely to produce weaker results.

Table IV

Ordinary Least Squares Regression Results of Firm Debt to Value Ratio[A] on Firm and Industry Measures of Volatility[B], Non-Debt Tax Shields[C] and Advertising plus Research and Development Expenses[D] for All and for Non-Regulated Firms.

	All Firms		Non-Regulated Firms	
Firms	821		655	
Industries	25		21	
	Without Industry Means	With Industry Means	Without Industry Means	With Industry Means
Constant	.330	.432	.202	.124
	(19.96)	(16.80)	(11.24)	(2.32)
Volatility	−1.73	−0.658	−0.806	−0.583
	(−12.33)	(−4.23)	(−5.85)	(−3.83)
Non-Debt Tax Shields	.370	.312	.423	.317
	(7.61)	(5.86)	(8.51)	(5.93)
Advertising and R & D Expense	−2.42	−0.989	−1.34	−0.971
	(−13.13)	(−3.99)	(−7.53)	(−4.06)
Industry Means:				
Volatility		−3.11		−0.843
		(−11.59)		(−2.46)
Non-Debt Tax Shields		.126		.526
		(1.30)		(3.44)
Advertising and R & D Expense		−2.36		−0.189
		(−6.74)		(−0.42)
R-SQRD	.342	.464	.236	.270
F-Statistic	141.78	117.41	67.11	39.84

[A] Firm Debt to Value Ratio is calculated as 20-year (1962–1981) sum of annual book value of long-term debt divided by the sum of long-term debt and the market value of equity.

[B] Firm Volatility is calculated as the standard deviation of the first difference in annual earnings before interest, depreciation and taxes over the period 1962–1981 divided by the average value of total assets over the same time period.

[C] The level of firm Non-Debt Tax Shields is calculated as the ratio of the 20-year (1962–1981) sum of annual depreciation plus investment tax credits divided by the sum of annual earnings before interest, depreciation and taxes over the same period.

[D] The level of firm Advertising plus Research and Development expenses is given by the 10-year (1971–1982) sum of annual advertising, plus research and development expenses divided by the sum of annual net sales over the same period.

variables, we replace the matrix of dummy variables with the industry means of the three independent variables. The results of this regression are reported in Table IV. The data in the first and third columns of Table IV are the same as reported in Table III. They are reproduced here only to facilitate comparisons. The second column reports the results of the expanded regression model where industry mean values of firm volatility, non-debt tax shields, and advertising and R&D expenses are entered as independent variables.

The significance of the coefficients of the industry mean variables (reported in the lower half of the table) indicates that these industry means are at least partially responsible for the industry effects accounted for previously with the industry dummy variables. The R^2 statistic falls from 59% (Table III) to 46% with this substitution. The lower R^2 indicates that there are industry factors in addition to industry means of firm volatility, non-debt tax shields, and advertising and R&D expenses that can account for some residual cross-sectional variations in firm leverage ratios. Note also that, while including the industry means reduces the magnitude and significance of our firm-specific variables, the latter are still significantly different from zero.

The rest of Table IV repeats the regression over the subsample of non-regulated firms. Each of the firm-specific variables bears the same relation to firm leverage as it does in the overall sample. Moreover, the addition of the industry means does not materially affect either the magnitude or the significance of any of the firm-specific variables. The industry mean of advertising and R&D expenses, however, is not significant in this regression. This suggests that the industry mean of advertising and R&D expenses is proxying for regulation in the overall regression.[16]

IV. Summary and Conclusions

This paper develops a model that synthesizes the modern balancing theory of optimal capital structure. This model incorporates positive personal taxes on equity and on bond income, expected costs of financial distress (bankruptcy costs and agency costs), and positive non-debt tax shields. We show that optimal firm leverage is related inversely to expected costs of financial distress and to the (exogenously set) amount of non-debt tax shields. A simulation analysis demonstrates that if costs of financial distress are significant, optimal firm leverage is related inversely to the variability of firm earnings.

The empirical section investigates the cross-sectional behavior of 20-year average firm leverage ratios for 851 firms covering 25 two-digit SIC industries. Several important results emerge. First, there exists strong industry influences across these firm leverage ratios. The cross-sectional regressions on industry dummy variables explain 54% of variation in firm leverage ratios. Excluding from the regression all regulated firms during the sample period, such as trucking, telephone, electric and gas utilities, and airlines, still yields an R^2 of 25%.

Our search for the specific economic sources of these strong industry influences on firm leverage ratios yields some noteworthy results. The volatility of firm earnings is an important, inverse determinant of firm leverage. It helps explain both inter- and intra-industry variations in firm leverage ratios. The intensity of R&D and advertising expenditures is also related inversely to leverage. Both of these results are consistent with the formal balancing model of optimal leverage.

---

[16] Regulated firms have inordinately low advertising and R&D expenses.

A somewhat puzzling finding is the strong direct relation between firm leverage and the relative amount of non-debt tax shields. This contradicts the theory that focuses on the substitutability between non-debt and debt tax shields. A possible explanation is that non-debt tax shields are an instrumental variable for the securability of the firm's assets, with more securable assets leading to higher leverage ratios.

A fundamental problem with the cross-sectional regressions is misspecification, which suggests a "missing variable" explanation for the perverse result on non-debt tax shields. The danger is that excluded variables are correlated with included variables, which can cause misleading inferences to be drawn from the regression results. Nonetheless, the strong finding of intra-industry similarities in firm leverage ratios and of persistent inter-industry differences, together with the highly significant inverse relation between firm leverage and earnings volatility, tends to support the modern balancing theory of optimal capital structure.

REFERENCES

1. Buser, S. and P. Hess. "The Marginal Cost of Leverage, the Tax Rate on Equity and the Relation between Taxable and Tax-Exempt Yields," Ohio State University Working Paper (October 1983).
2. Chaplinsky, S., "The Economic Determinants of Leverage: Theories and Evidence," Unpublished Ph.D. Dissertation, University of Chicago (September 1983).
3. Castanias, R., "Bankruptcy Risk and Optimal Capital Structure," *Journal of Finance* (December 1983).
4. Castanias, R. and H. DeAngelo, "Business Risk and Optimal Capital Structure," Unpublished Working Paper, University of Washington (1981).
5. DeAngelo, H. and R. Masulis, "Optimal Capital Structure Under Corporate and Personal Taxation," *Journal of Financial Economics* (March 1980).
6. Ferri, M. and W. Jones. "Determinants of Financial Structure: A New Methodological Approach," *Journal of Finance* (June 1979).
7. Flath, D. and C. Knoeber. "Taxes, Failure Costs, and Optimal Industry Capital Structure: An Empirical Test," *Journal of Finance* (March 1980).
8. Hamada, R., "The Effect of the Firm's Capital Structure on the Systematic Risk of Common Stocks," *Journal of Finance* (May 1972).
9. Harris, J., R. Roenfeldt. and P. Cooley, "Evidence of Financial Leverage Clienteles," *Journal of Finance* (September 1953).
10. Jensen, M. C. and W. H. Meckling, "Theory of the Firm Managerial Behavior, Agency Costs and Ownership Structure," *Journal of Financial Economics* (October 1976).
11. Kim, E. H., "A Mean-Variance Theory of Optimal Capital Structure and Corporate Debt Capacity," *Journal of Finance* (March 1978).
12. Kim, E. H., "Miller's Equilibrium, Shareholder Leverage Clienteles, and Optimal Capital Structure," *Journal of Finance* (May 1982).
13. Kim, E. H., W. G. Lewellen, and J. J. McConnell, "Financial Leverage Clienteles: Theory and Evidence," *Journal of Financial Economics* (March 1979).
14. Kraus, A. and R. Litzenberger, "A State-Preference Model of Optimal Financial Leverage," *Journal of Finance* (September 1973).
15. Marsh, P. "The Choice between Equity and Debt: An Empirical Study," *Journal of Finance* (March 1982).
16. Miller, M. H. "Debt and Taxes," *Journal of Finance* (May 1977).
17. Modigliani, F., "Debt. Dividend Policy, Taxes, Inflation, and Market Valuation," *Journal of Finance* (May 1982).

18. Modigliani, F. F. and M. H. Miller, "The Cost of Capital, Corporation Finance, and the Theory of Investment," *American Economic Review* (June 1958).

19. Modigliani, F. F. and M. H. Miller, "Corporation Income Taxes and the Cost of Capital: A Correction," *American Economic Review* (June 1963).

20. Myers, S. C., "Determinants of Corporate Borrowing," *Journal of Financial Economics* (November 1977).

21. Remmers, L., A. Stonehill, R. Wright, and T. Beckhuiser, "Industry and Size as Debt Ratio Determinants in Manufacturing Internationally," *Financial Management* (Summer 1974).

22. Schwartz, E. and R. Aronson, "Some Surrogate Evidence in Support of the Concept of Optimal Financial Structure," *Journal of Finance* (March 1967).

23. Scott, D. F., "Evidence on the Importance of Financial Structure," *Financial Management*, (Summer 1972).

24. Scott, J., "A Theory of Optimal Capital Structure," *Bell Journal of Economics* (Spring 1976).

25. Scott, J., "Bankruptcy, Secured Debt, and Optimal Capital Structure," *Journal of Finance* (March 1977).

26. Titman, S., "Determinants of Capital Structure: An Empirical Analysis," Unpublished Working Paper, UCLA (1983).

27. Titman, S., "The Effect of Capital Structure on a Firm's Liquidation Decision," *Journal of Financial Economics* (forthcoming)

28. Trzcinka, C., "The Pricing of Tax-Exempt Bond and the Miller Hypothesis," *Journal of Finance* (September 1982).

29. Trzcinka, C. and S. Kamma, "Marginal Taxes, Municipal Bond Risk and the Miller Equilibrium: New Evidence and Some Predictive Tests," Unpublished Working Paper, State University of New York at Buffalo (December 1983).

Index

About the Author

AHMED RIAHI-BELKAOUI is CBA Distinguished Professor of Accounting in the College of Business Administration, University of Illinois at Chicago. Author of more than 30 Quorum books and coauthor of several more, he is also a prolific author of articles published in the major scholarly and professional journals in his field, and has served on numerous editorial boards that oversee them.